D0722964

The Habit of Lying

The Habit of Lying

Sacrificial Studies in

Literature, Philosophy,

and Fashion Theory

JOHN VIGNAUX SMYTH

DUKE UNIVERSITY PRESS

DURHAM AND LONDON

2002

© 2002 Duke University Press
All rights reserved
Printed in the United States of America on acid-free paper ∞
Typeset in Aldus by Keystone Typesetting, Inc.
Library of Congress Cataloging-in-Publication Data
appear on the last printed page of this book.

To Eowyn Nilson
without whose love this
might have died the death

And for Amy Cook whose
love showed the truth

And for La cane enchaînée
whose amazing love
clarified everything
beyond all doubt

And for Gregory Goekjian,
another Armenian
who saw it all:
the genocide.

CONCORDIA UNIVERSITY LIBRARY
PORTLAND, OR 97211

The struggle against deceit
works to the advantage of
naked terror.
—THEODOR ADORNO

There are only two things.
Truth and lies. Truth is
indivisible, hence it cannot
recognize itself; anyone who
wants to recognize it has to
be a lie.
—FRANZ KAFKA

Contents

Acknowledgments
I am exceedingly grateful to
Eowyn Nilson, Jonathan Burt,
and Reginald McGinnis for
their sensitive readings of
various drafts of this book, to
Stanley Fish for originally
soliciting the manuscript at
Duke University Press, and to
Barbara Herrnstein Smith for
her untiring support of its
publication.

Introduction

*"It is not necessary to accept everything as true, one must
only accept it as necessary." "A melancholy conclusion," said K.
"It turns lying into a universal principle."*
—FRANZ KAFKA

*And when it comes to neglecting fundamentals, I think I have
nothing to learn, and indeed I confuse them with accidentals.*
—SAMUEL BECKETT

Interpreting the famous parable "Before the Law," Kafka's K. observes
that lying is a universal principle.[1] It is virtually self-evident—to put
the point in a more pedestrian way—that lying and concealment are
fundamental to the structure of most or all human societies. "Yet," as
one recent commentator puts it, "despite its ubiquity, antiquity, theoretical interest and, if Hobbes is right, its human specificity, most
social scientists and philosophers have given lying comparatively little

attention," and "by far the greater part of what philosophers have written treats lying as a form of deviance."[2] Moreover, deception is clearly crucial to much animal interaction too, perhaps most strikingly in mimetic or mimic behavior—from "elementary" (but often extraordinarily sophisticated) forms of chameleonlike behavior up to, and including, the human versions of mimesis which will be important to this study. Joseph Brodsky's claim that "the real history of consciousness starts with one's first lie,"[3] whether true or not, implicitly puts in question the definition of consciousness and its relation to mimetic signs. Umberto Eco has even proposed that "the definition of a 'theory of the lie' should be taken as a pretty comprehensive program for a general semiotics."[4] This at the very least suggests how complex and ambitious any serious approach to the topic would have to be.

The Habit of Lying, as its title suggests, is devoted in part to lying and concealment as such, aside from issues surrounding fiction or literature. In the first chapter, for example, I address the problem of lying in moral philosophy, and in the final chapter I address the topic of fashion in relation to dress-concealment. These chapters are crucial to the structure of my overall argument because they situate the "narrower" problem of fiction in a more general social landscape, which is indeed the ultimate focus of the book. But the central section of the book concerns fiction—first (philosophically) in its analytic relation to falsehood and subsequently (literarily) in its relation to both witting deception, which makes it akin to lying, and unwitting deception or error. In this sense (though without necessarily endorsing any of his other implications) my project is in harmony with the most basic thrust of Edward Jayne's "theory of negative poetics . . . based on the simple principle that misrepresentation is fiction's *sine qua non*, its distinctive and most irreducible feature."[5] Jayne "reject[s] Sir Philip Sidney's notion that a [poetic] text tells no lies because it makes no attempt to tell the truth and instead agree[s] with Gerald Graff's argument in *Literature Against Itself* that the distinction between true and false propositions . . . cannot be arbitrarily excluded from literary experience."[6]

My basic claim about the theoretical problem of fiction can be stated equally in the language of Continental philosophy and/or literary theory, for instance that of Paul de Man, and in the logical terms of analytic philosophy, from Russell and Wittgenstein onward. I argue that the problem of fiction casts the opposition between truth and falsehood in a particularly provocative light, showing not only that the issue of falsehood is central to both fictional theory and practice, but also that any attempt to rescue fiction from questions of truth and falsehood only recasts the problem in terms of the even more general opposition between law and arbitrariness. Combining the theoretical work of such authors as René Girard and the fictional practices of Daniel Defoe, Stendhal, and Samuel Beckett, I further claim that the history of the novel demonstrates that this opposition is thoroughly "sacrificial" in character, entailing sacrifices sometimes symbolic and sometimes literal, sometimes explicitly directed against fiction, sometimes seemingly in its favor. As my authors show, the theoretical issues at stake are moreover inseparable from the social and psychological problem of violence more generally, and the abstract relationship between law and arbitrariness, as well as truth and falsehood, devolves here onto the fundamental problem—at once theoretical and practical, philosophical and social—of the relation between rationality and unanimity. In the modern philosophical tradition stretching from Kant to Habermas, this relation is notoriously crucial to conceptions of both theoretical and practical reason, but it is a specific kind of imitative social and/or intellectual unanimity, nota bene, that Girard's theory postulates as the basis of sacrificial violence and the sacred, both in the history of religion and in the putatively secular relation between philosophy and literature.

What has all this, it will be asked, got to do with lying? Well, in such philosophers as Kant and Sissela Bok we discover that the moral problem of lying is defined in remarkably similar terms. These terms not only put in question—and indeed, I will argue, misguidedly beg the question of—the relation between rationality and unanimity, but also link this abstract elation, lo and behold, to the social problem of violence. We shall see, in addition, that the violence characteristically directed both in theory and in practice against the figure of the liar finds its sacrificial-cum-scapegoating counterpart in that violence equally characteristically directed against those who display certain aspects of the truth. I claim that the proscription of lying and the prescription of concealment, in short, are fundamentally complicit, and that the moral problem of deception more generally cannot be properly understood without recognizing that this complicity is fundamental both to most theoretical treatments of the subject and to the basic structure of social practice. Now the prescription of concealment is very obviously illustrated by the history of dress, and by the shifting relation, equally moral and fashionable, between clothing and nudity. Hence the interest of concluding my study with a chapter on theory of dress, which extends the net cast by my investigation to the realm of cultural studies more generally. The topic of fashion clearly brings us back to the issue of mimesis. Moreover, in Shakespeare, whom I use alongside such fashion historians as Anne Hollander and Daniel Roche and theorists such as Roland Barthes, we discover the structure of fashion to be defined in frankly sacrificial terms, organized around mimetic scapegoating. I hope that the very possibility of constructing a theoretical synthesis that extends over such a variegated set of social, literary, and philosophical landscapes, as well as such a far-flung group of thinkers and writers, provides a compelling reason to read on.

My subject, *in nuce*, could thus be said to boil down to relations between three modes of potential falsification: lying, concealment, and fiction. Each domain can of course be studied on its own terms: my treatments of lying in moral philosophy, of fiction in analytic philosophy, of three novelists, and of concealment in fashion theory can be considered to some degree independently. But how they can be compellingly interlinked determines the overall organization and argument of the book. Though my materials are diverse, my overall perspective (more a consequence than a premise of my readings) belongs to an interdisciplinary field that can conveniently be labeled "theory of sacrifice." Sacrifice first and foremost refers to ritual or sacred violence, notably the killing of a human or animal, and does not immediately relate to lying or fiction—symbolic rather than physical acts. But it seems generally agreed that one of the essential structures of sacrifice is that of surrogacy or symbolic substitution—of the sacrificial victim for the whole people, for example, or of the animal for the human— and in writers like Emile Durkheim and René Girard, sacred and sacrificial substitutions can scarcely be separated from the general emergence of symbolization (including language) itself in human development. I shall speak in the following pages of "symbolic" as well as physical sacrifice. Symbolic sacrifice can be conveniently imaged by the Christian mass, where the reenactment of the sacrifice of the Word (Christ) is no longer dealing with human blood or its animal substitutes, but with the symbols or "fictions" of bread and wine. We will see this pattern in Beckett, where the process of fiction-making itself is imaged as a kind of sacrificial behavior, and where fiction is not only associated with falsehood but also metaphorized specifically in terms of a symbolic cannibalism like that of the mass. Though this represents a comically extreme sacrificial formulation, an important part of my project is to develop a theoretical and interpretive net wide enough to clarify what is at stake in texts of this kind.

Aside from authors like Beckett and Kafka, there is a very diverse field of philosophical and theoretical writers—including Kierkegaard, Adorno, Bataille, Derrida, Girard, Serres, and Žižek, among others—who apply sacrificial terminology to essentially symbolic behavior, even, as for instance in Adorno and Horkheimer's *Dialectic of Enlightenment*, to the philosophical construction of "rationality" as such. It is in this general context that I situate my opening thesis that the relation between lying and truth-telling has been characterized, in the West at least, by strongly sacrificial features. According to Horkheimer and Adorno, for example, "so long as individuals are sacrificed, and so long as sacrifice implies the antithesis of collective and individual, deceit will be a constant of sacrifice." Moreover, according to the same authors, "the transformation of sacrifice into subjectivity occurs under the sign of the artifice that was already a feature of sacrifice. In the untruth of artifice, the deceit posited in sacrifice becomes an element of the character."[7] Sacrifice characteristically entails a scapegoat or victim on whom "good violence" is practiced to cure the evil variety. We shall see how insistently Western tradition metaphorizes mendacity as a particularly virulent sort of violence, one that demands punishment by an equally excessive counter-violence. The advocator of lies has certainly been thought of as a violent sacrificer of the most sacred thing—truth—but my emphasis in chapter 1 lies primarily on the problematic dimension of the counter-sacrifice, the scapegoating of the liar.

This scapegoating is revealed in the most theoretically sweeping way when we are confronted with philosophical arguments that condemn all lying without exception. Accordingly I devote the first chapter to Kant, who takes this position on the putative grounds of reason itself, and who even bizarrely argues that liars should be held accountable for murders they did not commit. Here, as we shall see, it makes common sense to say that liars are scapegoated, "sacrificed" on the altar of reason, and indeed threatened with a violence that is far from merely symbolic. (Kant's position is doubtless complicit in the kind of sacrificial rationality criticized by Horkheimer and Adorno in *Dialectic of Enlightenment*.) But beyond common sense—and here is the place to introduce the minimal and rather well known technical vocabulary of my project—the structure of sacrifice and the status of the victim are also strongly characterized by what Durkheim called, in general, "the ambivalence of the sacred," and, more specifically, by the kind of ambivalence that Derrida has diagnosed in the Platonic term *pharmakon* (meaning both poison and remedy, as applied, par excellence, to writing and by extension to the mimetic poetry Socrates expelled from the

Republic) and that the theory of René Girard has generalized to the ambivalence of the *pharmakos*, the sacrificial victim as such, regarded as the source of both evil and its cure.[8] I shall rehearse some of the main features of these relatively well known interpretations in a moment. For the present it suffices to say that both modes of potential deception, lying and concealment, can profitably be regarded as sacrificial *pharmaka* in my account, as mimesis and poetic fiction appear in Plato. The fortunes and reputation of fiction, in addition, have been closely tied to the scapegoating of the liar almost equally when fiction has been arbitrarily conflated with lying, and when it has been categorically opposed to it. In the first case, we may say that fiction appears as the poisonous and guilty side of the *pharmakon/pharmakos* (as we shall see in Defoe for example); in the second (as in Sidney's defense), it is sometimes whitewashed as innocent by definition.

My second opening thesis is that generalized condemnations of lying, such as Kant's, also reveal particularly clearly how—fiction aside for the moment—deception can be regarded as a *pharmakon* whose "bad" side is mendacity, but whose "good" side is a certain sort of concealment. Lying in Kant appears as a "universal principle" of deception condemned as such; it is the form of concealment that is *never* approved. There are obviously forms of concealment such as modesty of dress, on the other hand, that claim quasi-generalized or unanimous approval. What is interesting in Kant is not that specific deceptions are approved or disapproved, but the fact that the liar is made principal scapegoat for all the evils of deception, and that the categorical imperative against lying is a model of Kant's moral imperative in general. While the distinction between actually telling a lie and simply *not* telling (or showing) the truth is often casuistical and tendentious enough in ordinary morality and practice, Kant's absolutization of the principle might be regarded as its philosophical reductio ad absurdum. The scapegoating of the liar is suspect both in itself and in its tendency to evade the question of why such a general condemnation of lying should not also be applied to other forms of deception (such as any kind of concealment that leads to deception), or conversely why, if some kinds of deception are good, why some kinds of lies are not good too. It is also important to my argument, however, that even reasonable and intelligent people who readily admit the latter, like the philosopher Sissela Bok, are not by any means necessarily free of the basic Kantian problem. Beautiful as the truth can be, generalized "biases" in favor of truth are suspect even when they are not nominally absolutist.

It is hardly novel to claim, as has been argued since Plato, that fiction can profitably be considered as a mode of deception either intentional or unintentional. Indeed all three of the novelists I take as exemplary in this project in different ways confirm that position, and oppose the "aesthetic" whitewashing of fiction. However, the simple conflation of fiction (in the literary or colloquial sense) with lying or deception is obviously inadequate or only part of the story: we are concerned with so-called fictions in this study because they reveal as much as they conceal. Before jumping to conclusions on the terrain of literary theory, it will therefore be important to clarify the logical and empirical status of fiction as such, extraliterary as well as literary—the very definition of which, unfortunately, is hardly agreed upon by either logicians or literary theorists. Fiction's logical status will be treated in chapter 2, via Bertrand Russell, Ludwig Wittgenstein, Elizabeth Anscombe, Richard Rorty, and Nelson Goodman, inter alia. Its empirical (as well as theoretical) status will be investigated primarily via Defoe, Stendhal, and Beckett. My general position is that literary fiction offers a particularly exemplary way into the cultural problem of sacrifice, especially symbolic sacrifice, in part because as a mode of "nontruth," like lying, its own definition and situation is strongly marked by sacrificial features. Beckett's *Malone Dies*, for example, offers us a sacrificial model of human symbolisms in which fiction is presented as an essential part. Beckett also provides us with sartorial imagery pointed enough to force us to reconceive the traditional analogy between fiction and dress, considered as modes of concealment, along similarly sacrificial lines.

Though most of this book is derived from texts and authors wholly independent of them, I turn now to certain intersections between Girard and Paul de Man (and to a lesser extent Derrida). I make this aside, first, because it provides an economical way of indicating the general terrain encountered in the subsequent readings, even where my readings are not orthodox to the schools spawned by these theorists. Second, because these readings themselves provide a way to test and (re)interpret some of the central and now rather unfashionably global claims made by de Man and Girard in particular—claims that are not obviously compatible with any of the varieties of contemporary cultural studies or literary postmodernism currently in vogue.[9] And lastly, because—while much of this book could conceivably have been written without reference to either Girard or de Man—I wish to acknowledge an intellectual debt. My results are at least sufficiently both "de Manian" and "Girardian" to confirm their direct relevance to the issues at hand, and perhaps also to put in doubt the opposition (or indifference) between the schools of theory they are generally taken to represent.

I begin with de Man's definition of fiction because it offers us a sacrificial model which hinges on a strictly analytic definition of fiction as arbitrariness (specifically, as we shall see in a moment, between utterances and their referents). Translation and transformation of this definition into the terms of analytic philosophy, which I undertake in chapter 2, confirms de Man's position that fiction (both literary and, just as importantly, extraliterary) is more generally and consistently definable in terms of the relation between law and arbitrariness than merely in terms of truth and falsehood, or of any conventional (for example, "realistic") view of fiction's relation to truth as such. That such a translation is possible is a result worth arguing in itself, inasmuch as it leads to one of those relatively rare results which can be clearly stated in both "Continental" (or "literary") and "analytic" (or "philosophical") language. We shall also see that the threat of arbitrariness is directly related in Kant to the moral problem of lying. Total arbitrariness, one might say, is the consequence of pandemic or fully generalized falsehood, since from a single falsehood it follows in any fully articulated system (such as arithmetic) that everything is true. Only this kind of consideration, as we shall see, can explain Kant's bizarre arguments about liars and murderers, his horror of mendacity—however well-intentioned or happy in its consequences— not only as a breach of law but as a threat to its very coherence. In Defoe, as I have mentioned, we will see a similar horror directed at fiction.

Though (or because) he is invariably emphatic on the subject of literature's deceptive power, de Man's definition of fiction is primly logical. It must be emphasized that the accent here falls as much on system or law as on arbitrariness or chance. (If the world were governed by pure chance, as C. S. Pierce remarked, it would be much more orderly than it is.)[10] Indeed, de Man's own characterization of what he means by textual truth lies wholly on the side of necessity as opposed to chance. Specifically, for example, he cites Hölderlin's "what is true is what is bound to take place," and defines truth as an "empirical and literal event," where "what makes a reading more or less true is simply the predictability, the necessity of its occurrence."[11] Fiction is opposed to truth here, not as falsehood is, but as arbitrariness is opposed to necessity or law: "What makes a fiction a fiction is not some polarization of fact and representation. *Fiction has nothing to do with representation but is the absence of any link between utterance and referent,* regardless of whether this link be causal, encoded, or governed by any other conceivable relationship *that could lend itself to systematization.*"[12]

This definition has nothing directly to do with the problem of nonexistent entities, or with fiction in the usual literary and colloquial sense. De Man accordingly illustrates his point, not by a fiction in any conventional sense, but by a lie recounted by Rousseau in his *Confessions*—the famous lie in which he ruins a servant's life by accusing her of theft. This lie, we are told, differs from ordinary lies in first occurring arbitrarily or accidentally (Marion's name being the first thing to enter Rousseau's head on being accused himself). What matters from our point of view is not the correctness of this interpretation of Rousseau but the model of "fiction" it suggests in relation to both lying and sacrificial violence. The moment of fiction, nota bene, differs from lying only inasmuch as it coincides with a scapegoating of Marion that is entirely arbitrary, aberrant, and unmotivated (which de Man calls a "random lie" as distinct from a lie motivated to deceive). Only in the second moment, that of the cover-up, must this "fiction" be bolstered by Rousseau's lies in the ordinary sense.

Counterintuitive and even bizarre as it appears at first, we will see that de Man's definition of fiction in terms of such a "random lie" finds surprisingly exact parallels in Defoe, Stendhal, and Beckett. Reading these authors reminds us just how little the colloquial notion of fiction—as a basically unproblematic literary category—conforms to the problems that appear in actual literary history. In rejecting fiction understood in terms of the "polarity between fact and representation," we see that de Man's definition effectively redefines fiction in nonliterary terms that could apply to any semiotic field at all—for instance, fashion. His model of fiction also suggests, as it happens, a compelling connection with theoreticians of sacrifice for whom both mimesis—in the imitative sense of fashion rather than the literary sense of representation—and arbitrariness are central topics. De Man's model of fiction is "sacrificial" in the Girardian sense precisely because of the strict arbitrariness of its scapegoat. I have made Girard's theory my central reference as regards sacrificial theory, partly because its basic mechanisms are easily summarized and directly relevant to much of my analysis, partly because he explicitly shares with Derrida the *pharmakon/pharmakos* figure, and partly because his interpretation of Stendhal serves as a specific starting point in chapter 4. But others—notably, for example, Adorno on the subject of sacrificial mimesis in *Aesthetic Theory* or on the relation between sacrifice and aesthetics in *Kierkegaard: Construction of the Aesthetic*—could also serve as reference.[13]

Though I utilize Girard's basic mimetic-sacrificial models, I do not presuppose his most ambitious hypotheses concerning the sacrificial origins of human societies (anthropological hypotheses that lie beyond the scope and competence of this study). For my purposes, which apply his models more locally, we need neither accept nor reject his most controversial hypothesis that the origin and foundation of the sacred, of all primitive religion and social order, is to be found crossculturally in a process of arbitrary scapegoating (an arbitrary mimetic polarization of hostility), which is the basis of sacrificial ritual and myth.[14] It should be mentioned that Girard's early work on the novel, *Mensonge romantique et vérité romanesque*, developed the literary, social, and psychological logic of "mimetic desire" (desire triggered by imitation of others' desires) independently of his subsequent anthropological hypothesis. In his well-known model of "triangular desire," he emphasized the double bind of mimetic desire, since model and obstacle will tend (for instance in erotic love) to coincide: the person whose desire is imitated functions as a *pharmakon* which is both poison and remedy. The later Girard's full-blown mimetic-sacrificial theory is a more ambitious synthesis, stating that when mimetic rivalry observed in the primates became too strong to be governed by animal mechanisms of dominance and submission, when the already proto-human society was threatened by its own increasing mimetic powers and reciprocal violence, it developed a new mechanism—the "curative" experience of mimetic unanimity directed against an essentially arbitrary scapegoat. For Girard, whatever else it may be, human history is the history of the legalization, in every sense, of sacrificial arbitrariness.

The mimetic ambivalence of the Girardian *pharmakos* or scapegoat—the problem of whether it should be imitated or not—derives from its (mis)interpretation by the sacrificers both as malign source of the original "mimetic crisis" and as incarnating its transcendent cure. In Girard's anthropology, the false transcendence of the sacred scapegoat (made sacred to the extent, often, of being divinized in myth) is never entirely false. Source of sacred ambivalence, in Durkheim's sense, of good and evil, order and disorder, and so on, the foundational principle is interpreted by so-called primitive man (by "sacrificial" man more generally) in terms which are both true and false—and which, in Girard's hypothesis, are basic not only to the original development of conceptions of true and false, but also to the relations between truth and falsehood in primitive fiction or myth.[15] The truth of the primitive interpretation that the sacrificial process is at the heart of sacred order depends on the blindness that mistakes the arbitrariness of that process for law: law derives from arbitrariness, as truth derives from insight into the original error. As in de Man's definition of fiction, only as insight into this error develops is the sacrifice in need of bolstering by lies. Girard's sacrificial process turns out to be the history, as de Man puts it in his exposition of Rousseau's theory of language, of "a lie superimposed upon an error"[16]—a history, in short, in which the truth of sacrifice leads to what we might call *the sacrifice of truth*.

The essential aspect of Girard's theory for this project is the mimetic model, since it is this that determines the arbitrariness of the sacrificial process, where an arbitrary origin takes on the character of law by sheer force of imitative unanimity. We will see that the issue of unanimity (and the double binds associated with it) is important to relations both between falsehood and fiction, and between lying and concealment. As he himself stresses, however, we do not need Girard to encounter models of sacrificial violence in which mimesis is quite central and explicit. Beckett is a case in point, as is, perhaps to a slightly lesser degree, Stendhal, one of the main players in Girard's own early work. Defoe, Stendhal, and Beckett are my major literary examples because each shows in a different way, and with increasing self-consciousness and complexity, how his fictions (and lies) function in the more general symbolic order of sacrifice. Shakespeare, similarly, plays an important role in my final chapter on fashion because he provides an exemplary mimetic scapegoat model of fashion itself. This chapter can be regarded as a kind of empirical application or test of my philosophical and literary interpretations in the domain of cultural studies at large. A theory of fashion—which is by definition mimetic—is obviously crucial to the field of cultural studies if it is to have any authority over mimetic phenomena more generally, the phenomena by which any culture is transmitted.

It is worth stressing that the Girardian-Derridean moral of "Plato's Pharmacy"—concerning the emergence of philosophy out of the sacrificial expulsion of mimetic fiction—raises the mimetic dimension of Girard's account to the second power, since mimesis itself has become both the name of the expelled and the model in the name of which the expulsion takes place. This raising to the second power is also true of de Man's conception of fiction, since fiction is not only identified with an arbitrary scapegoating, it is also subject to the kind of *pharmakon*-ambivalence that characterizes the scapegoat, judged alternately as "the most cruel" and "the most innocent" (as de Man cites Hölderlin) "of all activities."[17] On the other hand, I by no means wish to exaggerate the theoretical harmony between de Man, Girard, and Derrida. On the contrary, what I emphasize about their intersection is all the more striking if we bear in mind their otherwise significant differences. It is worth observing, in particular, that my rapprochement of de Man and Girard can be contrasted with and even opposed to Derrida, with whom de Man is usually compared.[18]

For example, in "The Theater of Cruelty and the Closure of Representation," Derrida's conception of the relation of fiction to violence stresses the *"closure of representation"* as "fatal," as a kind of "play [which] is cruelty as the unity of necessity and chance";[19] while de Man's definition of fiction as arbitrariness, he insists, *"has nothing to do with representation"* (my emphases). Indeed, while de Man and Derrida are often regarded by fans and detractors alike as the major representatives of Deconstruction, it is well to remember that de Man also defined irony (a key term for him) very pointedly, in the closing lines of *Allegories of Reading* (1979), as the "undoing of the deconstructivist allegory of all tropological cognitions"[20]—the undoing, in short, of deconstructive understanding. De Man further defined irony, directly associated with the "random lie" in Rousseau, as "permanent parabasis" (a definition lifted from Friedrich Schlegel)—the continual or omnipresent entrance of the real into fiction.[21] De Man's conception of irony therefore reverses the popular conception of Deconstruction as endlessly unmasking the fictional or metaphysical constitution of supposed "truth" or "reality." "Permanent parabasis" implies, rather, that it is "fiction" more than "truth" which is the fiction. Moreover, like Girard's conception of sacrificial scapegoating in terms of the origin of signification as well as its consequence, de Man's appeal to "the implications of the random lie in the Marion episode"[22] concerns, not simply the intentionally false representation of Marion as guilty of theft, but what he calls "the absolute randomness of language *prior to any figuration or meaning.*"[23] This establishes a strict homology with the Girardian model of sacrificial origins. Fiction is imaged here in the stark act of nomination—in the name Marion, designation of the scapegoat—rather than any particular false or fictitious representation as such.

Before moving to the body of my project, I should perhaps emphasize that neither fiction nor the sacrificial process, respectively so conceived by de Man and Girard, leads *only* to distasteful consequences. On the contrary, like lying and concealment themselves, both not only underlie many of the pleasurable aspects of psychological experience and social life, but also provide a practically indispensable basis for theoretical insight. Since I am aware that my coupling of Girard and de Man will likely remain controversial with some readers, I should mention that their relation is further briefly discussed in an appendix, and again in my conclusion. What matters here is not to harmonize their projects as a whole, but to illuminate specific aspects of the model they share in common—which is not something that can be accomplished merely in the abstract. Defoe, Stendhal, and Beckett will provide successive illustrations of de Man's conception of fiction as "random lie" that become more complex in proportion to the degree of historical development and self-reflection that the novel attains in different periods—prerealist, realist, and postrealist (to put it very roughly and provisionally, since the inadequacy of the concept of realism will be implicit throughout)—and to the complexity, variegation, and systematic character of the more general sacrificial landscape these authors unfold. Finally, Shakespeare's depiction of fashion as an arbitrary indictment (or scapegoating) will provide a rather spectacular basis for the generalization of this conception of fiction to cultural life more generally.

PART ONE

PHILOSOPHY

1

The Liar as Scapegoat:

Rationality and Unanimity

■

He who does not have the good intention to tell a lie is hopelessly lost.
—ROBERT WALSER

Kant, an important guide to the broadest issues in this study, provides us with a brilliant model of what I have called the theoretical scapegoating of the liar—one that is particularly exemplary inasmuch as it occurs at the threshold of "enlightened" modernity. By indicating that it is ultimately not deception as such that is at issue in his condemnation of lying (one might mislead the potential murderer as to the whereabouts of his victim, to take Kant's example, as much by concealment or other means as by outright mendacity), but rather irrationality or arbitrariness, Kant also provides us with a framework generalized enough for a systematic study of the relation between lying and fiction. In brief, Kant's extraordinarily analytic stress on the arbitrariness of mendacity will prepare us for the analytic arbitrariness of fiction explored later.

Since Kant's position on lying may now seem eccentric to say the least, it is equally important to my argument to show in some detail that much saner and more plausible philosophers on the subject do not escape the basic Kantian problem that leads to what I have called the "sacrifice" of the liar. Hence Sissela Bok, whose *Lying* has been called a "seminal book"[1] in modern theory, is almost as important as Kant to the present considerations. I have taken her as a friendly scapegoat, so to speak, precisely because her work is so useful, especially on the subject of lying and violence.

I have also chosen these two authors because they represent putatively rational philosophies of mendacity which appear to some degree orthodox, normative, or representative of ordinary opinion in their periods and local contexts.[2] Admittedly, Kant's position that mendacity is *never* justified could hardly have been accepted quite literally even by most of his own contemporaries, except perhaps insofar as it was grafted onto a Christian conception of inevitable or original sin. However, while Kant's view may now appear to us frankly lunatic, I shall argue that it nevertheless—or for this very reason—gets to the theoretical heart of the matter. This is the relation so stressed by Kant between rationality and unanimity, and between the rule and the exception.

Whereas Kant takes exception to lying in an almost fanatical way, Sissela Bok, by contrast, seems eminently reasonable in arguing that we should lie only in exceptional circumstances and for good reason. If one desires a practical moral guide to mendacity, Bok is doubtless much to be preferred to Kant. But for theoretical clarity—however tragicomic in its practical upshot—Kant remains exemplary, and Bok's central arguments remain open to Kantian objections. Her very good sense in rejecting Kant, one might say, partially blinds her to what she shares with Kant and his most important insights.[3] But as an erudite and intelligent exponent of what is a morally normative and common-sensical point of view, she teaches us a great deal about lying, and especially, as I have said, about its relation to violence.

Though Bok's *Lying* contains little about fiction as such, it does represent the commonsensical view that the problem, at least in this context, is easily disposed of by "the fact that fiction does not *intend* to mislead, that it calls for what Coleridge called 'a willing suspension of disbelief,' which is precisely what is absent in ordinary deception."[4] In conclusion I evoke a tradition which puts this view in doubt. But the general problem of fiction must be postponed until chapter 2.

Lying

Kant and Bok strive in contrasting but comparable ways to justify the common view (perhaps more preached than practiced) that lying should "in general" be proscribed and avoided. What "in general" means is the crucial issue. For Kant, this prohibition meant a rule without exceptions, like a scientific law, a paradigm of the categorical imperative (which he defined as a synthetic a priori law). For Bok, it means a "general" rule punctuated by exceptions: "a presumption against lies," on the grounds that "trust in some degree of veracity functions as the *foundation* of relations among human beings."[5] Though this "foundation" is presumed rather than demonstrated—and the claim to "*some degree* of veracity" is in any case a very weak one—Bok nevertheless shares with Kant the positing of a supposedly general or fundamental rule against mendacity.

My aim here is not to justify mendacity "in general"—though I am resigned (if I can escape a lynching) to the likelihood of being suspected of such a project. Instead, I maintain it is the very concept of generality and unanimity that is problematic in this context, and that neither the practical nor theoretical problems associated with lying can be grasped adequately in isolation from conventions surrounding concealment and fiction—conventions, such as modesty of dress and the "suspension of disbelief," that also characteristically claim and depend on quasi-unanimous acceptance. The distinction between lying and concealment, in particular, is one dear and indeed indispensable to self-proclaimed truth-tellers and their theoretical champions. It allows them to get away with theoretical murder—and sometimes murder, as we shall see, that is more than a mere figure of speech. Typically, lying is violently proscribed in almost the same breath (as we shall see in Defoe, for example) that concealment is violently prescribed. The absolute Kantian proscription merely crystallizes the issue by making lying into the unambiguously poisonous side of the *pharmakon* of concealment generally, considered alternately as poison and remedy.

Concealment of course differs formally from lying, regarded as an attempt to deceive by the actual articulation of falsehood, but all lying in this sense is a form of concealment (of the truth). Conversely, even the values of privacy and discretion, forms of concealment usually praised, typically encourage deception: "No man can be secret, except he give himself a little scope for dissimulation; which is, as it were, but the skirts or train of secrecy."[6] If Francis Bacon is correct here about the necessary relation of concealment and dissimulation, no moral condemnation of dissimulation or deception can justify a general condemnation of mendacity unless it goes for concealment too (including, of course, "lies of omission"). No general rule can state in advance which mode of concealment (mere concealment or actual mendacity) might lead to greater deception in given circumstances—though it has been claimed that habitual liars and impostors seem often to engage in self-defeating behavior, making them bad deceivers, whereas concealers may often be more successful.[7] Kant's tragicomic prohibition of lying under *any* circumstances is illuminating because it elevates to transcendental purity a more commonplace scapegoating of the liar, who now plays the role of intellectual *pharmakos* at the hands of reason itself.

Bok's *Lying*, though in almost every conceivable way distant from the sacrificial terrain we have borrowed from Girard, de Man, and Derrida, nonetheless makes the initial point needed for my argument when she repeatedly draws attention to the striking "parallel between deception and violence" in Western thought: "Both violence and deception are means not only to unjust coercion, but also to self-defense and survival."[8] Her claim that "deceit and violence . . . are *the* two forms of deliberate assault on human beings"[9] illustrates how lying is considered not only as a *kind* of mental or symbolic violence, but as the very *model* of such violence. This is economically summed up by the clown in *Othello*: "for one to say a soldier lies, is stabbing."[10] Shakespeare's triple pun suggests a direct relation between violence and mendacity (to accuse a soldier of lying is like stabbing him), as well as forms of symbolic violence (the "stabbings" and "lyings" associated with intercourse), and also a witty *pharmakon*-ambivalence: to accuse a soldier of lying is like stabbing him, but so is revealing where he *lies* concealed from potential stabbers. This, as we shall see, is the very same kind of example used by Kant.

Bok aligns herself with what she presents as the moderate view of Aristotle, taking "as an initial premise Aristotle's view that lying is 'mean and culpable' and that truthful statements are preferable to lies in the absence of special considerations."[11] The generalization that lying is mean and culpable admittedly hardly approaches the generalized violence we can find elsewhere directed against lying. Take Martin Buber, for example: "The lie is the specific evil which man introduced into nature. All our deeds of violence and our misdeeds are only as it were a highly-bred development of what this or that creature of nature is able to achieve in its own way. But the lie is our very own invention."[12] Though nature regularly exhibits pretty spectacular displays of deception, not to speak of deceptive behavior that has all the appearance of intentionality,[13] Buber insisted on lying as *the* human sin. By implication, lying is worse than mere violence, which is shared with the animal world; it is the distinctively human violence. Similarly, though his view was supposedly deduced from reason not religion, Kant could not resist pointing out that Satan had to lie before Cain was able to kill. Even Montaigne, usually so moderate and urbane, made a show of violence against the liar: "If we recognized the horror and gravity of lying, we should persecute it with fire more justly than other crimes."[14] Montaigne also notes the properly sacrificial character of religious responses to lying: "Certain nations of the new Indies offered to their gods human blood, but only such as was drawn from their tongue and ears, in expiation of the sin of falsehood, *heard as well as uttered.*"[15] The apogee of this scapegoating tendency is perhaps represented by Defoe's Robinson Crusoe (discussed in chapter 3), who condemns lying more harshly even than murder.

The idea that mendacity is, so to speak, the deepest source of human violence, *more violent than violence itself*—and should thus be countered by maximum "good" violence—leads in a seamless manner to the classic Enlightenment question of whether one should lie to murderers. Kant's categorical "no" to this question, as I have said, elevates the problem to the level of tragicomedy. But, as Bok recounts, the murderer example was notorious and merely inherited by Kant. A conspicuously sane Dr. Johnson, for example, adduced it as an exception to what he called the "general rule" against lying. Cardinal Newman, on the other hand, later argued that Johnson would probably not have followed his own theory, preferring rather to fight the murderer than lie to him! In Kant, unjust violence is seemingly preferred (permit murder rather than lie); in Newman, just violence.[16]

These manly sacrifices to the gods of truth find a more amiable parallel in St. Augustine's account of a man who lies for others' benefit. While Augustine admits that such a man is probably unusually good, he nevertheless feels compelled to define his lies as sins, thus reversing the model of mendacity Bok associates with Machiavelli, where lies do good to the deceiver and evil to the deceived. One feels in St. Augustine something akin to Robinson Crusoe's position on clothing, which might be described as the paradox of original sin: perfect human beings would not need the "good evils" of dress-concealment or benevolent lies. Augustine's recommendation that such lies be simultaneously condemned and pardoned has all the ambivalence of the *pharmakon.*[17]

Bok's keen eye for the violent aura of the lie is consistent with her laudable philosophical aim to desacralize and defetishize the morality of mendacity. On the other hand, her claim that lying and violence are *the* "two forms of deliberate assault on human beings" may be accused of exaggerating the analogy in a manner that resembles the irrational and sacrificial perspectives she criticizes. Judith Shklar's *Ordinary Vices*, by contrast, emphasizes the distinction and even opposition between violence and mendacity in its plea for a reversal of the conventional tendency to rank the prohibition of lying and hypocrisy over the prohibition of cruelty.[18] Doubtless avoiding cruelty would rank high, too, among the more protean "special considerations" invoked by Bok as justification for lying—though I shall later point out a significant moment in her account where the values of force and truth seem ominously dependent. The connection between lying and violence is so deep, as we shall see, in part because *truth and force are both modalities of law.*[19]

Another disappointing aspect of Bok's excellent emphasis on the "striking parallel between deception and violence" is her tendency to define this relation in terms of the opposition between two basic attitudes: one, "seen from the perspective of those affected by lies and by assaults," which attempts to prohibit or at least limit violence and deception by law and other means; the other a "celebration" of violence and lies associated by her with Machiavelli, for example, and Nietzsche.[20] That affirmations of cruelty and lies are frequently linked in Nietzsche cannot be denied. It is accordingly tempting to regard Kant and Nietzsche as neatly summarizing *pharmakon* violence on each side of the truth/lie polarity in post-Enlightenment philosophy—whether in terms of the malingering sacralization implicit in Kant's "sacred decree of reason"[21] to tell the truth, or of the openly Dionysiac and sacrificial appeals of the self-styled Anti-Christ.[22] But the trouble with Bok's emphasis is that, when push comes to shove, she associates "celebration" of the liar *generally* with oppression and the victors' point of view, and the celebration of truthfulness *generally* with the victims' point of view ("those affected by lies and assaults"). Far from being a "universal principle" (as we saw in Kafka), lying is universally "presumed against" by Bok on the grounds, as we have seen, that "trust in some degree of veracity functions as the *foundation* of relations among human beings." But doesn't it follow that "trust in some degree of mendacity" must also function as the foundation of such relations? ("According to Marie Vasek [1986], a psychologist who has studied the development of lying in children, 'The skills required in deception are also used in being compassionate and co-ordinating our actions with those of others, and without them human society might not exist.' ")²³ But Bok provides no "presumption" against truthfulness on this account—perhaps because she somehow assumes the "degree of veracity" to be greater than 50 percent?²⁴

In contrast to Kant's universally valid categorical imperative, which claims unanimous consent of all rational beings, Bok's general rule is punctuated by "special considerations"; but no convincing argument is given why these exceptions are not quite as general in their application, whether quantitatively or qualitatively, as the rule itself. Bok appeals to Aristotle, and why not? But then why not equally cite Plato's appeal to noble lies as the foundation of the republic? I shall argue that Bok's appeal to a spurious "foundational" generality, like Kant's to a spurious unanimity, is really only a pseudorational counterpart of the sacrificial identification of mendacity with violence (and its symbolic equivalent, moral and intellectual chaos). It does not even guide us out of the classical opposition represented by Plato and Aristotle.

Though she appeals to Aristotle, Bok's position might also be described as a kind of democratized Kantianism (though of a kind that Kant would naturally have found untenable).²⁵ Her rationale for telling lies, "as a last resort," appeals to the principle of hypothetical public justification: on each occasion Bok's liar is to imagine a vindication of his or her lies before a court of rational public opinion. The absolute and actual rational unanimity demanded by Kant's categorical imperative is thus watered down into a hypothetical, democratic one. Bok does not go into hypothetical detail, but her utopian model seems to be an imaginary supreme court of wise men and women who unanimously, or at least by majority vote, approve all deceptions secretly revealed to them; or perhaps an imaginary court composed of all rational men and women, past, present, and future.

Were not the relation of "good" men and women to "rational" ones so obviously at stake in this scenario, the apparently commonsensical upshot of Bok's view might be regarded as a secular variant of St. Augustine's: if you lie, lie in a good cause and as little as possible, given your other moral concerns. But since what is at stake is not only the coincidence of morality and rationality, but also the relation between rationality and unanimity so crucial to Kant, it is appropriate here to consider Kantian objections—which would, I think, be at least twofold. First, such an imaginary Bokian court is obviously a surrogate for oneself, the liar, idealized as a purely rational being. Second, even if this were not so, no such court of public opinion could shuffle off the problem of the unanimity demanded by reason, even if such a court happened to be unanimous in any given case (since this might be fortuitous), or if first-level disagreement were always democratically resolved in the metalevel unanimity that recognized the court's voting authority. Of course, if we imagine a public composed of people so enlightened as to always agree, this objection would be weakened, but only at the cost of returning Bok squarely to the first objection (since now every rational person, including oneself, is imagined as partaking in such enlightened unanimity). Kant's point, by contrast, would be that Bok's projection of the problem of the relation between the rule and the exception to the arena of public justification really only evades facing this problem, as Kant certainly does head on, in the private one. For Kant, as we shall shortly see more dramatically, there can be no "exceptions" to law except unlawfulness and arbitrariness.

Bok's admission that lies are sometimes desirable in intimate and cordial relations, and her suggestive comparison of this situation to a game in which both sides agree on the rules,[26] demonstrates that she is as concerned as Kant with unanimity—and with metalevel unanimity where first-level agreement and transparency are lacking. But where Kantian unanimity follows from rationality, Bokian rationality seems to follow from the exercise of public justification. In this context, we may recall Kant's admonitory definition of pure democracy as a form of despotism, indeed the most arbitrary form, since " 'all,' who are not quite all, decide, and this is a contradiction of the general will with itself and with freedom."[27] Sensitive to the objection that a purely hypothetical appeal to the rational public is not likely to improve upon an actual appeal to oneself in the putative guise of reason, and proposing to supplement her imaginary court with actual consultations among relevant groups, Bok admits that this kind of objection based on the "tyranny of majority" argument is "extremely important," particularly when the actual as opposed to a hypothetical (rational) public is appealed to. But, she argues, "it matters only for certain kinds of deception, for no public can discriminate against dupes in general without also discriminating against itself."[28] There, once more invoking the slippery loophole of "generality"—and, crucially, without specifying how these "certain kinds" are to be limited in their generality—her basic theoretical argument seems to rest.

Despite the insane practical consequences of Kant's own general prohibition of lying, I think that Kantian objections to Bok's theory must be accepted in some form or another. For even if we accept, as Kant did not, that moral relations between truthfulness and mendacity, between Bok's rule and exception, could be decided by appeal on a case-by-case basis to "rational democracy" (supposing such a thing were convincingly defined), Kant would respond that precisely this appeal demonstrates that the prior "presumption" against mendacity cannot be assumed to be general, presumptive, or foundational in the sense (or senses) Bok insists on. Moreover, her limitation of the danger of majority tyranny to what she rather vaguely calls "certain kinds of deception" is itself potentially deceptive inasmuch as the quantitative and qualitative range of such "kinds" cannot be specified in advance, or independently of the imagined process of public justification itself. From the Kantian point of view, Bok's axiomatic presumption in favor of truthfulness—precisely the point where she seems most Kantian, and where indeed she might well receive the *overt* blessing of the public majority—must thus be condemned as theoretical despotism.

I have no wish to scapegoat Bok for harboring any more despotic motive than I in approaching this difficult subject. Yet if we compare her to Judith Shklar, as I have mentioned, we find both that Shklar recognizes mendacity as an alternative to violence as well as analogous to violence—suggesting what we are calling its *pharmacological* possibilities—and that no condemnation of mendacity in general is theoretically affirmed (her moral target being, rather, cruelty in general). Interestingly enough, moreover, there is at least one significant place in Bok's discussion of the legitimacy of "paternalistic lies" to children where one may imagine a sharp protest from Shklar: "Crises . . . should call forth paternalistic deception only if persuasion and *force* are useless."[29] Force is not yet cruelty, of course; but in this generalized appeal to force, we may suggest, Bok returns for a moment to the basically Kantian roots she appears to bypass via Aristotle. What is especially Kantian here is the complicity of force and truth as modalities of law—a complicity highlighted by the fact that both the categorical imperative and causality are synthetic a priori in the Kantian system.

Despite virulent objections, Kant might have accepted Bok's position as at least barely rational (since denial of the synthetic a priori, according to him, can never lead to a contradiction) if she gave up both her presumption of truthfulness and her appeal to merely hypothetical rational unanimity. (But this, of course, would be to give up the twin foundations of her own claims to rationality.) The Kantian conception of rational unanimity is especially crucial in this context, not only because it is the social equivalent of a law without exceptions, but because *mendacity itself posits a cognitive discrepancy or non-unanimity between subjects.* This is essentially why Kant's demand for unanimity coincides with an absolute prohibition of mendacity, and why, moreover, this particular imperative appears as a paradigm of the moral imperative in general.[30] For Kant, the claim to rational unanimity on any given topic makes no sense unless it is an *actual* claim—and here, I think, we are forced to agree with him, even though his generalization of the idea of rational unanimity in truth-telling is one of the main targets of this analysis. For if we concede that reason demands unanimity of "rational thinkers" by definition (whether in the orthodox transcendental sense of Kant, or, for that matter, in the sense of those modern pragmatisms that define "reasonableness" in terms of consensus), this is nevertheless applicable only to definite, actual judgments—the claim that others should agree, after all, is made by everyone who purports to be making a decisive argument—not to situations in which hypothetical grounds for unanimity are merely "presumed." The Kantian error lies not in equating rationality and unanimity in the abstract, but in generalizing an actual claim to unanimity in transcendental terms that are rationally unacceptable (and practically damaging). It lies not in denying the coherence of a Bokian rule or presumption with exceptions, but in refusing, as we shall see, all *exceptionality* in the sense of arbitrariness or contingency. With a kind of insane lucidity, Kant indicates what must be given up to construct any alternative at all to his position: what must be given up is the "general" presumption against lying as such.

Were it not for its practical implications, as I have said, the global structure of Kant's argument would be ideally comic. Surely his prohibition of mendacity in *any* circumstances was intended as a joke—or, better, as a "noble lie" constructed out of fear of mendacity's mimetic contageousness! He not only vehemently prohibits lies to murderers, but claims that lying reduces human beings to an inhuman status.[31] We could hardly hope for a more explicitly sacrificial account of reason and mendacity both, where unanimity is explicitly demanded as an essential ingredient of the sacrifice—including, by implication, the assent of the murder's victim. Emile Durkheim was surely on target to imply, in *The Elementary Forms of Religious Life*, that the unanimity demanded by Kant's imperative is more readily connected to that mimetic unanimity which is (according to Durkheim) a general goal of primitive ritual, than to the individualistic tendencies of eighteenth-century Protestantism with which Kant's philosophy is often understandably associated.[32] Kant's "sacred command of reason" to tell the truth, as he himself says, cannot be reduced to any particular religious belief, but has the sacrificial form of the sacred in general.

Kant's argument has the theoretical virtue of outlining the relation of rationality and unanimity with exemplary clarity. The *Critique of Practical Reason* makes universalizability into a negative test of the imperative: one should not act on principles that would be invalid if everyone acted upon them, as if they were laws of nature. Since synthetic a priori laws cannot be proven according to Kant (their denial cannot lead to a contradiction), the legality of the imperative is established instead in terms of the consequences of unanimous acceptance of the law, *as if everyone imitated everyone else*. Because Kant's ethics are notoriously and indeed sacrificially anti-utilitarian, indifferent to *actual* consequences, "consequences" here means "consequences for reason." But the principle of unanimity has also been extended to utilitarian modes of analysis, for instance in R. F. Harrod's "Utilitarianism Revised," which offers a "refined utilitarianism" claiming to embody the Kantian principle: "an act which is expedient in the circumstances but would be inexpedient when done by all in precisely similar circumstances must be judged to be wrong."[33]

Without stopping to interrogate what is meant by "precisely similar circumstances" in the utilitarian scheme, we may note that Lewis White Beck criticizes Kant's anti-utilitarian *Critique* for speaking of universalizable "actions" instead of "maxims," the locution employed in his *Foundation of the Metaphysics of Morals*:

> This is an inaccuracy in the *Critique*. If lying were universal, we should be able to get along far better than in this world, where it is only frequent; we should simply interpret affirmative sentences negatively and negative ones affirmatively. But if the *maxim* is to deceive another person, the best way of doing it is by sometimes telling the truth and sometimes not. . . . A maxim like "I should lie" depends for its effectiveness upon the fact that it is not universal, that its theoretical correlate "I lie" is not universalizable into a judgment, "All men always lie"; for, if it were, there would be no such thing as a lie at all. One's lies show mendacity and cleverness only *because they are exceptions* to a general rule. But general rules which have exceptions are not laws of nature; the latter have no exceptions.[34]

Though Beck's main point about maxims and actions is crucial, it is nevertheless worth adding that we might or might *not* "get along far better" in a world of universal mendacity where "we should simply interpret affirmative sentences negatively and negative ones affirmatively." For not only does this presuppose that being permanently confronted with truths (deduced by negation) would mean "getting along better," but it also implies, assuming that deception were not entirely abolished in such a world, that replacing the deceptions of outright mendacity with more devious modes of concealment would necessarily improve matters.[35] The preference for concealment over mendacity, as I have said, belongs to a package of social, moral, and intellectual strategies which often pass without adequate analysis. Beck's main point, however, is precisely on target, and his use of Kant's term "maxim" seems to translate as "aim" or "desire" (as in "the maxim to deceive"). Shorn of its a priori foundation, the imperative might thus be described as concerning itself *with the consequences for practical reason of unanimous desire*. No wonder, then, that the imperative exhibits the kind of double bind that Durkheim and Girard associate with mimetic unanimity.

Note, moreover, that Beck's Kantian alignment of deception with exceptionality should not be mistaken for Bok's. For even supposing we grant the coherence of her idea of a general "presumption" over Kantian objections, there is no reason that the general presumption should not favor lies, with truth-telling as the exception. (This is indeed proverbially the case.) Nor need we deny the social importance—as distinct from its theoretical validity—so often stressed by psychologists and sociologists, of "a general norm of truthfulness"[36]—even, or perhaps especially, if the putative norm were itself a lie, a falsification of the actual state of affairs. A "schizophrenic" attitude, as it has been called,[37] is to be expected toward deception.

Here we come to the rub. Nowhere is the concern with *exceptionality* in every sense more evident than in Kant's notorious reply to Benjamin Constant, "On a Supposed Right to Lie from Altruistic Motives":

> [The] benevolent lie *may*, however, by *accident* (*casus*) become punishable even by civil laws; and that which escapes liability to punishment only by accident may be condemned as wrong even by external laws. For instance, if you have *by a lie* hindered a man who is even now planning a murder, you are legally responsible for all the consequences. . . . It is possible that whilst you have answered Yes to the murderer's question, whether his intended victim is in the house, the latter may have gone out unobserved, and so not have come in the way of the murderer, and the deed therefore not have been done; whereas, if you lied and said he was not in the house, and he had really gone out (though unknown to you), so that the murderer met him as he went, and executed his purpose on him, then you might with justice be accused as the cause of his death.[38]

This is surely a passage of comic genius rather than rational philosophy. (It seems to confirm the old jest that philosophy is best considered as a branch of satire, and resembles, for example, Flann O'Brien's *The Third Policeman*, wherein the murderer is accused by the police of murder quite by accident.)[39] What is at stake here, in short, is an extraordinarily overt affirmation of a sacrificial mechanism which *legalizes accident*. Once arbitrariness has been introduced in the guise of falsehood, Kant implies, there is no stopping it: lying "vitiates the source of law itself."[40] Note particularly, moreover, that his own response consists essentially *in reproducing the thing it fears*—the very legalization of accident and contingency that he rejects outright in benevolent lies. If the victim is killed perchance as a result of the benevolent lie, says Kant, the liar may be held accountable for murder. And to cap the entire masterpiece of logic, Kant's first sentence here allows us to hold the benevolent liar accountable for the victim's death even if the victim by chance escapes unharmed!

This passage demonstrates beyond all doubt to what extent Kant identified the principle of lying with arbitrariness as such. That total unanimity should be demanded to approve such a purely arbitrary sacrifice by Kant—of both the liar himself and the murderer's victim— also confirms the suggestiveness of Durkheim's view of the Kantian imperative. Since Kant's "good" or "sacred" argument consists in reproducing and developing the arbitrariness of its "bad" target to the utmost degree, we have here, elevated to the terrain of reason, precisely the kind of sacrificial *pharmakon* structure identified by Girard and Derrida, a structure that is also linked by Girard to Durkheim's notion of sacred ambivalence.[41] Nor can Kant's argument be considered a mere reductio ad absurdum of the liar's position, since elsewhere in the same passage even the Kantian truth-teller is defended on the grounds that he might have saved the victim *by chance*!

Denied by his own synthetic a priori theory the possibility of a genuine reductio ad absurdum of the argument of the "good liar," Kant opts for a kind of homeopathic equivalent that amounts to sacrificial exclusion.[42] What is truly extraordinary about this, however, is the almost heroic way in which he seems to go out of his way to elaborate the consequences of his moral theory in their most unacceptable form. (We will see something similar in Defoe's theory of fiction.) Far from evading, as Bok arguably does, what is at stake in conceiving lying as fundamentally "exceptional," Kant does everything to highlight the problem. Whereas Bok leaves unsolved at best how rationality and public opinion are to be reconciled, Kant stresses to the utmost not only the incommensurability of moral rationality and empirical concerns in his sense, but also the practical contradiction between rational unanimity and actual opinion. The worlds of speculative and practical reason in Kant's framework are simultaneously absolutely compatible and absolutely incompatible. (Durkheim remarks on Kant's perspicuity in making "the speculative reason and the practical reason two different aspects of the same faculty," but also stresses the "violence" of the contradiction between the individual and the collective determinations of reason that escapes Kantian explanation.)[43] However unfortunate the practical consequences, Kant's system has the merit of stating this double bind logically, since neither affirmation nor negation of the imperative can lead to a contradiction. Both incompatible possibilities (that truth-telling is a "general" rule, or the negation of this) are logically valid, and it is against this generalized kind of threat to reason, regularity, and conventional morality that not only Kant's but also Bok's neo-Aristotelian position can be seen a defense.

Finally in this connection, since I am arguing that the broader issue of concealment is crucial to understanding the sacrificial dynamics of lying, it is worth considering how a phenomenon like dress-concealment—as governed both by law or morality, and by mimesis, fashion, or habit—might fare in the Bokian court. Note that dress, unlike lying, is governed *quite actually* by Bok's principle of "public justification," and indeed by more coercive forms of public prescription and proscription. But the "rationality" that derives from this publicity is dubious to say the least, and Bok's approach to the justification of mendacity would seem more obviously circular if extended to dress-concealment. We will see that Defoe's Robinson Crusoe admits to just such a circularity when, failing to provide adequate positive arguments for modesty, he deduces a "rational" presumption in favor of *habit* (pun intended). In these terms, one wonders whether Bok's approach to mendacity does not similarly boil down to a kind of unintended conservatism—whereas Kant's, if taken seriously, would be impossibly radical.

Fiction

We do not have the space or resources here, unfortunately, to consider Kant's position on fiction in the *Critique of Judgment*, which would be necessary to follow our overall topic, the relation of lying and fiction, through to the end in Kant. It is worth recalling, however, that Kant himself conceived pure and practical reason as a duality in need of mediation by judgment. (Beauty as "symbol of morality" and the sublime, its violent twin,[44] are primary mediators in Kant's system between freedom and necessity, between the synthetic a priori laws of practical reason such as the imperative, and those of pure reason such as causality or force.) Thus the overall architecture of the system implies that moral issues in general, and the paradigmatic imperative against lying in particular, cannot be properly dealt with in abstraction from the problem of artistic fiction, since this is part of the problem of aesthetic judgment more generally, and emphatically cannot be solved in Kant merely by appeal to notions like Coleridge's "suspension of disbelief."

Sissela Bok's appeal to Coleridge, however, deserves brief consideration here, since it is central to her contention (tacit and not so tacit) that the "general" problem of lying and deception can be adequately understood without considering fiction a very significant issue. The danger of confusing fiction with lying is mentioned by Bok in connection with telling children stories, or "sharing their leaps between fact and fancy." Admittedly, a lengthy footnote explains that "the confusion of fiction and deception has long antecedents," from Plato on, and that fiction and deception can of course be mixed. But however much the court of public opinion matters to her in other contexts, the impressive lineage of this theoretical "confusion"—which must surely have had practical consequences for how fiction-makers, including Plato, actually practiced their art—does little to modify her view that "fiction and lying are in themselves quite separate."[45] Even if this is meant to be a purely technical distinction, it clearly presupposes an adequate definition of fiction "in itself"—the thorny problem I address in chapter 2. But, that presupposed, it still does not explain how the technical distinction is relevant to actual practice. For even if fiction is absolved "in itself" of "practicing any actual deception," it might nonetheless or for that very reason be an effective vehicle for the kind of goal stated, for example, by Kafka: "My sole concern is with the human tribunal, which I wish to deceive, moreover, without practicing any actual deception."[46] Kafka states his "wish to deceive" outright. But his remark perhaps also implies that deception is inevitable, independently of the wish or the "actual practice" of deception. Coleridge's "willing suspension of disbelief" has two essential elements, the suspension and the willingness—the latter of which is implicitly denied here.

One of the wittiest responses to the kind of position represented by Bok's or Coleridge's formula is Oscar Wilde's "The Decay of Lying." This famously defines fiction as "lying for its own sake"—a more amusing version, nota bene, of the "arbitrary lie" formula we encountered in the introduction. Wilde dealt with the problem to his argument posed by Bok, just as de Man did, by questioning the relation of fiction to representation. The formula "lying for its own sake" belongs to the same pattern as his ironic reversal in the same essay of the classical mimetic dictum that art imitates nature. The point, of course, is that mimetic relations between art and "human nature" should not be regarded merely in terms of representation, but in terms of a dynamic system of reciprocal imitation, of specular mimesis, between the two terms. Wilde's joke that there was no fog in London until Turner painted it destabilizes the meaning of Bok's and Coleridge's "willing suspension of disbelief," since the point is that Turner's fictional fog can make people see the real thing willingly *or unwillingly* (and perhaps inaccurately) his way. What is at stake in the convention of "willing disbelief" is not fixed in advance by some abstract and unvarying definition of fiction, but is the product of reciprocal interactions between readers and texts, leading to states of belief and disbelief *more or less* willing (and more or less unanimous); and how much fictions deceive or are intended to deceive may or may not reflect the conventional agreements of any given group or period.

The depth and significance of what Bok calls the "confusion" of fiction with lying is further illustrated in her own terms, which identify lying with symbolic violence par excellence, by a plethora of models of fiction that associate it too with violence. This is not the place to go into detail on this matter, since I have already introduced it, and since my readings of Defoe, Stendhal, and Beckett will confirm fiction's association with both lying and violence in a more precise way. But for epigrammatic brevity we can hardly do better than André Breton's characterization of the simplest surrealist poem in terms of a man, pistol in hand, *who shoots at random into a crowd.*[47] Just as Wilde's and de Man's sallies against fiction-as-representation resulted in a definition of fiction as random lie, so Breton's seeming abandonment of representation in this context results in a definition of surrealism as random victimage. Breton speaks of "the simplest surrealist act" rather than of fiction or poem as such; but while this may be understood as an assault on the conventional opposition between art and life, fiction and nonfiction, Breton's image is presumably itself a fiction rather than a recommendation to murder. The image here, we trust, concerns an arbitrary *symbolic* violence, though nothing in its form prevents the reader from (mis)taking it literally, or acting it out. In our readings of Defoe, Stendhal, and Beckett, we will see that this kind of danger is omnipresent in fiction, and, moreover, that it is explicitly in terms of the aberrant literalization of metaphor that Shakespeare also chooses to define the scapegoating consequences of fashion.[48]

I conclude here with a detail from an actual fiction by Shakespeare, *Othello*, in part because it is a work which Bok also cites on the subject of lying and violence, in part for its own suggestiveness.[49] Whereas Bok naturally stresses the violence done by Iago's mendacity, I naturally stress the scapegoating of the liar himself. At the end of the play, when Iago has admitted his guilt and killed his wife, he then announces that "from this time forth I will never speak word."[50] But while the Venetian state might simply have executed him, capital punishment is by no means enough for the forces of justice and truth, including the average audience seeking its tragic catharsis. Torture must, beyond the close of the play, open the liar's lips and force him to speak the truth. In my view, Shakespeare is certainly on Iago's side in this matter, not merely because he is opposed to torture as such, but because he wants us to ask ourselves what on earth the torturers expect Iago to say. They, like the literary critics, are perplexed by his motive—they have a "presumption of truth" with a vengeance.

That Shakespeare wishes us to focus on the scapegoating significance of this torture is confirmed by the fact that, in *Much Ado about Nothing*, the torture of the villain Don John (bastard and thus orthodox scapegoat par excellence, who is Iago's structural equivalent in this play) is pointedly arranged in the very last line of the play to coincide with the wedding music. Sacrificial violence, in short, coincides with the music of legitimated love—or "lying" (to recall Shakespeare's own pun) in the erotic sense—and by extension with the structure of all orthodox legitimacies.[51]

2

The Analytics of Fiction

■

All the characters in this book are real and none is fictitious even in part.
—FLANN O'BRIEN

Here we expand the purview from lying to the logical problem of fiction. Understanding this problem is essential if we are to give a clear analytical meaning to the kind of identification of fiction with arbitrariness that we have encountered in Paul de Man, and that we will encounter just as emphatically in our three novelists. For logic to be genuinely pertinent to literature, we must address the problem of fiction in the broader logical sense, which may include aspects of literary fiction but also includes much else. Accordingly, my primary focus here will be epistemology of fiction in the so-called analytic philosophical tradition, beginning with Bertrand Russell's famous insistence that all fictions are falsehoods.[1]

This logical point goes not only for literary fictions but also for such apparently innocuous statements as "if it had been 100 degrees, the water would have boiled" (since its antecedent is false). Because this kind of problem seems at first very distant from the concerns of literary theory, its genuine relevance requires demonstration. To be sure, as in the case of literary fiction, we *want* to say that applying the logical yardstick here misses the point; that, in appealing to merely technical falsehoods, both this and literary fictions can convey perfectly true things. But this, unfortunately, does not grasp the full nature or extent of the problem. Pursuing two distinct but interlinked trajectories in twentieth-century philosophy—from Russell to Richard Rorty, and early Wittgenstein to Nelson Goodman—my central aim will be to demonstrate how, where fiction in the logical sense can be rescued from mere falsehood (as we feel it should be in the above example), the problem of falsehood reappears transformed into the problem of arbitrariness. This will confirm the pertinence of de Man's definition of fiction to logic as well as literature. Indeed, as we have seen, de Man's definition is startling precisely because it has nothing directly to do with nonexistent entities, and thus with fiction in the usual literary or colloquial sense. Rather, both fiction and nonfiction in the colloquial sense are faced with this threat to their truth systems.

The classical defense of fiction has been, of course, that fiction is a mimesis or representation of actuality, or more generally an allegory of the truth.[2] Since allegory in principle covers any conceivable kind of system governing the relation between the fiction and its referent, or the letter and the figure, de Man's definition of fiction would apply to the randomness in the system. Aristotle's dictum that poetry concerns what is true "by possibility and by necessity"[3] similarly ties fiction to truth and reality (though raising the problem of the relation between possibility and actuality mentioned above). It is only when possibility is taken to include not only actual possibility, past or future, but anything conceivable (in the loose sense of the term), that we approach the kind of license evoked by Bok's and Coleridge's "willing suspension of disbelief," or more specifically by the convention that, provided all fictions are properly labeled "fiction"—and imaginatively prefaced "Imagine that"—all will be well in the court of truth. I shall return later to an updated technical version of this position in Thomas Pavel's appeal to modal logic as a model for fiction theory, as well as to Goodman's critique of this model.

Although lying will be left largely in the background in this chapter, the conceptual landscape is directly relevant. This goes for my continuing emphasis not just on the conceptual relation of law and arbitrariness, but also on its social equivalent, the norm and the exception, unanimity and non-unanimity, the group and the individual. It is significant to my argument, for example, that while Richard Rorty pragmatically dismisses "the problem of fiction" as inherited from Russell et al., including the kind of opposition between fiction and truth that informs conventional views of the opposition between art and science, he nevertheless attempts to maintain the latter distinction on the basis of the opposition between non-unanimity and unanimity. We concluded in the last chapter, with Durkheim, that Kant's condemnation of lying amounted to a sacrificial assertion of unanimity. Rorty is far from condemning literature; but that does not alter the parallel fact that, in disposing of the problem of "fiction," he reintroduces the problem of (non)unanimity in terms of "literature" more generally. Nor is it an accident or mere joke, we conclude, that in his related consideration of contemporary relations between the disciplines, Rorty somewhat playfully recommends to poets a strategy of deception or concealment.

Exploring what is entailed in Rorty's putative dissolving of Russell's epistemological problem is extremely useful even if we do not accept his solution of the problem as such, since he leads us directly back to themes that dominated the previous chapter. Why his solution is difficult to accept will be addressed via Wittgenstein, whose early "picture theory" of reference Rorty takes as the basic target of his critique. A different kind of solution, via Pavel's appeal to modal logic, will then be considered. However, we find that Pavel's treatment, like Rorty's, also turns out to be more useful in leading us back to the theme of unanimity than in solving the problem as such. Pavel is especially useful because his treatment of unanimity is explicitly mimetic, thus transforming the abstract problem once again into a pragmatic, potentially "Girardian" form.

I conclude, via Nelson Goodman, that no solution to Russell's problem of falsehood can evade the larger problem of arbitrariness that it ultimately evokes—an arbitrariness that can be expressed equally in logical terms and in the social terms of mimetic unanimity. The very pressure to resolve the unresolved epistemological issue of fiction in fact encourages generalized appeals to common agreement or unanimity. But generalized appeals to unanimity, as we shall see succinctly expressed by Goodman, themselves characteristically produce a kind of logical equivalent to Girard's mimetic double bind.

Russell to Rorty

We must now survey some of the territory that lies between Russell's posing of the problem of fiction and Rorty's putative dissolving of this problem. Russell seems to have held consistently, through the various phases of his philosophic development, that fictional statements (or statements that include reference to fictional entities) are logically false, and that there is no satisfactory epistemological way around this fact. Naturally the falsehood "Mr. Pickwick lived in London" can be turned into the truth "In Dickens, Mr. Pickwick is said to live in London," but this does not alter the logical situation, since a truth is now simply affirmed about a falsehood.

It is nowadays common to dismiss the early Russell's and early Wittgenstein's "picture theory" or "picture picture" of reference (as Rorty and the later Wittgenstein call it) as blinded by a kind of positivist "reality fixation"[4] that misguidedly attempts to reduce theory of language to a propositional logic whose referential structure is that of pure "correspondence" between language and the world. No doubt there is truth to this criticism, and I am not advocating any early Russellian or early Wittgensteinian epistemology.[5] On the contrary, inasmuch as Russell's position on fictional reference remained consistent throughout his changing philosophical career,[6] even in his later "antirealist" phase,[7] it is wise not to insist too much on any particular epistemology in this connection. Russell's point is perhaps best presented as tautology: since fictions do not by definition exist, it is impossible by definition to "refer" to them. (And like many other tautologies this one may appear, at various levels of reflection, alternately trivial and deep.)

While Nelson Goodman's epistemological emphasis is very different from Russell's, we will see that his famous "actualist" critique of modal ontology (the latter inspired by the modal logic of "possible worlds" developed by Saul Kripke and others), essentially generalizes this tautology from fiction to possibility, insisting in *Fact, Fiction, Forecast* on the truism that "all possible worlds lie within the actual one."[8] The moral, once again, seems to be that "fiction" is itself a fiction (as the epigraph from Flann O'Brien in this chapter also wryly asserts).

The question of whether fiction can be considered a bona fide distinct category in which ordinary constraints of truth and falsehood are "suspended," aesthetically or otherwise, dominates one tradition of twentieth-century philosophy. In her *An Introduction to Wittgenstein's "Tractatus,"* G. E. M. Anscombe astutely analyzed Russell's opposition to Strawson—for whom fictions were, not false, but logically "spurious" or entirely without truth-value—in terms of the early Wittgenstein's opposition to a central aspect of Frege's philosophy of language. Aligning Strawson's view with Frege's famous distinction between "sense" and "reference," Anscombe shows why, from the Russell-

Wittgenstein perspective, "the Frege-Strawson position on the possibility of sentences without truth-value appears to be a waste of time."[9] As Wittgenstein put it: "Every proposition must *already* have a sense [by which he means both sense *and* reference in Frege's terminology]; assertion cannot give it one."[10] I shall return to his radical position later.

Thomas Pavel also criticizes Strawson (and Ryle) for adopting what he calls a "segregationalist" approach to fiction.[11] The cognitive apartheid posited in such segregation between discourses with and without truth-value (without truth or falsity) exceeds any logical threat to literary fiction posed by Russell, inasmuch as falsehood possesses profound logical respectability whereas segregationalist fiction is expelled from the realm of logical truth altogether. For this reason it seems misleading to describe Strawson and Ryle, as Pavel does, as belonging to "Russell's orthodoxy" (however much they may have been influenced by him in other respects), and still more misleading to label Russell himself as a "segregationalist."[12] Pavel points out that like "most educated people, Russell does not deny fiction, as an institution, a certain importance in our lives."[13] In fact it is the supposed dichotomy between Russell the educated person and Russell the logician that seems proof of segregationalism to him. But this shifts the meaning of the term. For while we may plausibly entertain a tension between these two Russells, and while one may tentatively agree that Russell's "philosophy provides little encouragement for research on the semantics of [literary] fiction,"[14] none of this alters his radically "anti-segregational" refusal to release fictions from truth-value in the strictest sense. It is this which is shocking about his position.[15]

Pavel nevertheless provides a useful account of later efforts to bypass "the Russell problem," including speech-act theory, several varieties of what he calls "conventionalism," causal theories of meaning, and modalism (a "relaxed" version of which he himself adopts).[16] Echoing the well-known critique of J. A. Austin by Derrida, Pavel finds in speech-act theory a diminished version of segregation in which fictional discourse tends to be treated as "parasitic" or "marginal."[17] Rorty similarly accuses John Searle of "falling between two stools,"[18] like the segregationalists, simultaneously pro- and anti-Russell. It should be noted that, segregationalist or not, speech-act and causal theories of meaning essentially evade the Russell problem by defining language as an action or event.[19]

The more technically elaborate causal theories of meaning, represented by Kripke, Hilary Putnam, Hartry Field, and Keith Donellan, are faulted by Rorty for dispensing with Russell's view only at the cost of great technical difficulty and ultimately incoherence.[20] But whatever one's view of causal theories, it is worth observing that inasmuch as the ultimate "meaning" of all discourse is to be located within the reality of the entire cause-effect complex, this perspective offers a place for fictional reference no more than Russell does—unless fiction, à la de Man, is identified with arbitrariness and, as such, an unstable supplement to the closure of causal systems.[21] Similarly, Pavel concludes that "by transferring the puzzle of fictional beings from ontology to the domain of discourse, the speech-act theory of fiction remains consistent with the Russellian orthodoxy and can dispense with non-existent beings in its ontology."[22]

Pavel ultimately maintains that all alternatives to Russell are unsatisfactory, on the grounds that they all circumlocute rather than solve the problem of fictional reference, except the modal analogy or model of fiction he derives from Kripke (though unlike Kripke, he does not propose a causal theory of reference).[23] Rorty's survey of the Russell problem goes even further than Pavel's, and in the opposite direction, proposing the abolition of the notion of reference altogether. Having rejected the "realism" of causal theories as a genuine alternative to Russell, Rorty proceeds to reject modalism, singling out in particular the Meinongian possibilism represented by Terence Parsons, in which fictions are conceived as "incomplete, possible, non-existent objects."[24] Rorty's conclusion, moreover, is that all putative epistemological alternatives to Russell fail to relinquish some form, however oblique, of the "picture picture" of reference-as-correspondence. Rorty thus finally offers us a single alternative: either to relinquish "the philosopher's" concept of reference and epistemology altogether (now identified rather grandiosely with the entire tradition following Parmenides), replacing it with the "amiably simple-minded" view (associated with Dewey, Sellars, and the later Wittgenstein) that no "light will be shed on the nature of fictions by analytic philosophy of language"; or to adopt a rigidly causalist and physicalist philosophic project that will hope to reduce all reference to "some up-to-date counterpart of 'atoms and the void.'"[25] Rorty plumps squarely for the first of these alternatives and claims to become amiably simple-minded. But the story is not quite over, and it is an educational one, which leads us once again, as in Kant, from the problem of falsehood to that of unanimity.

I note first that Rorty's invocation of Derrida as a kindred soul also "trying to do away with the notion of 'referent' "[26] is dubious, and returns us to the kind of problem outlined in the introduction. As a matter of fact, Derrida sometimes uses the term in the most emphatic manner, as for instance (to take an extreme example) when he claims that "the absolute referent of all possible literature is on a par with the absolute effacement of any possible trace" and that "the only referent that is absolutely real is thus of the scope or dimension of an absolute nuclear catastrophe that would irreversibly destroy the entire archive and all symbolic capacity."[27] To be sure, this has little apparently to do with the "picture picture" of reference; but whatever it is accused of meaning, it can hardly be accused of amiable simple-mindedness! As noted in the introduction, Andrew McKenna cites these passages in support of his contention that the Derridean referent is consistent with Girard's conception of the ultimate referent of sacrificial systems (totally indiscriminate and undifferentiated violence).[28]

Besides this appeal to the likes of Derrida and the late Wittgenstein (whatever Wittgenstein himself says)[29] in support of "amiable simple-mindedness," there is also something almost comically sacrificial in Rorty's offer of a binary choice between the amiably simple-minded and the entire epistemological project of Western philosophy since Parmenides—sacrificed simply as "absurd."[30] The choice offered (to be "absurd" or "wholeheartedly pragmatic") has an eerie echo of the early Wittgenstein's view of propositions—either true or false—which Rorty rejects. But while he provides an excellent summary of the basic problems involved in the analytic tradition, I would not make so much of Rorty here did he not also offer a further argument that provides an excellent model for our purposes, returning once again to the intersection of deception and unanimity.

Having suggested that much of the ironic power of modern literature (Borges, Nabokov, Mallarmé, Valéry, Stevens, et al.), and of philosophic critics like Derrida and Foucault, derives from their attacks on the "straight men" who believe in the "picture picture" of reference, and especially "common-sense realism" (as contrasted with those "who impugn the distinction between the scientist and the poet"), Rorty concludes:

> The modern revolt . . . suggests the poet, rather than the knower, as the man who realizes human nature. But this is dangerous; the poet needs to be saved from his friends. *If the picture picture is as absurd as I think it, it would be well that this absurdity should not become widely known.* For the ironist poet owes far more to Parmenides and the tradition of Western metaphysics than does the scientist. The scientific culture could survive a loss of faith in this tradition, but the literary culture might not.[31]

This passage is ideal for our purposes because it makes the entire upshot of the abstract problem of fictional reference into a kind of concrete mimetic rivalry between artist and scientist—analyzed, moreover, in terms of pragmatic deception. The differentiation maintained between poet and knower—originally via the poet's knowledge of the philosopher's error, now via the recommended deception to maintain that error—offers a very specific pragmatic transformation of traditional epistemology, such that the abstract problem devolves pragmatically (as in de Man and Girard) *into the knowledge of lies or concealments superimposed on errors*. Note, for example, that regardless of whether Rorty's poet and Rorty are correct about the absurdity of foundational epistemology, the recommended concealment of his view would in both cases conceal an error—either someone else's or the poet's own. It is significant from a structural point of view that Rorty's text yields this pattern regardless of whether we accept or reject his own wholesale rejection of "the problem about fictional discourse." In a certain sense, despite everything, he thus confirms the core of Russell's view—since while he impugns the distinction between science and poetry on the basis of their epistemological relation to truth, his account maintains a pragmatic distinction *on the basis of their relation to falsehood*.

We may wonder whether the joke is not on Rorty when he claims that "it would be better to see these people [Nabokov, Valéry, Stevens, Derrida, etc.] as using the Parmenidean tradition as a dialectical foil, *in whose absence they would have nothing to say*."[32] His picture of the relation between literature and science is nonetheless highly suggestive, as I have said, for my contention that the problems of both lying and fiction systematically devolve into that of unanimity in this study. For having denied any fundamental epistemological difference, he suggests "the literary culture" might not survive, not the insight itself (on which it has thrived), but *unanimous acceptance* of this insight. The literal sense of Rorty's "witty" recommendation to poets that "this should not become widely known" is thus to recommend maintaining, by concealment or lying, the lack of unanimity on which he predicates modern poetic force. In fact, it is not merely a matter of maintaining the disagreement between modern poets and realists, but apparently of establishing a new rift between poets and their friends from whom they must be saved. The force of literature, like lying, seems to reside in mutual miscomprehension.

That this is more than a witty sally is demonstrated in the subsequent chapter of *Consequences of Pragmatism*, where he offers a "crude" definition of literature as opposed to science in terms of "the areas of culture which, quite self-consciously, *forgo agreement* on an encompassing critical vocabulary, and thus forgo argumentation."[33] Literature is thus explicitly defined in terms of non-unanimity.

I am in agreement with Rorty that Russell's problem about fiction cannot be avoided in some form without rejecting almost all of Western "philosophy," but I do not think such a blanket rejection can be anything but arbitrary and sacrificial. I am accordingly in agreement with Nelson Goodman that this and related problems cannot "simple-mindedly" be conjured away without falling into the kind of dogmatism Rorty seeks to displace.[34] In particular, we must now question Rorty's identification of the problem of fiction exclusively with the problem of reference-as-correspondence (the identification explicitly denied by de Man in his rejection of the polarity of fact and representation). We must also question his conclusion that forgoing agreement on "an encompassing critical vocabulary" necessarily means forgoing "argumentation" *tout court*. On the contrary, one would have thought that a "wholeheartedly pragmatic" view would not so easily ignore the fact that arguments about literature in this sense *do* continually occur (and that the criteria for what counts as "encompassing" in this context would have to come uncomfortably close to the criteria of the kind of foundational epistemology Rorty rejects).

We also need not accept Rorty's surprisingly Kantian identification of unanimity (concerning an "encompassing critical vocabulary") with rationality or the possibility of argument as such; since while every rational or pragmatic argument entails an appeal to rational or pragmatic unanimity in part, it is equally true that the very need for such arguments presupposes nonunanimity to be resolved. Both "argument" and "literature" in Rorty's senses are oriented toward *the novel*, which makes it questionable why literature rather than science should be defined in terms of non-unanimity or novelty. While this "crude" definition is presented in a positive light for literature—and while his highlighting of the issue of unanimity as such is very useful to my argument—Rorty's denial of literature's right to "argumentation" seems to relapse into the kind of dubious logical segregation to which one might have thought he was, by his own account, immune.

Early Wittgenstein
We have seen that de Man's claim that the problem of fiction has nothing to do with "any supposed polarity of fact and representation"

confirms Rorty's rejection of "representationalism."[35] But it also denies that the problem of fiction can be reduced, as Rorty claims, to reference-as-correspondence in this sense, and accordingly dissolved. It is this problem that we must now pursue. In particular, we must question Rorty's own picture of what he calls the early Wittgenstein's "picture theory" of reference.

Admittedly, when Russell's position about fiction is stated as Rorty and Pavel, and indeed Russell himself, usually state it, in terms of the nonexistence of a Mr. Pickwick-fact to which the representation "Mr. Pickwick" might truly refer, the matter of correspondence seems clear enough. Yet if we recall Anscombe's astute alignment of Russell's rejection of Strawson's segregationalism with both Russell's and Wittgenstein's rejection of Frege's distinction between "sense" and "reference," things immediately become more complex. For if we accept Anscombe's view that Russell and Wittgenstein have essentially the same reason for thinking that "the Frege-Strawson position on the possibility of sentences without truth-value appears to be a waste of time,"[36] the reason lies in a refusal to grant "the picture theory" of representation in its usual sense—entailing a polarity between fact and representation (reference and sense)—any validity. As Anscombe summarizes Wittgenstein's reaction to the Fregean position:

> Frege was sure that a well-formed sentence whose names were not empty had a truth-value. But is it not strange to be sure of that? Is it not as if there were a great metal wall with holes in it, and we had some way of casting metal objects, and were absolutely certain that each object that was properly cast would fit into a hole in the wall one way up or the other (the well-formed proposition or its negation is true) *though no connection had been shewn between the principles of casting objects and the character of the metal wall.*[37]

It is precisely this notion of reference-as-correspondence that *both* early and late Wittgenstein oppose:

> Wittgenstein holds that what already has a sense must already be true or false; he is attacking Frege's idea that in judging we "advance from a thought to a truth-value."
>
> Wittgenstein remained on this side of the fence all his life; for in the very passage of *Philosophical Investigations* in which he attacked the ideas about complexes which he expounded in the *Tractatus*, he asked: "Am I really prepared to say what, and how

much, has got to turn out untrue before I give up my proposition about Moses as *false*?"[38]

If Anscombe's estimate of the early and late Wittgenstein's consistency on this point is correct, Rorty's relegation of the problem of fiction to Russell's and the early Wittgenstein's "picture theory" must be invalid. Rorty himself admits that the opposition between language treated respectively as "a picture" and as "a game" corresponds only "very roughly" to the opposition between the early and late Wittgenstein.[39] But when it comes to citing the *Tractatus* on the very topic ("sense") we have been discussing—"If the world had no substance, then whether a proposition had sense would depend on whether another proposition was true"—Rorty resorts exclusively to this paradigm:

> The language-game approach of the *Investigations* abandons this "picture picture" of language precisely in allowing that whether a sentence has sense (i.e., can be intelligible and true or false) *may* be dependent upon whether another sentence is true. Since this possibility is paradigmatically actual in the case of fictional discourse (taken at face value and neither "analyzed" à la Russell nor assigned special referents as in Searle and Parsons), philosophical problems about fiction simply do not arise once the picture picture is dropped.[40]

We have seen, however, that the picture theory does not "hook" language to the world (to use Rorty's locution) as Fregean sense has to be hooked to reference. Rather, "what Wittgenstein means by calling the proposition a picture" is that "it is we who 'use' the sensibly perceptible signs as a projection of a [logically] possible state of affairs."[41] The duality here is not between fact and representation (to use de Man's locution), or reference and sense, but between reference and the sign in its materiality—which is why "names [have] no sense but only reference"[42] for Wittgenstein, and why de Man also predicates his definition of reference on the utterance of a name (Rousseau's Marion). *Pace* Rorty, both early and late Wittgenstein have a basically nonrepresentational conception of reference.[43]

Wittgenstein's radical denial of representationalism in the polarity of sense and reference, his claim that all meaningful propositions are *already* true or false, is in fact an essential prerequisite of his "picture picture." He does not get rid, of course, of reference-as-correspondence in the "amiably simple-minded" sense of naming, but nor can Rorty or anyone else. What makes the "picture picture" incompatible with any ordinary representationalism, however, is its denial of modality or possibility *tout court*: "Thus the part of his views which seems to be nothing but a dogmatic consequence of the 'picture theory' is in fact his rejection of modality. Any sense of 'may,' 'can,' 'possible,' other than '*logically* possible,' would be unamenable to explanation in terms of the picture theory."[44] Wittgenstein's logic "represents" the world only insofar as all arbitrariness in the sense of modality is banished from the system, a drastic consequence entirely of a piece of his antirepresentationalism. So far from offering a genuine polarity of fact and representation, Wittgenstein presents a "correspondence" about which there is nothing whatever arbitrary or free—unlike Frege, for whom "empty" forms wait to be placed in correspondence with facts—and which is no more genuinely dualistic than the relation between effect and cause, or conclusion and premise.

In the *Tractatus* the world stands in an essentially undetermined relation to logic; it is just whatever happens "to be the case."[45] But having thus hygienically compressed the devil of pandemonium into a bottle at the origin of the world—into the abyss between what can be spoken of and what cannot, science and the transcendent— Wittgenstein's argument reveals just how much must be sacrificed to expel arbitrariness from his system. Though some detail has been required to make this articulate, we now see that Rorty's definition of the (false) problem of fiction in terms of a (false) view of reference-as-correspondence must give way to a further problem, which, as in de Man's rejection of the polarity between fact and representation, turns out to be the problem of arbitrariness. This is a problem that belongs equally to the early and late Wittgenstein, just as Russell's position on fiction survived both his realist and nonrealist phases.[46]

Finally, in this context, it is worth remarking that what supposedly transcends the world-mirroring logic of the *Tractatus*—what cannot be (philosophically or scientifically) spoken of, but only "shewn" and imitated—takes us once again from logical to social mimesis. The unanimity demanded by logic gives way to a demand for a transcendental unanimity that cannot be logically represented in the *Tractatus*, but only imitated and enacted.

Pavel's Modality and Mimesis

We are now in a position to explore further how fiction figures into the logical (and scientific) problem of modality—how Russell's and Rorty's problem, in short, can be transformed into Nelson Goodman's. Before coming to Goodman's critique, it will therefore be helpful to summarize Pavel's view of modal logic as a convincing model or metaphor for literary fiction.

Pavel's appeal to modal logic is made in the conviction that "the moratorium on referential issues has by now [1986] become obsolete"[47] in fiction theory. Targeting structuralism alongside analytic segregationalism, as we have seen, for bracketing and ultimately ignoring the problem of reference, Pavel cites with approval de Man's emphasis on allegory as a "central topos of literature": "The logic of fictional worlds vindicates his [de Man's] results, by suggesting that allegorical reading provides for the most general pattern of decoding relations or correspondence within fictional structures."[48] Pavel's own view is that the "notion of [possible] worlds as an ontological metaphor for fiction remains too appealing to be dismissed."[49] We are told that were it not for certain "intuitive" difficulties, only "the presence of contradictions [in fiction] effectively prevents us from considering fictional worlds as genuine possible worlds and from reducing the theory of fiction to a Kripkean theory of modality."[50] Instead of attempting to clarify the logical situation, however, Pavel steers a course that recalls his attitude to Russell's problem: logic must again be "relaxed," we are told, to make way for a more "tolerant" theory in which logic is merely a "*distant* model" or "metaphor" for fiction.[51] In short, from the strictly logical point of view, his metaphor does not achieve much more than adding some contemporary analytic glamour to Aristotle's venerable dictum about poetry and possibility.

Since our emphasis, when we come to Goodman, will be on the problems that do arise for a theory of fiction based on modality, and indeed for modal theory as such, we can hardly complain that Pavel does not push his position more aggressively. Yet only a more stringent approach, like Goodman's, brings these problems to light (problems, as we shall see, extending far beyond the merely technical difficulty that fictions may contain logical contradictions). Indeed, Pavel retreats from the difficulties he poses in a rather dramatic manner, restricting himself "to propos[ing] models representing the user's [reader's] understanding of fiction."[52] Not only does this mean retreating from what he calls the "external" logical problem of fiction (represented, for example, by Russell), but also from the "internal" authorial perspective.[53] Though we need hardly quarrel with the restriction for the purposes of his illuminating analysis of reader-response, the approach can thus not be said to address the general problem of fictional reference as he initially poses it. In fact his internal/external dichotomy risks providing a new version of just the kind of "segregation" he criticizes elsewhere.

As in the case of Rorty, however, we do not need to accept Pavel's epistemological conclusions as such to find him illuminating. For, like Rorty, Pavel takes up the topic of fiction and unanimity—and specifically *mimetic* unanimity—at the very pragmatic juncture where his logical investigations cease. Consider, for example, his comparison of the fiction/reality duality to that of sacred and profane (into which the universe is divided by "the religious mind"),[54] and his example of the mime who mimics a religious blessing: "Since cult and fiction differ merely in the strength of the secondary universe, when sufficient energy is channeled into mimetic acts, these may leave the fictional mode and cross the threshold of actuality."[55] The relation between fiction and actuality is not here mimetic in the abstract sense of representation, for the difference between enactment and mere mimesis is said to be a matter of "energy," not accuracy. Rather, imagining a crowd "deprived of any religious ceremony for so long that even an imitation of the precious forbidden gestures can be electrifying,"[56] Pavel comes very close to defining mimesis in its Girardian sense, in terms of the mimetic unanimity of the crowd that binds it together and "validates" or "actualizes" the mime. No less Girardian is his example of the lover who, pretending to love his friend's wife in order to seduce her, and spurred on by her resistance, concludes by believing his own lie.[57]

Given this emphasis on mimesis and mutual "identification" as a key to the relation between fiction and actuality, it is hardly surprising to find Pavel cheerfully admitting to the "complex and unstable relation between texts and worlds,"[58] since "the threshold of actuality" is on this account determined no more predictably than the threshold between genuine and feigned love, or genuine and feigned religion. It is in the context of the "incompleteness" stressed by several philosophers as a "major distinctive feature of fictional worlds" that Pavel stresses the arbitrariness of fiction—but his mimetic models arguably provide better and more pointed illustrations than his modal ones. Reminding us that indeterminacy marks other fields too, such as quantum physics, he claims that nevertheless "at least the indeterminacy that governs specific domains seems to obey definite constraints. *In fiction, indeterminacy strikes at random.*"[59]

Nelson Goodman

Goodman's now classic *Fact, Fiction, and Forecast* (1954), which has been called "one of the few books that every serious student of philosophy in our time *has* to read,"[60] gives us reason to be nervous about the "definite constraints" supposedly operating in "specific domains" (in Pavel's phrase). It also provides us with a means of formulating the relation of fiction and arbitrariness in extraliterary as well as literary terms. Having confirmed the generality of the problem, which extends across philosophy of science as well as art, we will arrive at Goodman's formulation of the relation between the two—which once again (now almost predictably) turns on the issue of unanimity.

Goodman begins his deconstruction of conventional philosophy of science with a discussion of ordinary "counterfactual conditionals" ("If that water had been heated to 100 degrees centigrade, it would have boiled"):

> The analysis of counterfactual conditionals is no fussy little gram-matical exercise. Indeed, if we lack the means for interpreting counterfactual conditionals, we can hardly claim to have an ade-quate philosophy of science. A satisfactory definition of scientific law, a satisfactory theory of confirmation or of disposition terms (and this includes not only predicates ending in "ible" and "able" but almost every objective predicate, such as "is red"), would solve a large part of the problem of counterfactuals.[61]

We begin, thus, with the problem of fiction-as-possibility in its seemingly most anodyne and unproblematic aspect—one, however, which, as we noted earlier, has the same logical form as Russell's (since the antecedent of every counterfactual conditional is false, all such counterfactuals, including contradictory ones, are "true"). Failing to find a logically general way of specifying the kind of conditions that must obtain to exclude unwanted counterfactuals ("Even if the match lighted, it still wasn't scratched"), while admitting innocent ones ("Even if the matched had been scratched, it still would not have lighted"),[62] Goodman generalizes the problem to defining the kind of causal laws that must obtain for correct counterfactual inference. The problem here is not limited to the grammatical form of counterfac-tuals, which can easily be translated into propositions in which "mo-dality is removed from the predicates." ("If the statement 'the water was 100 degrees at time t' were true, then the statement 'the water boiled at time t' would be true").[63] Indeed, Goodman favors a deter-minedly "actualist" analysis of all possibles (as for instance in the example of a color that would be seen at "place p" in the visual field only if both eyes were open at time t, though in fact only one is open): "To speak of the 'fictive' or 'possible' place-time p + t is not to speak of a new non-actual entity but to say something new about (i.e. apply a new predicate to) the old actual entity p + t."[64]

Goodman's objection to the kind of "possible worlds" talk favored by Pavel and others is that it is a mere formalist or technical abstraction:

> My main purpose here, then, has been to suggest that discourse, even about possibles, need not transgress the boundaries of the actual world. What we often mistake for possible worlds are just equally true descriptions in other terms. We have come to think of the actual as one among many possible worlds. We need to repaint that picture. All possible worlds lie within the actual one.[65]

Having failed to find any satisfactory analysis of counterfactuals, Goodman proceeds to generalize his failure to produce a satisfactory definition of law or "lawlikeness"[66] in general—a problem that applies not only to possibles (and dispositional terms, such as "flexible") in general, but to the problem of induction, and indeed finally to "the problem of projecting from any set of cases to others" (a fine definition of allegory).[67] Satisfactory interpretation of all these cases is found to depend on providing some way of distinguishing "lawlike from accidental statements" or "accidental hypotheses,"[68] of differentiating "accurately between causal laws and casual facts."[69] Goodman's illustration of the inductive problem in terms of projecting the predicate "grue" (green before time t, blue after t) is notorious in twentieth-century philosophy, as is his sympathetic critique of Hume's critique of induction (that it is based on habitual generalization from past regularity): "To say that valid predictions are those based on past regularities, without being able to say *which* regularities, is . . . quite pointless."[70]

Goodman's "new riddle of induction," his generalization of his and others' failure to distinguish "lawlike or projectible [from arbitrary] hypotheses . . . on any merely syntactical grounds or even on the ground that these hypotheses are somehow general in meaning"[71] has had, as the author justly boasts, an "effectiveness as an irritant [that] seems not to lessen through the years. Attacks upon it do not decline in volume or vehemence or futility."[72] As the author and others have pointed out,[73] canonical attempts in the philosophy of science to formulate a noninductive account of scientific rigor do not escape the "new riddle":

> Thus Goodman's paradox shows clearly that it is not sufficient to define a law, as Popper does, as "a statement that must be falsifiable." For even though "All emeralds are gred" [green at time t, otherwise red] is a statement that can in fact be falsified, no one would seriously consider it to be a genuine law. Accord-

ingly, Goodman's paradox pertains to inductionism and falsifica-
tionism alike.[74]

We see now more clearly not only why Wittgenstein prohibited
modality from the *Tractatus*, but why the problem of arbitrary projection extends to the problem of fiction in general, understood as the
"projection from any set of cases to others" (whether the system of
projection be allegoric, realistic, possibilistic, inductive, or any other).
This is in full accord with de Man's definition of fiction as arbitrariness
defined in relation to *any* conceivable systematic relation between
utterance and referent. "Fiction" is therefore not an entity; rather we
may say that the *truth power* of a text lies not in its truth but in the law
of its interpretive system, and that its *fiction power* lies not in its
falsehood but in the arbitrariness of its system. This is the result I
anticipated in my introduction, now stated in terms that are fully
analytic as well as literary.

Unanimity: Jest or Earnest?

Goodman, whom Rorty compares in this respect to the later Wittgenstein,[75] proposes to solve his own problem by constructing an
"actualist" account of inductive (and more generally projective) practices based on their "entrenchment" in our history—an entrenchment
which neither guarantees their objective validity nor condemns them
to mere subjectivism. The technical details of his construction do not
concern us here: procedures are outlined for deciding between apparently competing projections in a given tradition (Western science),
and to produce a hierarchy of projective metalevels. Goodman does not
claim to provide a solution to all these details; indeed, that the matter
is by no means merely technical is demonstrated by the fact that such
fundamental problems as the interpretation of "kind," "kinship," and
"likeness"—not to speak of "a random sample"—are left explicitly
unsolved.[76] But his general point is that actual tradition provides our
only guide to the "warrantability" of any given projection.

The fact that traditions are not necessarily commensurable or
consistent later provoked, in *Ways of Worldmaking* (1978), Goodman's pluralist trope, as Rorty calls it, of there existing "many actual
worlds."[77] Here Goodman duly extends his actualist account of fiction
more generally to literary fiction as such. Whereas Pavel is inclined to
speak of the "possible world" of Don Quixote, Goodman speaks of Don
Quixote as "referring metaphorically" or "figuratively" to the actual
world, that is, to Don Quixote-like people and situations.[78] He regards

literary fiction in the same general light as the nonliterary fiction of *Fact, Fiction, Forecast*: "The so-called possible worlds of fiction lie within [and refer to] actual worlds."[79] This means that literary fiction is a priori no more necessarily problematic than any other fiction (or induction, or counterfactual) as regards its truth content. But since the problem of kinds and likenesses was one of the outstanding logical problems left unsolved at the end of *Fact, Fiction, Forecast*, the appeal to "Don Quixote-likeness" may be said to state rather than solve the problem as it applies to literature. We know that Goodman resolves this problem, in principle, by appeal to projective entrenchment—presumably in the relevant literary (or other) tradition. But his choice of *Don Quixote* as example states the issue to ironic perfection, since Don Quixote, whose entire library his friends wished to burn, is probably the most entrenched embodiment in Western literature of the danger of projective entrenchments.

Though Goodman states the theoretical problem of fiction with great force and in a way that is exemplary for my project, he has rather less to say about literary fictions, or about what kinds of entrenchment they represent in relation to philosophic or other discourse. It is quite striking how briefly literature is *actually* treated in the "actualist" analysis of *Ways of Worldmaking*, and how little of his more extensive treatment in *The Languages of Art* bears on its fictional or projective character. Despite his admirably argued insistence on the difficulty of distinguishing "cleanly" between the goals of knowledge and aesthetic satisfaction,[80] at no point is the relation between literature and philosophy developed in the radical way that his theory potentially opens up. This is very understandable insofar as the relation can no longer be understood a priori, but would depend on a very detailed study of literary (and philosophical) works or "entrenchments" themselves.

The problem is nevertheless naturally acute in Goodman, as in Rorty, where the relation of art and science (or literature and philosophy) is directly addressed. Like Rorty, Goodman appears to downplay the significance of the opposition in general, aligning himself against the traditional "two cultures." But in Rorty, we remember, things were complicated by his joke about the advisability of literary deception—and further complicated, moreover, by the problem of how far we take that joke or "fiction" seriously. We have seen that Rorty seriously maintains no "foundational" differentiation between art and science, let alone literature and philosophy, while his joke is that differentiation, promulgated by deception, should nonetheless be maintained by poets for the health of modern literature. But even this joke seems to have the serious intention of making sure that no new foundational differentiation is made between the poet and "the knower," this time reversed in the poet's favor as "the man who realizes human nature."[81] Rorty's recommended pragmatic differentiation comically contrasts with his affirmation of serious theoretical indifference between the two.

I have claimed that Rorty's analysis is most problematic, but also most illuminating for us, when it links the problem of literature to unanimity. This is also the case in Goodman, though Goodman does not, for good reason, make the Rortian move of identifying art with non-unanimity or novelty. Instead, in *Ways of Worldmaking*, he addresses the question by way of a concluding joke:

> I am not claiming that rightness in the arts is less subjective, or even no more subjective, than truth in the sciences, but only suggesting that the line between artistic and scientific judgment does not coincide with the line between subjective and objective, and that any approach to universal accord on anything significant is exceptional.
>
> My readers could weaken that latter conviction by agreeing unanimously with the foregoing somewhat tortuous and in a double sense trying course of thought.[82]

Like Rorty's denial of a foundational epistemology which could distinguish art and science a priori, Goodman's serious claim here—that the difference between the arts and sciences is *not* that between subjective and objective—is a very weak one (especially for the conclusion to a book as powerful as *Ways of Worldmaking*). As in Rorty, it is rather Goodman's witticism that is of compelling interest, where he invites us into an elegant double bind concerning unanimity. If we disagree with him about the rarity of unanimity, he will be inductively confirmed in his claim, while if we agree en masse, he will be inclined to change his mind.

This is an inductive paradox that resembles the famous deductive "liar" paradox, only it entails unanimity and non-unanimity about truth and falsehood instead of truth and falsehood as such—the very kind of translation from theory to practice that we have seen throughout. What is more, Goodman's joke relies on the fact that the inductive hypothesis of non-unanimity is self-fulfilling. Girard labels self-fulfilling prophecies of this kind "masochist induction"—where in this case agreement leads inexorably to disagreement, and vice versa.[83]

That analytic theory of fiction as well as the moral philosophy of lying systematically devolves on the problem of unanimity—and mimetic unanimity—is significant enough for our purposes. It provides a further link between the de Manian definition of fiction, confirmed here in other terms, and the basis of Girardian mimetic theory. From this point of view, Goodman's witticism merely emphasizes what we have suspected all along—that generalized appeals to unanimity are always potentially subject to what Girard calls the mimetic double bind. It may be, however, that Goodman's joke in its specific context also suggests something more: that the ancient rivalry between "literature" and "philosophy," "art" and "science," "fiction" and "nonfiction," even "comedy" and "seriousness," is best characterized precisely in these *seemingly* paradoxical—and thus potentially duplicitous—terms. If this is the case, Rorty's own joke about establishing literary differentiation on the basis of deception carries serious force.

PART TWO

LITERATURE

3

Lying for No Reason:

Lying and Obscenity

■ in Defoe

And his name was called Friday.
—DANIEL DEFOE

Leslie Stephen's attribution to Defoe of "the most amazing talent on record for telling lies,"[1] if remotely true, makes Defoe a crucial case for students of both lying as such and the relations between lying and fiction. He is also important to my project because neither he nor his readers were foreign to the "naive" equation of lying and fiction (something that cannot be so obviously said for later periods when the conventions of the novel were more entrenched). The relation of lying and fiction is directly addressed in Defoe, who defines fiction in ("de Manian") terms of the random lie. He also rather spectacularly confirms the sacrificial landscape we encountered in chapter 1, particularly regarding what we called the *pharmakon* relation between lying and concealment.

Defoe is all the more exemplary since he has so often been credited with such a significant contribution to the development of the novel or "fiction" itself, and since the modes of deception practiced in his political and other so-called nonfictional activities and texts cannot be neatly distinguished from the modes of deception practiced in his fictions. He invites our attention both because he defined what we would call fiction—what he calls "romance" or, more generally, "story" or "invention"—as a species of lying, and because his work did not presuppose for its original audience (since such a thing did not yet exist) any shared conception of the novel which putatively transcended problems of mendacity by appeal to "aesthetics" or to "realism." Such concerns in Defoe interpretation have persisted, as Michael Seidel observes, despite the subsequent development and general acceptance of fictional convention: "The shrewd criticism of William Hazlitt and Samuel Taylor Coleridge seriously explored [Defoe's] techniques for lying while seeming to tell the truth. These are still matters of supreme interest to the current crop of Defoe critics."[2]

I have said that Defoe's own definition of fiction, not merely as lying, but as "lying for no reason," returns us squarely to de Man's definition and the problem of fictional arbitrariness. Defoe also extends that problem to the morality of concealment, something we will pursue specifically in terms of juxtaposition of two chapters in *Robinson Crusoe*, on obscenity and lying.

I concur with Lincoln Faller that Defoe "had a good basic grasp of what we'd call narrative theory"[3]—or, even if not, that by following the fault lines of his position we can arrive at a good grasp of some significant problems.[4] Some of these may be globally relevant, but they take off from a specific historical context, one in which a book like *Robinson Crusoe* could genuinely deceive readers as to its historical authenticity, and be savagely attacked (by Charles Gildon, for example) as immoral lies.[5] We must therefore heed Faller's warnings against reading into Defoe's work "meanings (or absences of meaning) it could never have had for him and his original audience,"[6] something the following assessment by Seidel, for instance, seems to risk: "Defoe could not abide the notion that narrative invention is primarily a lie; it is, instead, a carefully crafted simulacrum, a stand-in for or mimicry of truth whose value lies in its *as if* quality."[7] Seidel's claim that "in his clumsy grappling with his first naive critics, Defoe was beginning to form a basis for the defence of realism"[8] may do slightly more justice to Defoe than earlier views of his ill-controlled realism represented by Ian Watt and Wayne Booth.[9] But it ignores Defoe's own repeated usage of the words *invention* and *story* as synonymous with falsehood, as well as the fact that his own appeals to "allegory" or "parable" differ very significantly from the defense of realism sustained according to Seidel (in a rather broad sense, one supposes) "by critics . . . from Coleridge to Georg Lukács."[10] Maximillian Novak and G. A. Starr both recognized this difference when they wrote, respectively, that Defoe's "defense of lying establishes a basis for any type of fiction which contains serious ideas, social commentary, or even a tag moral" (though this can "hardly be used to justify those parts of Defoe's fiction from which no moral whatsoever can be drawn"), and that "his theory of fiction does not really rest, as one recent critic [Novak] maintains, on a 'defense of lying', but rather on a traditional distinction *between* lying and beneficial deception."[11] The quibble over whether beneficial lying should be called lying pales before Novak's and Starr's agreement that Defoe viewed fiction—including his own "good" fiction or allegory—as a kind of deception. Seidel resists this conclusion on aesthetic grounds: "To call Crusoe a lie is to intimate that the process of fiction is incapable of producing an experience that, because it seems so true and powerful, is, in a sense, real."[12] But Defoe's own position, officially at least, seems to be that it is for precisely this kind of slippery confusion between being "seemingly true" and being "in a sense, real" that fiction, as opposed to allegory, must be feared and condemned. Better a coherent lie, thoroughly tied to reality, than something only real "in a sense."

That Defoe's deceptions still affect current Defoe scholarship is readily illustrated by the fact that the basic Defoe canon remains as contentious as it has ever been. More than one text I shall mention is still seriously disputed, and far from being restricted to his own period, the confusion continues to have serious consequences for the findings and careers of scholars and historians. Thus *A General History of the Pyrates* (1724), for example, was presented as (at least nominally) authored by Captain Charles Johnson until the 1920s, and, despite its confident attribution to Defoe by J. R. Moore, remains in doubt.[13] Similarly, Captain George Carleton, nominal author of *Memoirs of an English Officer*, appeared in nineteenth-century editions of the *Dictionary of National Biography*, and was taken seriously by historians as an eyewitness to the Peninsular Campaigns, before being attributed to Defoe's invention—an attribution now again disputed.[14] If Furbank and Owens are to be believed, even *Memoirs of a Cavalier* (1720)—which "instinct tells us . . . is a work of fiction by Defoe," and which provides a basis for significant critical assessments of Defoe—is not beyond suspicion.[15]

Despite the confusions of his bibliographers—confusions he apparently delighted in[16]—critical assessments of Defoe have developed considerably since the 1980s. No longer is debate largely divided between advocates of the naive and unruly protorealism described by Watt and Booth (in which irony was either absent or uncontrolled), and advocates, like Novak and Starr, of a narrowly controlled allegory in the Protestant tradition of spiritual autobiography. Stereotypes of the intellectually naive Defoe have not disappeared, however, any more than moral conflations of "the nastier aspects" of his characters with a picture of their author as a greedy opportunist.[17] Nor have the basic terms of the Watt-Booth/Novak-Starr opposition been clearly superseded.[18] Seidel, for example, regards the prefaces to *Robinson Crusoe* (which we will address later) as amounting to "a potent theory of realism,"[19] while Boardman views them as producing an "indeterminate measure of complication," and the novel as a whole as embodying "an impossible formal 'request,' that the reader experience [it] as both true and fabricated."[20] Boardman's overall view, summarized and questioned by Katherine Armstrong, is that "the inconsistencies and discrepancies in [Defoe's earlier] narration" are "a sign of Defoe's ideological confusion which only gave way to clarity of vision and purpose in *Roxana*."[21]

My analysis is perhaps best situated, though it differs significantly from both, between the contemporary views of Armstrong (1996) and Faller (1993). Armstrong regards *Memoirs of a Cavalier* (1720), *Colonel Jack* (1722), and *Moll Flanders* (1722) as "sustained exercise[s] in irony" that "are more lucidly understood as political interventions than as experiments in narrative form impelled by purely aesthetic and formal considerations."[22] Even *Crusoe*, though said to be "uniquely successful among Defoe's works (with the arguable exception of *Moll Flanders*) in going beyond the immediate occasion of its composition,"[23] is regarded as a contribution in part to immediate political circumstances (specifically to debate on the national debt). Though Armstrong's interpretive scheme may appear unduly restrictive, it provides a plausible defense of the basic consistency of Defoe's political views, and above all, from our perspective, interprets his irony in terms of genuine deception rather than merely as a literary or aesthetic device.

Faller resists, from another perspective, the "near incoherence" of Defoe's texts "implicit in the common notion that Defoe writes with a kind of 'journalistic' realism."[24] Against Laura Brown's view that Defoe's realism "[imitates] the randomness" of life and Watt's presumption of his "total devotion to the disorderliness of life," Faller pointedly reverses Watt's terms (while allowing that they "promiscuously intermingle"): "Defoe flouts the orderliness not of literature, but of life itself."[25] (Defoe's fiction, in short, exhibits an arbitrariness that is by no means "realistic.") Unlike Armstrong, Faller stresses the literary character of the work in terms of its formal, "musical," or "structural logic"[26]—and even in terms of the evocation of a gentlemanly "garden" of literary and conceptual play.[27] But this by no means precludes him from adopting an Armstrong-like conception of the deceptive management of men "by means of plausible and persuasive fictions."[28] For Faller, Defoe's fiction does not merely betray carelessness, naiveté, or bad faith in its disorder, though he calls Gildon perceptive to regard *Crusoe* as an "incoherent Piece."[29] Rather, he adopts Pierre Macherey's "theory of literary production"—"the disorder that permeates the [literary] work is related to the disorder of ideology (which cannot be organized as a system)"[30]—and concludes that Defoe conferred on the ideology of early capitalism "an essentially *unsystemizable* form."[31]

First in his prefaces, and then in *The Serious Reflections of Robinson Crusoe* (where the equation of fiction and random lying is explicit), we will see how Defoe's seeming "incoherence" nevertheless exhibits remarkable consistency or at least relentlessness. While "people usually think it easy to be arbitrary,"[32] this is not necessarily so, since, as the radical disagreements of his most perceptive critics continue to demonstrate, the achievement of genuine incoherence requires a firm grasp by negation (conscious or not) of every pertinent system of order. Faller makes the point "homeopathically": "Defoe's novels stimulate consideration of [the main faults of conventional criminal biography, facticity, and the unreliability of its narrators], almost homeopathically one might say, curing the disease by calling attention to it."[33] Indeed, we will see that this kind of *pharmakon* cure is explicitly recommended by Crusoe for liars and storytellers—though just how far Defoe consciously considered applying this principle to his own work seems unclear.

However, while Faller seems right on the money in his identification of the central problem in Defoe, I see no reason to assume that it can be circumscribed by the ideology of capitalism, early or late. For, unlike the *pharmakon* equation "tradesman = thief" that Faller discusses so intelligently,[34] the equations "fiction = falsehood" and "fiction = arbitrariness" cannot reduced to economic terms. The converse is perhaps rather the case.

Lying in the Prefaces

Because it would be misleading to consider the "theory" of lying, concealment, and fiction advanced in *The Serious Reflections* without at least some consideration of Defoe's practice of these behaviors, I begin with a consideration of his prefaces (since prefaces conventionally provide guides to the status, fictional or otherwise, of their texts). Admittedly, Defoe's prefaces may seem to do this, if at all, only by appearing even more unreliable than the texts themselves. But they do nevertheless provide a guide to his shorthand deployment of such synoptic terms as *History, Truth, Beauty, Virtue,* and so on; and though it is hardly news to find them wanting in coherence or reliability, it will be instructive to summarize some of their more peculiar involutions. To emphasize the characteristic rather than the exceptional, I have chosen several prefaces more or less at random from relatively well known works.

We begin with the relatively straightforward short preface to *A General History of the Pirates,* which opens with the claim that it derives directly from authentic accounts of pirates themselves or of those who captured them. If a lie is necessary, this would seem sufficient. But then immediately we are warned that though some of the details may seem to "divert" the reader like fictions, they are authentic nevertheless (with the apparently innocent implication that history can be at least as strange as fiction). This in turn, however, is directly followed by the suggestion of a tension between history and virtue, and soon it is admitted that "perhaps" some suppression of fact has occurred. Though Defoe's reminder that geographers make bad maps because they rely on illiterate eyewitnesses or informants who have reasons to conceal the truth hardly suggests that the text's distortion of history and geography is in the service of virtue, we are soon again reminded that truth, utility, and entertainment are not necessarily allies. After all this, the preface then returns to an even more barefaced version of the original lie—asserting that *all* the "facts" in the book are actually *provable.*[35]

Even supposing an irony directed at two audiences, one "naive," which needs to believe in the facts, the other aware that the most useful works are not always historical, it is hard to explain why the lie must be redoubled in this flagrant and implausible manner or how the other maneuvers fit together. (Moreover, unless indeed we regard this very flagrant incoherence as Defoe's particular signature, the uncertainty of attribution in this case makes clarificatory reference to other Defoe texts unreliable, even supposing these other texts were themselves clearer.)

Turning to the preface to *Memoirs of a Cavalier* (1720), a work more unanimously attributed to Defoe, we find that shadow-fictions and editorial mediations multiply. There are not merely an anonymous author (the cavalier himself) and anonymous editors, but also anonymous authors of the preface ("persons now concerned in the publication") perhaps or apparently different from these. Though we are told that there is no need to trace the origins of the memoirs, since their veracity has "sufficient sanction [from] all the Histories of the Times to which they relate," Defoe's "persons" go on to claim that the papers have been in their possession "above twenty years," and were found "by great Accident" in the closet of one of King William's secretaries of state. (In case we do not believe there is "no need," we are thus given to understand that it is "not proper" to inquire further into their origins.) Nevertheless, "no small Labour has been thrown away" on inquiring into the name of the author, and though only the initials of the son of a soldier who acquired the memoirs "as plunder" have been discovered (!), we are to be persuaded that all this gives "an authority" to the work.[36]

The authoritative assertion that the work "is a Confutation of many Errors in *all* the writers upon the subject" sits, however, uneasily with the confirmation earlier claimed from *"all* the Histories of the Times" (my emphases). Indeed, a change of tack emerges when it is admitted that while other eyewitness and contemporary accounts "perhaps have good Authority," they not only contain "less than half" the incidents, but also lack the "beautiful ideas" of the present work. This appeal to sheer quantity of historical data seems at first to rest on very different grounds than the appeal to ideas, let alone their beauty. But of course much of the data is in reality invented, so that the difference between so-called historical, ideological, and aesthetic merit is weakened if not erased by Defoe's forgery. By the end of the preface, such an erasure becomes virtually explicit. For the text now qualifies its truth claims— *"almost* all the facts, *especially* those of moment, are confirmed *for the general part* by all the writers of those Times" (my emphases)—and informs us that if the account is "embellished with Particulars, which are no where else to be found, that is the Beauty we boast of; and . . . it is that must recommend this work to all the men of Sense and Judgment that read it." In short, the wealth of so-called factual detail is now explicitly called an embellishment and identified with beauty, while the tension between beauty and truth appears speedily resolved in the claim that it is precisely this which recommends the work to men of sense and judgment.

Knowing that Defoe plagiarized much of his material from the likes of the republican-oriented Edmund Ludlow and Bulstrode White-locke,[37] as well as the Earl of Clarendon and others, may encourage us with hindsight to identify the particular beauties "nowhere else to be found" with Defoe's own inventions. Indeed, if we credit Armstrong's claim that "generally speaking, Defoe is less given to vivid detail than are actual histories,"[38] we may be inclined to revise the equation of sense, judgment, and beauty with the unique wealth of particular incidents, and return to the stress on "beautiful ideas." It is not impos-sible—though credulity may be stretched—to regard Defoe's irony as ultimately suggesting that his own ideological "take" on the history (the facts of which he has got entirely at second hand) is what distin-guishes his work. Certainly this would accord with Armstrong's thesis that a coherent anti-Jacobite irony controls the text as a whole.

On the other hand, the preface seems once again to indulge in quite needless and morally perilous complication. Though moral claims seem at first unusually absent, when they do appear—not regarding the moral of the story itself, but its relation to other texts on the same subject—they are compromising and equivocal, to say the least. After hearing that the *Memoirs* refute errors made by *all* other writers on the subject, special mention is made of the Earl of Clarendon's account of the English civil war, and we are further informed that the "editors were so just as to refuse" the request "above twenty years ago," by an author of an earlier refutation of Clarendon's royalist-inclined his-tory, to make use of some of the cavalier's own supposedly authentic details. This appeal to justice is all the more loaded, not only because it marks the sole intrusion of moral categories into the preface, but be-cause it risks being accused of quite concrete and gratuitous injustice—and toward those republican accounts, moreover, to which Defoe was especially indebted. For while suppression of the fact of Defoe's bor-rowing from such sources might perhaps be defended as necessary to the illusion of autobiography, it seems highly unnecessary for the supposed editors to pose as protecting the cavalier from being scooped by the very kind of author from whom Defoe has plagiarized most shamelessly. In a novelist like Sterne or Diderot, such a maneuver would be openly comic; but there seems little trace of "merriment" (to use Defoe's own term for what exceeds the "gravity" of history or allegory) in this context. Indeed, perhaps the story about the manu-script's being obtained as plunder is less wholly "merry" than first appears, serving as allegory of a more literary plunder. Such a pos-sibility, at any rate, is compatible with Crusoe's claim in *The Serious Reflections* that, rather than make the mistake of a realistic reading in which a certain amount of nonallegorical "invention" or "story" is taken for granted, readers should instead assume that *every* detail has allegorical significance. The trouble is that, while such teasing ambiguities may be, as Faller says, "no accidental qualities"—consequence of Defoe's "partly conscious, partly implicit 'theory of fiction' even current theorists might admire"[39]—we find ourselves faced with at once too many and too few editorial claims to resolve the matter in any satisfactory fashion.[40] In order to sort out the putative differences between merry and grave, literal and allegorical, fictional and factual in this preface, we seem to need another preface, more "editors," and so on.

It is thus not entirely surprising to find the "editor's" preface to *Colonel Jack* (1722) making the contradictory gesture of doing away with prefaces altogether. This work, we are told, needs one "as little as any before it"; and we are given to understand that its preface was written merely in deference to convention. Defoe nevertheless breezily exploits the opportunity to make some customary claims and justifications: that the text, for example, shows vice punished and virtue rewarded. This customary apology indeed now leads to another rather less conventional claim: that, provided the story as a whole is designed to fulfill such edifying aims, it matters not a jot whether it be "history" or "parable"—and thus, once again needs no introduction.[41]

Besides noting that the need for prefaces is here explicitly linked with the opposition between history and parable, we should underline that this claim is as radical and problematic as it is abrupt and undefended. For it seems obvious that it matters a great deal whether virtue is rewarded in history or in parable—despite Faller's generous glosses that "insofar as a history illustrates moral truth, it is in essence a parable; whatever difference remains is trivial," and that "trying to sift out the actual from the invented is not so important as looking for the meaning that stands behind both, and which makes both 'equally useful.' "[42] Faller's sympathetic aim is to "prevent the greatest danger to story-telling in Defoe's eyes, that fictions may become lies."[43] But we must consider, on this score, both how many lies Defoe tells elsewhere, and that the "naive" demand to know the difference between virtue's fate in history and in parable, or fiction, cannot be so easily evaded. If Defoe here relinquishes the "naive" lie which claims outright historicity, it is to replace it by an assertion whose mendacity is not so much diminished as more elusive. Far from rendering a preface superfluous, such a resolution of the disparity between history and parable in the interests of virtue would require, as Defoe himself implies, an almost interminable preface. The pleasant and delightful part of the book "speaks for itself," we are told, while the useful and instructive part would need a preface *as long as the book itself*. (If so, Defoe's "notorious verbosity,"[44] as well as his propensity to promise sequels to his books that might or might not materialize, may stem from a more interesting source than mere capitalist opportunism or poor taste.)

Faller notes that a similarly paradoxical proposal and withdrawal of the opposed categories of "story" and "history" occurs in the preface to *Roxana*, where, despite Defoe's claim to historicity, he goes on to call the novel a "story" seven times and "history" only twice. All this, according to Faller, must be "more than mere confusion or inattentiveness," and we may incline to agree that it signals "something *sui generis*."[45] Similar difficulties are found in the preface to *Moll Flanders*, which, though much discussed, still contains some twists worth emphasizing. Indeed, that preface is worth dwelling on here because it seems to exhibit a gratuitousness even more exemplary and perverse than has already been emphasized by critics.

Many critics have noted Defoe's coy challenge to the reader—having complained that in a world "so taken up with novels and romances it will be hard for a private History to be taken for Genuine"—"to decide as he pleases" about *Moll*'s status as fiction. But since the text is explicitly called a "Fable" with a moral, and defended in terms of the "usefulness" traditionally accorded to "Plays," it appears that decision has been made for us. The issue is complicated by the fact that "playing" or "jesting" is such an explicit object of critique in the novel itself, particularly "jesting" in the special sense that the border line between seriousness and jest is not clear (precisely as in Defoe's prefaces). Critics have been understandably quick to point out the salacious double edge, if not bad faith, of Defoe's exhortations to the reader to remain "serious" even where the story "might incline him otherwise," in a story supposedly "wrapped up clean" and "carefully garbl'd [sifted] of all levity and looseness."[46] Even a critic as sympathetic as Faller admits that "Defoe's writing may too often bring the modern sense of 'garbled' to mind."[47] Since it is immediately added that the "wicked part" of the story should be left for moral purposes as wicked as "the real History will bear," the moral process of "wrapping up clean" seems self-contradictory. As Armstrong puts it ("not wish[ing] to deny Defoe's disingenuousness"): "In a sense *Moll Flanders* capitalizes on the very sins it attempts to excoriate."[48]

Moll's "pretence" to penitence and the preface's claim to show virtue rewarded (though Moll, old and rich, "was not so extraordinary a Penitent as she was at first") have been extensively discussed without anything resembling critical unanimity. The enormous discrepancies between such views as Armstrong's (who compares *Moll* to *America's Most Wanted* and regards it first and foremost as a contribution to practical debate about crime)[49] and, say, those of the spiritual autobiography school seem even more exaggerated than is characteristic of critical debate.[50] Even so, no one, perhaps, has sufficiently emphasized the spectacularly bizarre and self-defeating trajectory of the preface's treatment of the relation between virtue and aesthetics, where quasi-random complications seem elevated almost to the level of a method.

Defoe's opening gambit is to blame the corrupt taste of the reader if the "penitent part" of Moll's story is not "so full of Life, Brightness and Beauty" as the rest—and we might wish he had simply left it at that. As it is, the penitent parts of Moll's story are not given the kind of space that would make such a caution against boredom particularly plausible; indeed, readers prejudiced against tales of virtue are more likely to be put off by the preface itself. Far from leaving well enough alone, however, Defoe draws our attention to the "fact" that Moll's story is left unfinished—the reason given, that no one can write up to the instant of death, being, as Faller says, "the ripest of red herrings"[51]—and takes the opportunity to advertise that two "of the most beautiful Parts [are] still behind" (that is, to come). Predictably, these will not provide beautiful accounts of penitence, but rather the adventures of Moll's "Governess," the abortionist, and her husband, the dashing highwayman. Moreover, while all this is often explained in terms of Defoe's opportunistic desire to leave room for best-selling sequels,[52] he seems inexplicably hell-bent on making life as difficult as possible for himself. Faller's suggestion that "perhaps (or so I believe) he didn't quite know himself what it all meant, and so escaped having to say so"[53] by writing a formal conclusion to the novel, may well be valid. But it doesn't explain why Defoe then admits or pretends, for no apparent reason, that there already exists a biography of Moll's final years. He is thus compelled to justify himself for not including it in the present volume or in a sequel to come, and for this purpose he now appeals—horror of horrors!—to its inferior "elegancy" or aesthetic merit.

The perverse pattern seems too gratuitous to be accidental: first one argues that texts describing virtue are the most beautiful; then, for no apparent reason, one invents such a text said to be too inelegant to merit publication. This level of self-defeating arbitrariness does seem, as Faller puts it, sui generis. Worse, we are told that the account of Moll's final years is part of the biography of Moll's husband, "written by a third hand" and very beautiful—thus suggesting that the *same* volume provides an inelegant account of virtue alongside a beautiful one of vice. We seem very close to turning Defoe's earlier accusations of readerly corruption against the author. For even if we generously suppose him to be denigrating some existing biography of the real criminal or criminals on whom Moll is based, no reason is given why the inelegant text of "not so extraordinary" virtue could not be just as well improved by the editor/author as Moll's own "loose" account.[54]

Defoe was surely no Gogol, another so-called father of realism, who starved himself to death when he found himself unable to describe paradise.[55] Yet it must be admitted that his text seems a model of rhetoric as self-frustration, not only in its perverse multiplication of difficulties, but in managing to suggest, just like so many of his critics, that the author himself may be the guilty party. Furbank and Owens are rather unusual among Defoe critics, but also apt, in speaking of a "self-lacerating quality in his vision," whose "tone is not irony . . . but something more original, for which rhetoric does not have a name."[56] We shall see shortly how the indictment of fiction is linked to a "lacerating" and "self-lacerating" pattern of victimage in *Robinson Crusoe*.

Lying for No Reason in *Robinson Crusoe*

Volume 1 of *Robinson Crusoe* is often presented as though volumes 2 and 3 didn't exist, and many readers of the celebrated novel have never heard of them. Critics also often ignore Crusoe's own admittedly rather shrill exhortations, in the preface to volume 3, that to ignore this volume is to misunderstand his whole project. For our purposes, however, *The Serious Reflections of Robinson Crusoe* is central, since Defoe's most extensive discussion of the relation between fiction and lying occurs there.

Readers and critics may perhaps be excused for this relative neglect not only because the *Reflections* appear a bit of a bore—perhaps exceeding volume 2 in this respect—but also because Crusoe's claim that it provides the key to the two earlier volumes seems obviously suspect. If, as we are told, the "first two volumes may be called the product" of the third, then this should very likely be attributed to divine providence of the kind that Crusoe experiences in volume 1, since it seems highly unlikely that Defoe had the idea of volume 3 in mind when he began the first. (It is often suggested, as I have said, that the "poor quality" sequels were born out of Defoe's unfailing instinct to capitalize on commercial success.) Laura Curtis's circumspect avoidance of a general "theory of fiction" in Defoe, as suspiciously ex post facto, seems confirmed here, as though the ex post facto "theory" were as mendacious as the texts it claims to explain.[57]

To highlight the issues of lying, concealment, and fiction as such, we will restrict ourselves to the prefaces to *Crusoe*, and to two consecutive chapters of volume 3—"Of Lewd and Immodest Discourse" and "Of Talking Falsely." In the latter, Crusoe proposes that lying is "mankind's darling sin and the devil's distinguishing character" since it so frequently accompanies "the concealing of all other crimes." But at least, he continues, in a well-known passage, "They that lie to gain, to deceive, to delude, to betray, as above [to murder, to rob, etc.], have some end in their wickedness; and though they cannot give the design for an excuse of their crime, yet it may be given as the reason and foundation of it. But to lie for sport, for fun, as the boys express it, is to play at shuttlecock with your soul, and load your conscience for the mere sake of being a fool, and the making a mere buffoonery of a story, the pleasure of what is below even madness itself."[58] Worlds away from Kant as Defoe is in most respects, "below even madness" is a thoroughly Kantian way to condemn lying considered not in terms of its motives or effects but in terms of sheer arbitrariness. Motivated lying, however heinous, is relatively rational, whereas the danger of those "white devils" who traffic in the "sport of lying" is that they not only mean no ill, but *"mean nothing at all"* (my emphasis). "They not only tell untruths, but 'the truth is not in them,'" and in lying for no reason, they achieve "a meanness below the dignity of commonsense": "This supplying a story by invention is certainly a most scandalous crime, and yet very little regarded in that part. It is a sort of lying that makes a great hole in the heart, at which by degrees a *habit of lying* enters in. Such a man comes quickly up to a total disregarding the truth of what he says . . . but commands the company . . ." (99).

The relevance of this to Crusoe's life is obscure, but its potential relevance to Defoe's invention of his "Surprising Adventures" is painfully obvious. While the essay begins by specifying its topic as this "strange liberty (*particularly in conversation*)" (my emphasis), it enumerates techniques to be found throughout Defoe's *writing*, and at least three times returns to make a defensive distinction between fiction as "sport" and as parable. Parable is a kind of *pharmakon* remedy for the evils of fiction, "this *other* jesting with truth" (my emphasis), of which examples are said to be the Scriptures, *Pilgrim's Progress*, and "in a word, the adventures of your fugitive friend, 'Robinson Crusoe.' "

Having been savagely attacked by such critics as Gildon, Defoe was clearly sensitive to the objection that "the preceding volumes of this work seem to be . . . condemned" by his own equation of fiction and lying. He therefore demands "in justice [that] such an objector stay his censure till he sees the end of the scene, when all that mystery shall discover itself" (103). But the discovery of the allegorical mystery seems to require, as we saw in *Colonel Jack*, a potentially interminable set of prefaces—the *Reflections* being, in effect, a whole book of them (concluding with an essay on angels that openly exacerbates rather than dispelling mystery, and can hardly be said to have produced amicable agreement among the critics).[59] Moreover, *Crusoe* offers us no less than four prefaces as such—the editor's prefaces to volumes 1 and 2, plus Crusoe's own preface and the "Publisher's Introduction" to volume 3—which need to be taken into account if we concede to Defoe's demand that we consider the status of his text globally. I will therefore do so briefly.

The brief preface to volume 1 begins with the equivocal claim that "the Editor believes the thing to be a just History of Fact; neither is there any Appearance of Fiction in it." Stressing the mere "appearance" of nonfiction, and overlooking (or minimizing) the editorial lie, Seidel regards this as a "manifesto of realism."[60] But while such a view may seem at first compatible with Defoe's claim that the diversion and instruction of the reader will be "the same" whether the text is believed to be history or fiction, the reason given for this—"because such things are dispatch'd" (hastily read or dealt with)[61]—is hardly the one preferred by enthusiasts of realism. The opposition between allegory and history may perhaps collapse in an edifying reading of any text, as *Colonel Jack* suggests, but their coincidence or reconciliation is hardly edifying when put down to mere carelessness or haste.[62]

In any case, the preface to volume 2 raises the stakes in a way that seems quite incompatible with such a laissez-faire attitude, doubtless because Defoe had recently learned from critics like Gildon that the problem of fiction so facilely "dispatch'd" can unfortunately matter a great deal. Six short paragraphs pack quite a few punches: first, against those "envious people" who have made "abortive" attempts, "as impotent as malicious," "to reproach [*Crusoe*] with being a romance, to search it for errors in geography, inconsistency in the relation, and contradictions in the fact"; and second, against the "scandalous . . . knavish and ridiculous . . . abridging this work," which does an "injury . . . to the proprietor" equivalent to "robbing on the highway, or breaking open a house" (for which the penalty was death). Since a specific implication seems to concern a possible abridgement by leaving out volume 2, modern editors and critics, who regularly do so, may feel relieved that Defoe cannot implement his threat that "nothing shall be wanting on his part to do them justice."

Despite the proprietorial language and comparison with robbery, Defoe is ostensibly concerned not with financial losses but with his claim that in abridging the work editors "strip it" of those moral and religious reflections which are its greatest beauties, leaving it "naked of its brightest ornaments . . . calculated for the infinite advantage of the reader." This, combined with "pretend[ing] that the author has supplied the story out of his invention," takes from the work "the improvement which alone recommends that invention to wise and good men." Yet despite his violent attack on those who give the lie to the "history" of volume 1, Defoe makes no effort to hide that a "part" of the story, at least, "may be called invention or parable," arguing that this is legitimated by its moral design. This admitted, we wonder why it is still perversely insisted that critics are criminal to "pretend" that the fiction is a fiction. After all, if their crime consists in a failure to draw Defoe's own distinction between invention as parable and romance, they are still correct to warn naive readers against taking, say, details of geography literally. Rather than helping such readers to make the appropriate distinctions between literal and figural, Defoe seems actively to encourage confusion, and it remains utterly unexplained here why a naively literal reading should be preferable if under the further delusion that it is engaged with a genuinely historical rather than a fictional or allegorical text. On the other hand, if lying for a reason, however bad, is preferable to lying "at random from the truth,"[63] then any referential reading, however false, is preferable to a reading that suspends the problem of reference in the name of pure invention. Falsehood is consistently preferred by Defoe to "free play" or "fiction," however realistic.

It may seem implausible to connect the preface's menacing and personal tone to such considerations, but a comparable virulence surfaces in contexts where no obvious personal interest is at stake. Defoe's general view is actually no more perverse than Paul de Man's characterization of fiction in terms of a random lie, or than Goodman's insistence that all fictions are actual. This is merely to say that every speech act may, at a minimum, be read as an allegory of its causal conditions, or that every fiction can be read as an allegory of autobiography.

In the preface to volume 3, where for the first time Crusoe writes his own preface, this principle actually becomes structurally explicit. Repeating accusations against the "envious and ill-disposed part of the world [which has] raised some objections against the two first volumes, on pretence, for want of a better reason, that (as they say) the story is feigned, that the names are borrowed . . . that there never were any such man or place, or circumstances in any man's life," he responds: "I *Robinson Crusoe* being at this Time in perfect and sound Mind and Memory . . . do hereby declare, their Objection is an Invention scandalous in Design, and false in Fact; and do affirm, that the Story, though Allegorical, is also Historical . . . [,] the beautiful Representation of a Life of unexampled Misfortunes, and of a Variety not to be met with in the World" (ix). Even if we ignore the literal implication of "not to be met with in the world" (an amusing figure with which to claim historical authenticity), this appeal by a fictional pseudonym to the language of legal oath has its own irony, since that language obviously supposes the authenticity of names as well as events. Crusoe's claim that "there is a man alive, and well known too, the actions of whose life are the just subject of these volumes . . . and to this I set my name" (x) thus conforms rather precisely to his own definition of fiction as "meaning nothing at all," since "Crusoe" merely signs his name to a declaration that it is not his name.

Comparing his story to *Don Quixote*, regarded as "an emblematic history of, and . . . just satire upon, the Duke de Midina Sidonia," he further suggests that his autobiography is really a disguised biography. But, if so, why could Defoe not sign his own name or initials, or at least hide more consistently behind third-party "editors" in making this declaration? The fact that no subsequent scholarship has managed to come up with this "well known" person suggests that there was little risk of the allegory being too transparent—unless, perhaps, that well-known man were Defoe himself. Pat Rogers's claim that no one has ever doubted Defoe was the "man alive" is highly exaggerated[64] (and he himself discusses the frustrations, confusions, and implausibilities that have attended every attempt to map out autobiographical correspondences in any detail), but there is no denying that Crusoe's language is insistently autobiographical, even perversely so, given the biographical claim. The extreme declaration that "there is not a circumstance in the imaginary but has its just allusion to a real story," for instance, makes it hard to imagine how the text could be anything but autobiographical, since no one could attest to the allegorical verity of every event in "the inimitable Life of Robinson Crusoe" except the inimitable author himself. This being the case, Seidel's claim that "in a very real way, *Robinson Crusoe* is a tale of telling"[65] would be true with a vengeance, insofar as *Crusoe* might have to be read as an allegory, not only of Defoe's life, but of its own production.

The text seems ridiculously opaque and ridiculously transparent at the same time. First Crusoe fobs us off with the notion that his edifying "deductions" from his life will make amends for his refusing to let "the reader into a nearer explication of the matter," that is, for not "having the emblem explained by the original." In a manner characteristically perverse, however, the verdict of autobiography becomes virtually impossible to resist at the very moment the text explains why the subject of the allegory must be concealed—"because the Teacher, *like a greater*, [has] no Honour in his own Country," and "Facts that are form'd to touch the Mind, must be done a great Way off, and by somebody never heard of." (Even this equivocal avowal raises "a Question, whether the Instruction of these Things will take place, when you are supposing the Scene . . . had its Original so near Home" [xiii].) Given the text's reflections on contemporary envy and obstinacy, no wonder the author would avoid proclaiming too loudly his pedagogical authority, let alone comparing himself explicitly to Christ. But at the same time, as Pat Rogers implies, we are hardly encouraged to believe that the teacher is really a third party, especially since it has been stressed that so much instructional value lies in the text's allegorical form, the work of the author. Indeed, when we are told by the "Publisher's Introduction" that "the author shows now, that he has learned sufficient experience how to make other men wise and himself happy," author and teacher appear again to merge.

Readers may find such complacent claims doubly irritating inasmuch as they are surrounded by such confusion, and inasmuch as the publisher's accusations against the "pirates" of the text—"shifting off the guilt, as well as they could, though weakly, from one to another"— seem to apply very well to Defoe himself, "weakly" shifting responsibility for his exorbitant claims from the editor to Crusoe, to the publisher, and back again. The text seems to be structured in such a way that the rationale for its deceptions becomes increasingly obscure the more attention is bestowed on them, continuing gratuitously to obstruct comprehension even when the general shape of the concealment is admitted.

This gratuitousness is particularly striking in Crusoe's listing of almost a page and a half's worth of details from his story, such as "the Story of the Print of a Man's Foot, and Surprise of the old Goat, and the Thing rolling on my Bed, and my jumping out in a Fright, [which] are all Histories and real Stories" (x). For while critics have been quick to seize on the more obvious possible parallels with Defoe's life, such as his imprisonment—"it is as reasonable to represent one kind of imprisonment by another, as it is to represent anything that really exists by that which exists not"(x)—many of the details seem so insistently literal as to be interpretable only as directly transposed to Crusoe's island from another geographical context, and others remain quite impenetrable. The procedure appears so gratuitous that one can imagine Crusoe repeating every detail of his account (like Borges's story of the word-for-word re-creation of *Don Quixote*) without anything becoming clearer.

We may nevertheless feel confident that at least one formal principle of the allegory remains crystal clear to the point of being trivial: the substitution of fictitious names (like "Robinson Crusoe") for real ones (like "Defoe" or his schoolmate "Cruso"). But unfortunately this is emphatically not the case: "It is most real that I had a Parrot, and taught it to call me by my Name, such a Servant a Savage [*sic*], and afterwards a Christian, and that his Name was called *Friday*, and that he was ravished from me by Force, and died in the Hands that took him, which I represent by being killed; this is all literally true" (x–xi). Though "Robinson Crusoe" is punctiliously presented at least once in quotation marks, note that Friday is not—and that the obvious editorial solution of adding them would simply render "and that his name was called '*Friday*'" utterly vacuous. Once again, Crusoe conforms remarkably well to his definition of fiction as "meaning nothing at all."

Assuming it highly unlikely that Defoe or some other person on whom Crusoe is modeled had a servant really called Friday (and even if so, we would still need to explain why the servant's striking name should be unconcealed when it seems so important that his master remain hidden), we may note further that since Crusoe supposedly named Friday "realistically" in memory of the day of the week on which they met, the problem is not merely nominal. On the contrary, inasmuch as the day of the week is regarded as strictly accidental, we would still need to explain how this corresponds to a naming in real life—something complicated by the fact that Crusoe exploits the "real" accident to assign his own allegoric meaning. For Friday, of course, is the day on which the Good Friday is "saved" by Crusoe, and underlines the resemblance between Crusoe and Christ. Thus the allegoric or meta-allegoric schema here has the singular characteristic of constructing an equation between the accidental character of the real (preserved in allegoric transposition) and the arbitrary character of the allegoric (which is precisely the arbitrariness of naming). Such an equation might certainly be ascribed to providence in Crusoe's terms (where the real and the allegoric must coincide just as we are told they should in a virtuous text), all the more so because only the providential Word could create reality by merely naming it—that is, imbue the arbitrariness of the sign with full causal efficacy. Here we may recall the merit of Faller's claim that "Defoe flouts the orderliness not of literature, but of life," as against Watt's view that he merely imitates life's disorder. For only in literature is naming characteristically providential or allegoric, whereas the orderliness of life precisely depends on distinguishing between the causal efficacy of ordinary accidents and the noncausal arbitrariness of naming, between the historic and the allegoric. Seidel's tendency to translate *allegory* as *realism* should thus be reversed. Flouting "life's orderliness" means flouting both its order and its mode of randomness, while literary order, if Faller is correct, is not incompatible with a most spectacular arbitrariness or disorder, sui generis rather than realistic. (The prevalence of disorder, as Peirce reminded us, is a sign rather of the intervention of law than the dominance of mere chance).

As a matter of fact, of course, "and his name was called *Friday*" is literally true only of his naming by Defoe—and thus a sort of reductio ad absurdum of Seidel's description of *Crusoe* as "in a very real sense . . . a tale of its telling." But it is worth pointing out that Defoe's peculiarly indefensible insistence on the truth of the name has a substantive and potentially sacrificial counterpart in later commentaries for whom Friday's very identity is problematic. Leslie Stephen, for example, claimed Friday is more like an English servant than a genuine "savage," rather as Dickens (who lamented the heartless lack of sentiment in Crusoe's attitude to Friday's death) viewed the women in the novel as "men without breeches."[66] Here the merely formal problem of nomination, as we have pursued it, extends from proper names to general names like "woman" and "savage," fully referential and ideological in implication. It is in such terms (also linking the treatment of Friday to that of women in Defoe) that J. M. Coetzee situates the problem of "the truth of Friday": "What is the truth of Friday? You will respond: he is neither cannibal nor laundryman, these are mere names, they do not touch his essence, he is a substantial body, he is himself, Friday is Friday. But that is not so. . . . He is the child of his silence, a child unborn, a child waiting to be born that cannot be born."[67]

As in Defoe's text, the very tautology that "Friday is Friday" leads to a radical negation of this proposition. Coetzee also offers a particular sacrificial gloss on his namelessness: his tongue has been cut out—perhaps by Cruso himself.[68] Though the detail is invented, it has eerie parallels in Defoe. First, the very syntax of "It is most real that I had a Parrot, and taught it to call me by my Name, such a Servant a Savage" unites Friday and the mimetic parrot (unable to name itself) in a sentence that combines his naming with the manner of his death. Second, while Crusoe's rationale for representing this death by murder might possibly be defended inasmuch as Friday's "ravishment" resulted in his death, such a substitution of effect for cause seems again strikingly gratuitous, emphasizing not so much the "murder" inflicted by the ravishers as that arbitrarily imposed by Defoe's text. In both Coetzee and Defoe himself the violence done to Friday is *literally symbolic*, a matter of naming (recalling de Man's account of Rousseau's Marion.)

I accordingly propose "And his name was called *Friday*" as a model of fiction in Defoe—like Valéry's famous model cited from Stendhal: "The Marquise went out at five o'clock." Where Valéry's model emphasizes the first-level arbitrariness of realism,[69] the imitation of randomness in life, Defoe's own "random lie" reveals a second-level or metalevel arbitrariness, a lie that occurs at the level of the allegoric explanation of the "realistic" substratum. Defoe's thoroughly Kantian gesture of condemning fiction, conceived as random lying, as worse than murder, is here fulfilled to perfection—gratuitous murder included. Faller's view of the systematically "homeopathic" function of Defoe's "incoherence" also seems confirmed. Indeed, one of Crusoe's own sacrificial or pharmacological solutions to the problem of the liar is that he lie on and on until no one believes a word.

Crusoe on Obscenity

We now arrive at the crux of my argument concerning the sacrificial *pharmakon* relation of lying and concealment in Defoe, which confirms in a more precise way what we saw in chapter 1—that an arbitrary scapegoating of the liar is mirrored by an essentially arbitrary affirmation of concealment. Allegory is itself conceived as a mode of concealment, but Defoe also deals with nonliterary varieties.

Despite difficulties detailed by Crusoe in converting the island inhabitants of volume 2, with their new women, to Christian marriage, obscene language seems hardly a major theme in the novel. Yet Crusoe's chapter "Of Lewd and Immodest Discourse" stands prominently before his chapter on lying in volume 3. His argument against obscene language is based on an analogy with clothing: what clothes are required to conceal should equally be concealed in speech. Immodest speech is said to be like "exposing the nakedness of Nature, the common mother of us all" (95). The argument against lying is thus directly preceded by an argument for concealment.[70]

Significantly, the chapter is not directed at those honest and unconcealed reprobates whose obscene words reflect their obscene behavior. Precisely, honesty in this case is regarded as irredeemable except possibly by "gaol or . . . hospital"—though an even more desperate solution is said to consist, just as in the case of the liar or fictionalist, in "go[ing] on" and "run[ning] their length till their carcass stinks as bad as their discourse, and the body becomes too nasty for the soul to stay any longer in it" (92). Just as no one will seek the body of truth beneath the mendacious clothes of the inveterate liar, so no one will seek the soul beneath the corrupt body and speech of the debauchee. Both the honestly immodest nonconcealer and the inveterate fictionalist require sacrificial treatment of an extreme order, the former "repent[ing] sometimes in that emblem of hell, a fluxing house, and, under the surgeon's hands" (92).

Though such harsh words may seem designed for precisely this kind of shameless reader, Crusoe instead directs his homily at more ambiguous men "of seeming modesty" who nevertheless use "lewd and filthy expressions" in a way that "has something in it of a figure which intends more than is expressed" (92). Either practice accords with speech, says Crusoe, or we must assume that "not being able yet to arrive to such a degree of wickedness as he desires, [such a man] would supply that defect with a cheat, and persuade you to believe he is really worse than he is." On the one hand, we are told that "he that desires to be worse than he thinks he is, is certainly as bad as he desires to be"; but on the other hand, he who "let[s] fly the excrescences of it at his mouth, is as wicked as the devil can *in reason* desire of him" (93, my emphasis). In the first case, the distinction between Crusoe's two classes of men seems to collapse; but in the second case, just as in his attack on fiction, it seems to turn around an opposition between wickedness without limit and wickedness constrained by reason, albeit the devil's. Either the "cheat" of immodest speech turns out not to be one after all (the man really is as wicked as his discourse implies), or it is lie commensurate with some degree of reason and thus, we may deduce—since (bad) reason is amenable to (good) reason—appropriate as the object of Crusoe's persuasion.

Crusoe pointedly distinguishes between religious and secular arguments for modesty, equivalent to the difference between sin as such and "sin against breeding and society" (93). Even his interpretation of Genesis occurs after he has already descended "from the wickedness to the indecency of the matter" (93)—implying that Genesis has a sociological as well as a theological significance. According to him, it is "a mistake when we say sin was the immediate cause of shame. . . . Shame was the effect of nakedness, as nakedness was the effect of sin" (93). Modesty is therefore perhaps not "an original virtue," though "it cannot but be allowed that sin has thereby brought us to a necessity of making modesty be a virtue"; and "sin would have a double influence upon us if, after it had made us ashamed, it should make us not ashamed again" (93). Both modesty and immodesty, clothing and nakedness, virtue and vice are things to be ashamed of. The virtue of modesty is shame itself, whereas wholly pure and irredeemably immodest people are said to resemble each other in being unashamed (93). Modesty and shamelessness are predictably *pharmakon* signs of both innocence and guilt, health and disease, remedy and poison.[71]

It is notable that Crusoe's attack on obscenity seems at least as obscene as its putative target, the bawdy talk of seemingly modest people. He calls talking bawdy "that sodomy of the tongue" (in comparison with which the modern "arse licker" seems quite mild); and such mere talkers are told that they ought to enact their discourse, "act the common requirements of Nature in the most publickest places of the streets, bring their wives or whores to the exchange and to the market-places, and lie with them in the street" (94). "Talking bawdy is like a man going to debauch his own mother . . . exposing the nakedness of Nature"(95). Crusoe seems hell-bent on revealing the worst possible obscenity lurking in the most innocent lewd figure "which intends more than is expressed," literalizing and enacting every linguistic form ("mother nature," for example) in a kind of obscene incarnation of figure. Like the nakedness of the saint and the sinner, God's reasons and the devil's are precisely alike in pharmacological form.

Yet, for all his violence, Crusoe admits that he has no fully convincing argument for modesty of dress except, ultimately, the inductive principle that where no rational argument can convincingly be brought against social custom and habit, the latter are presumptively validated. Whereas fiction, the "habit of lying," is condemned on the basis of its arbitrary irrationality and shameless exhibitionism, the habit of concealment—"habit" in the sense of dress—is defended on the basis of its habitual character. But if fully revealing otherwise concealed sacrificial arbitrariness is thus characteristic of fiction, no one can complain that Defoe's text does not do the job—not least in Crusoe's spectacularly gratuitous concluding argument that lewd talk should be avoided just as much as nudity is, *on account of the weather*! His trajectory from sodomy to the weather is not only splendidly British, but a paradigm of fiction in his own sense.

4

Lies and Truths:

Mimetic-Sacrificial

■ **Falsification in Stendhal**

Ce roman n'en est pas un.
—STENDHAL

Stendhal is exemplary here for several reasons. His well-known obsession with secrecy, disguise, and pseudonymity (he employed around a hundred and fifty pseudonyms and his diaries were written in a multi-lingual code) make him, like Defoe, an interesting liar and concealer in his own right. While his writerly career began with acts of genuine plagiaristic fraud, he developed into maturity by frankly incorporating lying and concealment, plagiarism, and inverse plagiarism (where the author's words are falsely attributed to others), as integral structural features of his fiction. Like Defoe, he was still in touch with fiction as genuine deception, but, unlike Defoe, he was working with a form (the novel) whose mimetic prestige was already well established. Whereas Defoe had to defend himself against bald accusations of lying, Stendhal took pains to more or less blatantly falsify what might have otherwise passed as quite innocent or merely "fictional." This is not to say that pragmatic motivations are not often involved in his deceptions, but that he also offers us (as Defoe could not) a complex reflection on the fully fledged conventions of novelistic mimesis that puts our basic problem in a new light.

Stendhal is also exemplary for us because the problem of mimesis-as-representation is inseparable in his work from social mimesis. As René Girard recognized, he makes explicit not only the relation between artistic-mimetic "form" and social-mimetic "content," but also the general mimetic-sacrificial landscape in which these mutually function. Symbolic sacrifice is everywhere illustrated, not merely in such evident "literal" features as Julien's death in *Le Rouge et le noir*, but also in terms of the functioning of symbolisms themselves. Neither truth-telling nor literary mimesis escape systematic sacrificial formulation in Stendhal; indeed, we may legitimately regard at least some of his "random lies" as quite conscious counter-sacrifices or *pharmaka* directed against the sacrificial dimension of "mimetic representation" or "realism" as he conceives it. Arbitrary mendacity here clearly means consciously "willed" or "judged" rather than accidental or merely haphazard.

A simple but exemplary case of such lying occurs in his own projected review of *Le Rouge et le noir* written under the pseudonym D. Gruffot Papera in 1832. Having praised his novel at great length for its mimetic fidelity to the period, Papera continues: "One thing will surprise the reader. This novel isn't one. Everything it recounts really happened in 1826 in the neighborhood of Rennes. It was in this town that the hero perished after having fired two pistol shots at his first mistress, of whose children he had been tutor, and who by a letter had prevented him from marrying his second mistress, a very rich girl. M. de S[tendhal] has invented nothing."[1] This is exemplary of the *pharmakon* relation between truth and lies in Stendhal, since at the very moment he reveals the real relation between the novel and the history of Antoine Berthet, on whom Julien's story is partly based, he simultaneously falsifies the date and place of Berthet's execution (which was really in Dauphine in 1827). Like Defoe's handling of the name "Friday," this falsification seems all the more gratuitous inasmuch as it concerns mere names and dates (for what does it matter to our understanding of the relation between fiction and reality whether Berthet was executed in 1826 or 1827?). As in Defoe, the random lie appears as a second-level or metalevel arbitrariness that occurs at the level of an explicit articulation of relations between fiction and the real: a gratuitous falsification of what seems already arbitrary or marginal in significance.

But whereas in Defoe, as we saw, such falsification often seemed to operate at the uncertain limits of authorial consciousness and control, in Stendhal it is both clearly willful and quasi-systematic, as though "the essence of the Stendhalian narrator . . . [were] the 'constant and exemplary transgression of the rules and functions apparently constitutive of the literary game.' "[2] This literary game does not so much entail a ludic, "postmodern" suspension of truth, however, as a kind of paradoxical affirmation of truth. Just as the potential falsehood of "realistic" truth is indicated by the accompanying lie, so the lie stands as a sacrificial index of truth—truth affirmed in the very moment of its sacrifice. We read in the autobiographical *La Vie de Henry Brulard*: "How many precautions must one not take in order not to lie."[3] Yet "paradoxically, it takes hypocrisy to protect integrity."[4] What matters to "truth" is not the individual truth or falsehood, but what we earlier called the truth-power of the system, its law. Despite Stendhal's famous liking for *le petit fait vrai*, as Ann Jefferson puts it, "factual accuracy is consequently irrelevant to truth, or even, at times, *thoroughly incompatible with truth*."[5] Truth itself appears as *pharmakon* in its successive manifestations as fact and law.

This chapter will analyze Stendhalian mendacity in terms that both follow and resist aspects of Girard's reading of *Le Rouge et le noir* in *Mensonge romantique et vérité romanesque* (1961).[6] Stendhal provides a model of fiction that is not only plainly situated in a more general mimetic-sacrificial landscape, but also compels us to modify and expand Girard's own exposition of how "truth" functions in this landscape. With so much intelligent work recently devoted to Stendhal, it will also be helpful to invoke some relevant aspects of contemporary debate.

Mimetic Pharmaka

Stendhal's oft-parroted formula that "the novel is a mirror" (which first occurs in *Le Rouge* as the epigraph to chapter 13) was often in the past taken, rather astonishingly, at more or less face value as a simple affirmation of realism. But no one, particularly after reading recent studies, can ignore the counterevidence. Ann Jefferson, for example, observes that the very repetition of the formula in *Le Rouge*, not to speak of Stendhal's other works, undermines "whatever authority the utterance in its epigraphic form might have had."[7] Stendhal's false attribution of the epigraph to the seventeenth-century historian Saint-Real, as Jefferson, Stirling Haig, and others have surmised,[8] is also a double joke, since a historian called "Holy Real" is made to appeal to the novel rather than to history as a model of mimetic fidelity (turning against himself, so to speak, in the mimetic and Aristotelean rivalry between history and fiction as claimants to truth).[9] The characteristic comic edge of Stendhal's appeals to literary mimesis makes it wise to stress, at least provisionally, that "the mimetic function operates within a ludic framework" in Stendhal's fiction, a framework which lays bare "the arbitrariness of narration."[10]

Jefferson's *Reading Realism in Stendhal* shows to what extent contemporary defenses of realism in Stendhal recognize its necessary complications, both because "Stendhal's novels turn the mimetic language into dialogic polyphonies of discourse" and because the problem of mimesis in Stendhal is always that of the mimetic double bind: "The novels impose a double bind of the most intractable kind. But it is a double bind that, far from spelling defeat for its victim, is actually promising a solution. Its fundamental contradictoriness is a sign that the very reading that allows representation to take place cannot itself be represented. . . . The reader who enables mimesis cannot her-/himself be mimetically figured, cannot consequently be emulated."[11] Jefferson here states the crucial complication of the relation between literary and social mimesis in Stendhal, which is that authentic individuality and insight are always initially defined in opposition to what can be imitated—both socially (in fashion, for example) and representationally. Her linkage of mimetic representation and emulation is taken a step further by Jefferson Humphries, for whom the very "ideology of realism" is "generated from that very tautology, or riddle" that "we can desire only those things that are desirable" (his summary of the mirror-logic of mimetic desire in Girard's sense).[12] Humphries's claim that "*The Red and the Black*, on the surface, observes all the proprieties of an unquestioning realism"[13] is surely overstated, unless such phenomena as the falsified epigraphs, the falsified date of composition, and so on—not to mention the fact that the number of Madame de Rênal's children varies from chapter to chapter—can be dismissed as peripheral or (in the latter case) accidental.[14] Nevertheless he agrees with both Girard's and Jefferson's observations that in Stendhal "imitation in the sense of mimesis [representation] always takes place in a context involving imitation in the other, pejorative sense,"[15] and that "realism itself is in danger of being caught up in this pattern of conformity, repetition and fashion" (Stendhal's pseudocompulsive plagiarism being the most succinct expression of this).[16]

Unlike many others, however, Humphries might be called an ultra-Girardian in that he sees no escape from mimetic desire: "The ironic stance of Stendhal's narrator does not constitute a real escape from mimetic desire, but starts from the premise that no real escape is possible: our desire is then not only vulnerable to manipulation, but is *defined* by manipulation—willing, conscious, or not."[17] While we will later need to clarify this in relation to the implications of Girard's own reading, Humphries here stresses the omnipresence of mimetic deception in Stendhal, denying the possibility of escape from what Jefferson, like Girard, calls the mimetic double bind. It is well known, for example, that the category of *folie* ("folly" or "madness") plays a quasi-comic, quasi-sacred role in the Stendhalian lexicon; it belongs with the Exceptional, the Unexpected, the Unpredictable, the Accidental, the Inexplicable, the Inexpressible, the Original, the Unique, the Singular, and so on, that make up his favored set of antinomies to mimetic law. But Jefferson and Shoshana Felman are "completely wrong," according to Humphries, to regard Julien Sorel's "folie," in *Le Rouge*, in terms of one " 'who has no language in common with his peers, and whose solitary word fails to make itself understood' "[18]— that is, to see his oft-affirmed singularity (especially at the end of the novel) as any genuine way out of mimetic "inauthenticity."[19] Similarly, Leo Bersani's view is that "unsayability is a sign of [the withdrawal's] impossibility, its status as myth and illusion." Christopher Prendergast—who cites Bersani, and for whom irony and silence (the "more powerful" escape) are also two ways that Stendhal withdraws from the "contract" of the *vraisemblable*[20]—restricts this impossibility to the limits of nineteenth-century intelligibility: "What Stendhal rejects is not the idea of representation as such, but outworn forms of representation."[21] But in either case, we would expect the kind of *pharmakon*-ambivalence that Prendergast himself explicitly invokes in his study.[22]

Despite Stendhal's own frequent appeals to accident and the unexpected, it is important to stress that the "arbitrariness" of his fiction cannot be reduced to a realistic mimesis of mere chance. Thus while David Bell's 1993 study of "chance, random, and disorderly phenomena in the context of the French realist novel" (including Stendhal's *La Chartreuse de Parme*)[23] has much to recommend it, its realist temptation was aptly predicted by Prendergast, who warned (in 1986) against "simply produc[ing] a new *vraisemblable* according to which 'life' is properly grasped in terms of the disruptive and aleatory movements of the *imprevu*."[24] Humphries also makes the obvious point that while coincidence and contingency may appear, in *Le Rouge*, "to structure the book's opening"—and more than its opening—they "are in fact extremely contrived."[25]

To clarify the tension between the critics on this subject, we may appeal to one of the novel's own explicit treatments of mimetic representation—in Mathilde's portrait of Julien, which conjoins mimesis in its double sense of representation and social mimesis, and arbitrariness in its double sense of willfulness and randomness. Stendhal's concern with the relation between mimetic representation and mimetic emulation could not be more pointed, since Mathilde (Julien's second lover) explicitly views the other young men around her as mere "copies" (288) of each other, while Stendhal puts her in the double bind of trying to make a mimetic copy of an original (as she sees Julien), a man not susceptible to imitation. Mathilde's first desultory effort, "at random," looks "remarkably like Julien"—a highly predictable Stendhalian first move. Transported by what she takes to be "conclusive evidence of a great passion," she attempts to produce a proper portrait, but "the profile penciled at random was a far better likeness" (288). Mimetic truth is seemingly produced "at random" instead of by mimetic law.

Humphries says this "suggests that there may be more of accident than of will in what we call successful originality in realistic art."[26] But "accident" is misleading, unless we are to believe that her successful portrait is strictly a product of chance (a most contrived coincidence on Stendhal's part indeed). Her randomness has nothing to do with the representation as such (since the "random" likeness is a good one), but must be defined in relation to habits of representation (the rules she imitates from past experience or her art classes), her mimesis of (the rules of) mimesis. Mimetic truth is achieved by means she is incapable of imitating—which is not at all to say by chance.

It is entirely nonaccidental, moreover, that Mathilde's portrait of Julien almost directly precedes Stendhal's famous discussion of his own portrayal of Mathilde. In Mathilde's portraiture he has given us, I suggest, a preliminary model for his own. This is the much-discussed narrative intervention in which "the novel is a mirror" formula occurs again, defending the novel's representation of the mud on the road in the interests of truth. But then, in a typical volte-face, the narrator interjects that Mathilde's "character is purely imaginary" (289): "Now that it's fully understood that a character like Mathilde is impossible in our age, no less prudent than virtuous, I am less afraid of distressing the reader by describing further the follies of this attractive girl" (290). Haig cites Prendergast in regarding this primarily in terms of an ironic preemption of the moral outrage, combined with critical accusations of implausibility, with which Mathilde's behavior was actually received by the novel's first readers.[27] Jefferson takes a similar tack, though distinguishing between what lies outside the (Parisian) reader's representational purview (Mathilde's "singularity") and his (im)moral refusal to recognize what lies within it (the erotic activity of modern women), and generalizing beyond morality to a mimetic "paradox" whereby "the nature of the society being represented prevents the representation of it from being fully perceived within it."[28] Humphries goes even further in the direction of realist generalization, arguing that since "to observe the proprieties of realism, a novel must be perfectly fictitious, and yet perfectly deferent to the real," "the ideology of realism . . . makes [Mathilde], and the novel, *and the real itself*, both and neither."[29] Stendhal's apparent self-contradiction, in short, simply states, according to Humphries, the general paradox of realist ideology as such.

This risks incurring Prendergast's criticism of "concern [in Stendhal criticism] with abstract categories [which] de-contextualises and de-historicises its object."[30] Certainly representational mimesis as such is not under fire in this episode, since Mathilde's portrait succeeds well enough. Rather, there is a structural parallel between the apparent randomness (actually unconsiousness) of her successful drawing and the "arbitrary" self-contradiction at the conscious level of the system of Stendhalian "truth" or law. We have stressed that Mathilde's own "randomness" is hardly to be confused with chance (to this extent her own "superstitious" interpretation is correct); but nor is Stendhal's falsehood to be reduced to abstract epistemological problems of representation: "Truth and the desire for truth make up together an uneasy mixture within which a contradiction ferments, and from which there never fails to emerge a falsified product. . . . So there are two ways of falsifying: one, by the labor of embellishment; the other, by an effort *to enact the truth*."[31] Valéry's summary here emphasizes the problem of falsification in terms of desire rather than epistemology. Mathilde's problem was not that she was incapable of a singular and accurate mimetic representation, but that she was incapable of imitating herself, her own accuracy. Stendhal, on the other hand, as Valéry observed, dared "write according to his character, which he knew, and even imitated, to perfection."[32] The problem of mimesis and truth in Stendhal therefore goes well beyond mimetic realism. Yet Humphries is nevertheless correct to claim that the latter is sacrificially constructed in *Le Rouge et le noir*: "The black point of the book is about, and situated upon, the red: the bloody, violent contradictions of mimetic realism."[33]

In the third preface to *Lucien Leuwen*, Stendhal himself provides a suitably violent and literally pharmacological allegory of the mirror. In this allegory, a man takes some quinine for his fever, grimaces at the bitter taste, sees himself "pale and even a little green" in the mirror, drops the medicinal glass, and hurls himself at the mirror. "Such will perhaps be the fate," we are informed, "of the following volumes." Though Jefferson sees here only the umbrage taken by the vain reader at the reflection of the way he is,[34] this ignores the "grimace" caused by the medicine. Realism is not only a mirror, but a medicine ("truth, bitter truth")[35]—a coincidence emphasized by the simultaneous (presumed) shattering of the two glasses. The glasses are *pharmaka*, mimetic medicines for a mimetic disease, whose inefficacy results in their "sacrifice."[36]

The upshot of this is not merely the deconstruction of mimetic realism, however. For Stendhal abruptly returns, after this mini-allegory, to his earlier complaint (in the second preface) that he will be accused—for "representing" both parties—of being both legitimist and republican, or that literary representation will inevitably be confused with political representation. The preface concludes, not with abstract paradoxes of representation, but by stating the double bind of mimesis in terms of the tension between literary and political judgment: "*To tell the truth, since we are forced to make such a serious confession for fear of worse,* the author would be in despair to live under the government of New York. . . . In the Nineteenth Century, democracy necessarily leads in literature to the reign of mediocre, rational, narrow-minded and flat people, literarily speaking."[37]

Realism and Striptease

We now move beyond the problem of realism, as conceived by the various critics mentioned above, insofar as Stendhal himself conceived truth not just as realist mirror, but as a mode of unconcealment. "Red" and "Black" are often identified by critics with the poles of honesty and hypocrisy, and the epigraphs to part 1 ("truth, bitter truth") and part 2 ("She isn't pretty, she wears no rouge") of *Le Rouge* suggest a similar opposition—though the alignment of rouge with mimetic deception destabilizes any simple color-coding. Red, sign of blood and the blush, is predictably a *pharmakon* sign, color of both truth and dissemblance.

Fielding was perhaps the first great novelist to accuse (Richardson's) realism of striptease; but Valéry's view of the falsified enactment of truth, in the context of Stendhal, makes the similar point that "eroticism is never far removed from truth-tellers," and that "a woman who strips naked is as if entering on a stage." Similarly, Stendhal's style, with its casual "tokens of *sincerity*," is compared by Valéry to "a great saint [who] knew this principle very well when he undressed in the public square."[38] This confirms Humphries's and Jefferson's Girardian contention that erotic desire and realist fiction belong to the same system in Stendhal.[39] It may also help explain why the first appearance of the mirror formula in *Le Rouge* occurs in the epigraph to a chapter titled "Net Stockings." The venerable comparison of fiction and truth to clothes and body takes us beyond fiction-as-representation to fiction as a relation between concealment and revelation.

I have already discussed the epigraph's attribution to Saint-Real, but not why the epigraph is attached to chapter 16, a chapter in which a friend first perceives that Mme. de Rênal is in love with Julien because she has put on net stockings. This is also a chapter in which Julien's concealed feelings are portrayed as particularly crass and cynical, in accord with the "truth, bitter truth" of realism. But we soon discover that this is only an appearance. At the end of the chapter we are told that because "Mme. de Rênal had never read any novels . . . no *gloomy truths* could freeze her spirit" (64, my emphasis); while at the start of the following chapter we discover that "happily for him . . . the depths of [Julien's] soul bore little relation to his crude language"(64). The whole deceptive maneuver parodies, in effect, that "realism" which believes the worst interpretation likely to be the true one.

The epigraph to chapter 17, moreover, offers the first version of a motif that recurs several times in the novel, emphasizing the gratuitous symmetry of mimetic operations: "A girl of sixteen had a rose-petal complexion and wore rouge" (64). In chapter 18, Julien is himself compared to this emblematic girl, and we have seen that the epigraph to part 2, attributed to that champion of realism, Saint-Beuve,[40] takes up the same motif ("she isn't pretty, she wears no rouge"). Having been initially linked to bitter truth, realism is now identified with mimetic concealment. Worse, by hiding the far from bitter truth of her complexion, by implying that things are worse than they really are, the emblematic realist risks making them so.

Just as realist Saint-Beuve is linked by Stendhal to the embellishment of rouge, so Saint-Real's mirror is linked to the "Net Stockings" for which it serves as epigraph. Both rouge and net stockings are embellishments, Valéry's first mode of falsification, but the latter embellish by revealing or "enacting the truth," Valéry's second mode of falsification. The stockings do indeed reveal the "naked truth," to her friend and the reader, that Mme. de Rênal is falling in love with Julien; but this is concealed from Mme. de Rênal herself by her natural modesty (a kind of moral clothing that she wears even when naked, like net stockings). According to the narrator, these stockings provide an almost irresistible temptation to the reader to conclude falsely that she is conscious of what she is doing. But the reality is that her mimetic or fashionable gesture is a sign both of the truth (her love) and of unconscious deception (modesty, which Stendhal elsewhere calls "a subtle habit of lying"). The double bind of the novel is not representational but practical: to be an accurate mirror it must reflect both nakedness and clothing at the same time, like net stockings. To take the analogy further, it must reveal the naked truth without losing the *force* of concealment. The power of Stendhal's imagery derives from the fact that rouge and net stockings are not merely metaphors for realism but incarnate models of fashionable mimesis, concealment, and revelation—of "fiction" in short—that are quite actual.

Sacrificial Boredom

We now turn more directly to the sacrificial dimension of mimesis in Stendhal, which René Girard uses as a kind of textbook for his theory of mimetic desire in *Mensonge romantique*. Though Girard had not yet formulated his theory of sacrifice as such, his treatment of Stendhal highlights what he would later call sacrificial features, especially in the domain of erotic sadomasochism. Girard conceptualizes the dynamics of mimetic desire in terms of "masochist induction." Because mimetic desire tends to produce rivalry, and thus often failure, the lover reasons after several failures that failure is the rule, the "true" model of desire (as Denis de Rougemont also concluded in *Love in the Western World*). "In . . . 'ordinary' desire the obstruction [is] a result of imitation; now imitation is the result of obstruction . . . [and] the masochist perceives the *necessary* relation between unhappiness and metaphysical desire." The "masochist's reasoning is irreproachable. It is a model of scientific induction; it may even be the archetype of inductive reasoning."[41] We met with this model, in a more abstract context, in chapter 2. Just as Nelson Goodman's inductive joke established self-fulfilling disagreement, so the Girardian sadomasochist concludes that love is always nonreciprocal. Accordingly, what Girard calls the first "moment" of mimetic *askesis*—properly sacrificial in that it is said to be a model of *"absolute gratuitousness"*—is defined as "the renunciation of desire for the sake of desire."[42]

There is no clearer guide to the generally sadomasochist dynamics of mimetic desire in *Le Rouge* than chapter 29 in part 2, titled "Boredom." This reads like a three-page vaudeville guide to the mimetic principle, and is treated as such by both Girard and later critics such as Prendergast.[43] It is the famous chapter where Julien attempts to regain Mathilde's love by writing love letters to her friend, Mme. de Fervaques, letters copied verbatim from those of a Russian count to a woman in England, and where Julien succeeds even though he forgets to change place-names from England to France. At the moment Mme. de Fervacques first responds to Julien's love letters we read: "It was a triumph for boredom" (337). Mathilde, having apparently tired of Julien, soon finds herself jealously repeating the "naive" emotion expressed forty pages earlier when he first spent the night with her ("You are my master, I am your slave" [291]): "Despise me if you will, but love me" (337). The epigraph to this chapter employs explicitly sacrificial language: "To sacrifice oneself to one's passions, well, maybe; but to passions one does not feel! Oh, the sad nineteenth century" (336).

It is more than plausible that "boredom" functions in *Le Rouge* not only as a realistic emotion but as a kind of code word for the sacrificial structure of mimetic reversals of this kind. There are in fact, significantly, *two* "mirror" chapters titled "Boredom" in the novel, the first dealing with the first meeting of Julien and Mme. de Rênal. To be sure, both chapters justify their titles by referring to boredom in the ordinary sense: Mme. de Rênal is said to be bored with her husband without acknowledging it in the first "Boredom," and something similar plausibly applies to Mme. de Fervacques in the second (in each case leaving the women emotionally susceptible to Julien). Even the ordinary sense of boredom identifies it with the possibility of passion, *pharmakon*-like. But the real focus of the second "Boredom" is of course not Mme. de Fervaques but rather Mathilde's catastrophic shift from indifference to self-abasing idolatry in a chapter that could hardly be less "boring." I suggest that Stendhalian "boredom" names a structure that reduces all objects of desire to indifference or mimetic interchangeability, whether this is experienced as boring, or, on the contrary, as a whirlwind of faster and faster oscillations between seemingly contrary states such as mastery and slavery, or pleasure and pain.[44] The two "Boredoms" themselves suggest such a mimetic pattern, as does the fact that the second contains two women, applies "boredom" to a secondary character, and results in Mathilde's falling for Julien for the second time.

Yet the very likeness of the two chapter titles, in typical Stendhalian fashion, seems at first only to signify their opposition. Unlike Mathilde, "blackly" self-conscious and susceptible to mimetic desire, Mme. de Rênal is described in counter-mimetic terms that are taken to amusing extremes. Not only is her blush the authentic counterpart to cosmetic rouge, but she has supposedly read *no* novels, forgotten her entire education, and "put[ting] nothing in its place . . . ended by *knowing nothing*" (29, my emphasis). On the other hand, even Girard (who affirms her "transcendent" authenticity at the end of the novel) stresses that she cannot escape unconscious mimetic dynamics at the start, as does Humphries.[45] Like Mathilde's, Mme. de Rênal's maid falls in love with Julien, and we are early on granted a grotesque, even quasi-sadomasochistic scene in which "Mme. de Rênal indulged in the delicious pleasure of pleading her rival's cause [to Julien], and of seeing Elisa's hand and fortune turned down, again and again, for an entire hour" (38). From the mimetic point of view, it is also significant that she asks herself "can I be in love?" (38) only after her mediation for Elisa.

Despite their apparently differing in every possible way, the first "Boredom" therefore begs to be read in light of the second, and vice versa. Though we cannot go into great detail here, it is possible to recognize in the first chapter a more diffuse and deceptive pattern of symbolic violence and mimetic reversal that the second makes explicit, self-conscious, and even programmatic. Though both Julien and Mathilde are more "advanced" in mimetic consciousness than the younger Julien and Mme. de Rênal, this only means that their mutual deceptions are more "advanced," not that the structural grounds of these deceptions are essentially different.

The first such structural ground occurs at the level of the text itself, since Stendhal almost certainly modeled the first "Boredom" to some degree on the meeting of Rousseau and Mme. de Warens in the *Confessions*, one of Julien's trinity of favorite texts. A first irony derives from the fact that Louise de Warens was called "Maman" by Rousseau—appropriate insofar as Louise de Rênal is insistently defined by her maternal qualities (she is introduced in the act of calling her children and dies in the final line embracing her children)—although he ends by being her lover, in a kind of parody of incest. But the overriding irony is that while Mme. de Rênal's special merit is associated with her having no textual models to imitate, she is here plagiarized from one of the three texts said to provide Julien himself with all his models. Precisely where innocence of mimetic mediation is stressed at the level of character, the text itself introduces concealed mimetic mediation to the maximum structural extent.

While the second "Boredom" is structured very simply and explicitly around the "triangular" mediation of Mme. de Fervacques, the first entails mediatory patterns that are all the more instructive for being less immediately visible. Above all, as the Rousseau subtext suggests, the mediation of children is crucial to the sacrificial pattern. Mme. de Rênal's first reaction to Julien is that he is "scarcely more than a child" (21). We are told that "a completely pleasant experience had never struck [her] so profoundly"(22)—*not* because she has been bored, as one might expect, but because she feared the new tutor would be an old priest who would whip her children. Violence is thus a central mediating principle in "Boredom" from the start, and the substitutive sacrificial possibilities of her children will later be more fully revealed when she interprets them as divine scapegoats for her own sin in loving Julien. She finds him good-looking only after her fears of violence have been allayed—while it is the cook (like her mistress, "a good girl and very devout" [26]) who first exclaims, "Oh, good Lord, what a pretty little priest!"

The pattern of child/adult substitution is connected, predictably, to a male/female one. Despite or because of the importance of feminine modesty in Mme. de Rênal's character, "Boredom" begins with a series of gender reversals that had been anticipated at the end of the previous chapter, where Julien is overcome by "timidity" (*timidité*) on entering the Rênal grounds, and Mme. de Rênal is equally apprehensive, since "feminine delicacy" (*timidité*) is carried to an extreme (*un point excessive*) in her character (20–21).[46] Owing to his pallor, eyes, and apparent childishness, Mme. de Rênal's "somewhat romantic disposition took him at first for a girl in disguise." His good looks are perceived by her in terms of the "almost feminine delicacy of his features," while "the blunt masculine air commonly considered necessary to male beauty would have frightened her"(23). She is said to be "completely deceived" (22) by both his eyes and complexion; and his "timid manner of a young girl" is mentioned no less than three times (anticipating his later resemblance to the emblematic young girl who wears rouge).

Patterns of reversal are thus just as unstable and deceptive here as in the second "Boredom." First we see Julien as a kind of lower-class "girl-child," defined in relation to three distinct hierarchies of power. Mme. de Rênal also begins timidly, before Julien's girlishness provokes her into assuming a kind of maternal authority. But soon Julien in turn resumes dominance, assuming "a particularly cruel expression" (23) that makes her beg him in an "almost supplicating tone" not to beat her children. He responds with almost parodic submission, "Madame, you shall be obeyed"—such repeated inversions anticipating, albeit in a different emotional key, the master-slave reversals of the second "Boredom." Moreover, once again, a strategy of wholly mechanical mimesis is prominent in Julien's citation of Latin texts (which he understands not at all) to impress M. de Rênal. This deceives the children into admiring Julien over their father (who, also duped, tries to show off his own Latin), prefiguring the kind of comparison between the two men that will later lead to their mother's infidelity. As in Julien's epistolary seduction of Mathilde via Mme. de Fervacques, *wholly mechanical mimesis is the road to success.*

Above all, however, we should stress the crucial element of child mediation in the lovers' meeting, not only because of Mme. de Rênal's subsequent vacillation between the roles of mother and lover, but because their (imagined) whippings and subsequent divine scapegoating introduce a sacrificial motif which will steadily expand its domain of influence as the novel progresses.[47] As though to emphasize the sacrificial and sadomasochist development, the following chapter, "Elective Affinities," offers as its epigraph (attributed to "A Modern"): "They can touch the heart only by bruising it." The chapter begins: "The children worshipped [Julien], he liked them not at all" (27).

Sacrificial Bullets

The most succinct statement of the sacrificial principle in *Le Rouge* is perhaps Mathilde's witticism that the only source of distinction in the modern world is a death sentence. Though formulated in connection with Count Altimira, whose letters are copied by Julien, this of course applies to Julien himself at the end of the novel.[48] It also applies more obliquely to Mme. de Rênal, whom Julien (seemingly) tries to murder after she has denounced him to Mathilde's father. To be the sacrificial victim, however arbitrarily, is to be transfigured. Mathilde's witticism dovetails perfectly with the later Girardian thesis that the purpose of sacrifice is to reenact the original differentiation produced by the scapegoat murder. It also reverses, incidentally, Humphries's generalization that "originality . . . works some sort of violence on what it repeats,"[49] since originality or distinction is produced by violence rather than vice versa.

Though the novel's sacrificial conclusion is in one sense entirely inevitable insofar as it mimics Stendhal's sources in the real executions of Berthet and Lafargue,[50] Stendhal goes to quite vaudevillian lengths to emphasize that it is also an unlikely demand in the service of literary catharsis. It is a grim pun, as Humphries and others have pointed out, that Julien's head is said to be most poetical (in both senses) when it is about to be cut off. Indeed Julien himself—who self-sacrificially insists on his guilt and refuses to appeal for clemency—"seems to accept [death] as an almost aesthetic necessity."[51] Humphries is not alone in emphasizing not just the aesthetic but also the quasi-sacred transformation characteristic of sacrificial phenomena: "After his death, his remains are treated . . . like those of a saint or a demi-god."[52]

Yet there is every indication that the sacrificial resolution may not be taken entirely seriously by Stendhal,[53] or that it is taken seriously only insofar as sacrificial effects apparently "work," however ludicrous they may be. Just before meeting Mme. de Rênal, for example, Julien leaves the church of Verrieres and picks up a scrap of paper on which he reads: "Details of the execution . . . of Louis Jenrel" (an anagram of his own name).[54] Observing that the "name has the same ending as mine" (as he will have the same end), Julien imagines he sees a pool of blood by the baptismal font, an effect produced by some red curtains erected for a festival (20). Some prophetic—and parodic—sacrificial festival of death and rebirth indeed!

The finale of *Le Rouge*, from the moment Julien attempts to murder Mme. de Rênal after she has denounced him to the Marquis de la Mole, is a traditional locus of critical controversy that we cannot ignore here, not least because it arguably stems from this sacrificial ambivalence as such. Many critics "have said that the attempt on the life of Mme. de Rênal is insufficiently motivated,"[55] while many others have made efforts to exonerate Stendhal from this charge.[56] By contrast, citing the illegibility of the letter Julien writes to Mathilde in this chapter en route to the murder scene, Ann Jefferson claims that "the illegibility of this letter prefigures that of the crime itself," and that, like Julien's death, the murder is part and parcel of his general withdrawal from intelligibility, "the lover's response to the violence perpetrated by the *doxa*."[57] This view seems supported by the fact that the finale appears as a kind of "non-novelistic" alternative or supplement to Julien's "novelistic" career—on his engagement to Mathilde and elevation to lieutenant, he famously remarks that "the novel of my career is over"—and that its last few chapters are the only ones to lack epigraphs (conventional guides to interpretation).

Against Jefferson, however, we need to balance Humphries's view that the shooting is novelistically "predictable, if implausible."[58] For the mimetic-sacrificial finale has essentially two main conditions: Mme. de Rênal's letter of denunciation (mimetic in the sense of dictated by her confessor), and the murder attempt itself. Since this leads to a renewal of Mme. de Rênal's love, it provides an eerie echo of the earlier "masochistic" episode in which Mathilde admires Julien for having threatened her with a sword, twisting Mathilde's witticism a further, sacrificial degree: one loves a man who has earned a death sentence for attempting to take one's life. Mme. de Rênal explicitly declares that "to die by Julien's hand is the height of bliss" (364).

The general opposition of "true passion" to mimetic law or *doxa*, as Jefferson puts it, is now seemingly extended to criminal law in particular. For it is the criminal law that victimizes Mme. de Rênal and "causes" her death (out of apparent grief) in the wake of Julien's, while it is mere accident (her being wounded instead of killed) that transfigures Julien into her lover instead of her killer. But it is important to observe that Julien is actually in formal complicity with the law in demanding his own execution. There is no doubt that such critics as Jefferson, Prendergast, and Haig are correct to interpret the finale, including the dropping of epigraphs, as gesturing toward what Haig calls "the *unsayable* realm"[59]—toward a singularity that falls outside conventional representation. But it is equally important to observe that the epigraphs disappear immediately after Julien has had the self-sacrificial thought: "Only these words: I feel I have been rightly convicted" (389). However technically correct, this acknowledgment coincides with Julien's adoption of a perverse and sacrificial legality that further tortures both Mme. de Rênal and Mathilde. Julien's stubbornness and the state's conspire toward a gratuitous multiplication of the original victimage, and his (and the text's) unstable gestures toward "transcendence" of deviated mimesis in fact coincide with his (and its) rigid adherence to a sacrificial solution. The "black" Abbé Frilair formulates not only the suicidal nature of Julien's behavior (397), but also an explicit sacrificial model to resolve his unintelligibility that ironically resembles Julien's own: "For me nothing should be inexplicable. . . . Perhaps we can make a martyr out of him" (371).[60] This sacrificial structure goes equally for the characters and for the text, since Stendhal can also be said to "martyr" Julien, and also Mme. de Rênal, by inventing (this time without realistic pretext) her singularly unlikely demise.

We must therefore now squarely face the possibility that the "unintelligibility" of the finale is a consequence neither of the protagonists' transcendence of the *doxa*, nor of Stendhal's genius for incoherence (depending on one's point of view), but rather of the sacrificial arbitrariness which structures it. Such arbitrariness is revealed no more wittily than in the scene of the shooting itself: "Mme. de Rênal was not fatally wounded. The first bullet had passed through her hat; the second was fired just as she turned around. The bullet struck her in the shoulder, glanced off her shoulder blade and fractured it, and then, rather surprisingly, went on to strike a Gothic pillar from which it broke off a big splinter of stone" (363). The bullet's path seems here no less "surprisingly" gratuitous than the apparently realistic sentence which redirects our attention from the relevant issue at stake, Mme. de Rênal's state of health, to the Gothic architecture. But though both Berthet and Lafargue fired two shots at their mistresses and thus provide a realistic pretext for the scene, Stendhal's treatment of the bullet's "accidental" trajectory is clearly no less strategic than Julien's "happening" to notice the Gothic architecture of his courtroom a few pages later. The architecture, in short, is of a (sacrificial) piece with the "gothic" pool of blood on the cathedral floor and Mathilde's "gothic" imitation of her ancestors when she buries Julien's head.[61] Moreover, inasmuch as Julien's action is insufficiently motivated (as both hostile and sympathetic critics observe), it blends with the randomness of the bullet itself—the arbitrariness both of sacrifice (rather than mere revenge), in the Girardian sense, and of fiction in the de Manian sense. On the sacrificial "accident" of the bullets' trajectories the whole meaning of the book depends.

Girard against Girard

While we have indicated the sacrificial economy of the novel to some extent independently of Girard (taking his mimetic insights as starting point), we should now confront Girard directly. Also, since Jefferson Humphries's elaboration of mimetic desire may seem close in many ways to both Girard's and my own, we should clarify their respective relations. Above all this concerns the sacrificial status of the text itself and its mode of deception.

Girard's remarkably original reading of *Le Rouge* recognizes the great subtlety of its dialectic of rule and exception, arguing that the advanced novelists of mimetic desire differ from "romantic" approaches in being able to conceive it on many planes at once.[62] Though insistent on the "true love" achieved in the finale, and on a relatively unequivocal opposition between Mme. de Rênal and Mathilde ("the real Mme. de Rênal is the one desired by Julien; the real Mathilde is the one he does not desire"),[63] he nevertheless underlines the novel's structural resistance to such a reading in a manner that takes us well beyond more conventional affirmations. The novelists of mimetic desire, we are told, "emphasize the analogies between [their] characters,"[64] and the formal resemblance between what Girard calls "deviated transcendency" and "vertical transcendency" (between advanced dialectical modes of mimetic desire and modes that genuinely escape the Girardian double bind)—said to be even clearer in Proust and Dostoyevsky than in Stendhal—is such that they can be distinguished only "by their fruits."

Though insistent on the true "peace" achieved in the final pages, when Julien is at last said to speak for his creator, Girard thus acknowledges the *pharmakon* resemblance between the *forms* of mimetic deviation and "vertical transcendence." Because writers "have at their disposal only the one language which is already corrupted by metaphysical [mimetic] desire and, by definition, *incapable of being used to reveal the truth*, the revelation of [the mimetic] disorder presents complex problems." "Even though it is the novelist's supreme reward, passion is *scarcely present* in the novel itself. Freed, it rises out of a novelistic world *totally* given over to vanity and desire."[65] Humphries's claim that "the ironic stance of Stendhal's narrator . . . starts from the premise that no real escape [from mimetic desire] is possible" is thus highly Girardian, at least from a formal perspective. Where Girard speaks of a mimetic language that is "by definition" incapable of revealing the truth, Humphries constructs the violence of the finale as a figure for "the bloody, violent contradictions of mimetic realism" as such. "The guillotine would thus represent the central governing metaphor for mimetic realism."[66]

But while we have seen that this view of realism finds some support in Stendhal's third preface to *Lucien Leuwen*, Humphries's analogy between realism and Julien's self-sacrifice is questionable: "By breaking the rules of mimetic desire (according to which the desire of Julien, to be a model of the desire of others, is illicit and transgressive), Julien breaks himself."[67] For the self-sacrificial fate of those who desire to be models is not necessarily subject to the paradox of mimetic realism.

(The primary paradox of mimetic realism, as Humphries implies elsewhere, is not that it could not represent such a fate, but that it is inevitably drawn into a specular interplay with history, or theory, from which fiction differentiates itself.)[68] Nor is desiring to be a model outside "the rules of mimetic desire" in Girard's sense; it rather constitutes an elementary form of what Girard calls "negative mimesis" (the desire for autonomy that Humphries himself elsewhere recognizes: "Mimetic desire enforces conformity by championing the individual").[69] To break the rules of mimetic desire, Julien would have to neither possess nor be a model.[70] The sacrificial finale therefore remains mimetic in structure whether Julien still desires to be a model, as Humphries claims, or whether it stems from his inability *not* to be one.

Girard therefore differs from Humphries not in proposing that mimesis can be transcended, but in proposing that Julien's final desire points to the very opposite of Humphries's conclusion that he desires to be a model. Instead, according to Girard, the aesthetic finale points toward the desirability of a religious *imitatio* which is affirmed despite the author's atheist intention:

> Stendhal attributes Julien Sorel's "German mysticism" to the extreme dampness of his prison cell. But the conclusion of *The Red and the Black* remains a meditation on Christian themes and symbols. In it the novelist reaffirms his skepticism but the themes and symbols are nonetheless present in order to be clothed in negations. They play exactly the same role in Proust and Dostoyevsky. We shall see everything which touches on these themes, including the monastic vocation of Stendhal's heroes, in a fresh light which the author's irony cannot hide from us.[71]

So what is to distinguish the sacrificial, sadomasochistic irony from genuine or "vertical" transcendence? Girard's insight into Stendhal is most powerful, but also most problematic, when it insists that "analogy between deviated transcendency and vertical transcendency is even closer than we first suspected" (156), since this allows him to stress the analogy to the maximum extent without giving up the opposition. Girard's Catholicism is of course relevant here, though he argues: "We should not treat the religious question externally but if possible look on it in a purely novelistic light."[72] Thus, relinquishing any transcendence in "the novelistic world" as such, and stopping short of an overt appeal to Christian faith, Girard regards the artistic product itself (or, more precisely, the author's capacity to produce it) as the only genuine proof or palpable fruit of "vertical transcendence."

But, as Paul de Man complained,[73] *Mensonge romantique* fails to provide a satisfactory account of the relation between intersubjective mimesis (the novelistic subject matter) and the hermeneutic structure of the work (its "free" control over this subject matter which enables its construction). Nothing in *Le Rouge*, at any rate, justifies Girard's substitution of the transcendence of the work for the intersubjective transcendence of its characters. Mathilde's successful portrait of Julien, for example, occurs when she is far from mimetically independent of him.

Girard is nevertheless correct that the structural ambivalence of Stendhal's irony is no more capable of demonstrating a skeptical truth behind his religious language than a pious one. His claim is that this irony, insofar as it cannot help but appear skeptical, must be either mendacious or deluded. But this would go equally, at least as far as the nontranscendent "novelistic world" is concerned, for any counterskeptical implication. Stendhal's irony is bound to be deceptive inasmuch as its "content" is invoked independent of its sacrificial structure. Indeed, the sacrificial theory of the later Girard, for whom the primary sacrificial effect is precisely an effect of (pseudo)transcendence, could itself be brought to bear on "vertical transcendence" in this context.[74]

But the problem is not merely that the sacrificial pattern extends to the level of the representation as well as its content (or, as Humphries puts it, that "the novel, as an instance of mimeticism, is bleeding from a myriad of small cuts").[75] It is that the pattern of sacrificial mediation remains consistent independently of problems of representation:

> Why does Stendhal still speak of passion [at the conclusion] when desire has disappeared? Perhaps because these moments of ecstasy are always the result of feminine mediation. . . . It is not so much a question of opposition between two types of women as two antinomic functions exercised by the feminine element in the existence and creation of the novelist. . . . In the great works, the transition from vanity to passion is inseparable from aesthetic happiness. It is the delight of creation that wins out over desire and anguish. The transition always takes place under the sign of the deceased Mathilde [i.e., Mctilde], the woman who had rejected him in Milan, and, as it were, as a result of her intercession.[76]

Girard's appeal to the "antinomic functions exercised by the feminine element" takes us beyond the realist problem emphasized by Humphries, as well as by his own earlier claim that it is the "real" Mme. de Rênal who is desired by Julien, and the "real" Mathilde who is not desired. But the supposed transition from desire to passion and "aesthetic happiness," as mediated by the dead Metilde (her importance is a commonplace originating with Stendhal himself), is hardly without sacrificial features. In the novel itself, of course, such "intercession" seems to be conducted under the sign of the dead Louise de Rênal—whose sudden death in the last line, as we have observed, might be regarded as its sacrificial precondition—while Mathilde (Metilde's namesake) lives on only to be wholly "vanquished," as Girard describes it,[77] a kind of butt of her own joke that only people with death sentences have genuine distinction.

Even if we resist the banal temptation to regard this as a kind of fictional revenge on the real woman who rejected Stendhal (indeed, precisely if we reject all explanations that fish for reductive authorial motivations), the sacrificial arbitrariness of the text is all too clear. Not only is sacrifice "idealizing," as Humphries suggests[78]—Mme. de Rênal, for example, is canonized as "Mother" when she is gratuitously killed off by Stendhal while embracing her children—it evidently scapegoats: Mathilde is not only asked to sacrifice her own child by Julien, but the latter actually has the temerity to suggest that she allow Mme. de Rênal, her arch-rival, to bring up the baby. The "antinomic functions" of lover and mother (which Stendhal brings together, as we saw, in his quasi-parodic allusion to Rousseau's *Confessions*) are here established on most cruel and arbitrary grounds, and there is no reason to divorce what Girard calls "aesthetic happiness" from this sacrificial gesture.

Stendhal himself described his finale as "asinus asinum fricat" ("ass rubs ass"), emphasizing comic mimetic symmetry.[79] But while every formal symmetry can be read as emphasizing a substantive asymmetry—like the two "antinomic" women Julien momentarily mistakes for one another in his prison cell—Girard's affirmation of Julien's choice of Mme. de Rênal is ultimately "Romantic" in his own sense, in that it has to ignore the sacrificial implications of its own analysis. To be sure, when Julien appeals to the "accident" of passion that occurs "only when superior people meet," the Girardian analysis warns us against mistaking this at face value (Julien says it deludedly to Mathilde at the very moment he is on the verge of returning his affection to Mme. de Rênal). But nothing essential changes even when he has rejected Mathilde, whom he then stubbornly tries to convince to marry M. de Croisenois after his death (having earlier commanded her: "Do not talk to . . . people . . . like de Luz" [365]): "The death of M. de Croisenois changed all Julien's ideas about the future of Mathilde; he devoted several days to proving to her that she ought to accept the hand of M. de Luz" (404).

The irony, of course, is that nothing whatever has changed: Mathilde is still being mercilessly sacrificed to interchangeable suitors. Girard's affirmation of Julien's "conversion" to Mme. de Rênal is accordingly no more convincing than Ann Jefferson's view that "Julien's crime and salvation cannot be imitated because they remain inexplicable."[80] On the other hand, her parallel view that "Mme. de Rênal's passion remains inimitable [should not be imitated?] because it is wrong" is surely on target precisely because the structure of that passion is so clearly sacrificial: whether Mme. de Rênal is in the business of regarding her sick child as divine scapegoat for her love, or dreaming of abasing herself in the market square, her models are "profoundly degrading."[81] At the finale, she still experiences her passion as a mortal sin that substitutes God for Julien, for whom she is willing both to die and to kill. Given this, it seems hard to see why her *folie* should be any more "transcendent" than Mathilde's, and we may suspect, to the contrary, that part of the attraction of Stendhal's religious heroines for his atheist heroes (and their atheist author) lies precisely in their exemplary "feminine" ability to substitute their men for gods.

Girard, as we have seen, wants to recuperate all such "irony" for his argument that the very "clothes" of religious negation maintain the centrality of the religious model. This is to a certain extent undeniable even in an atheist context (as for instance when Julien exclaims that he would fall down at God's feet if only God existed). But it is also true that the text continues to insist on purely secular mediations. For example, when Mme. de Rênal sends Elisa, her old rival, to Julien's jail, the jailor tells Julien "in the greatest detail everything he had learned about Mme. de Rênal, *but he said not a word about the visit of Mlle. Elisa*" (367, my emphasis). We may conclude our consideration of Girardian transcendence with this example, not only because it formally reintroduces the triangular mediation of their earlier relationship, but because the very arbitrariness of the concealment (why should the jailor care about it one way or the other?) is what makes it significant. Admittedly, there is the faint semblance of a realistic pretext for this, since Mme. de Rênal tells Elisa that Julien must not be told of her gift of money to the jailor. But she does not ask that Elisa's visit itself be concealed; and, worse, from the point of view of mimetic dynamics, she actually asks Elisa to go "as if on your own account" (364)—recalling her own pleading on Elisa's amorous behalf early on in the novel. In effect, Stendhal sends Elisa to Julien purely so that we know he doesn't know, an ignorance which seems to have absolutely no narrative significance (and which is therefore understandably never mentioned, to my knowledge, by the critics). The jailor's own moment of narrative *askesis,* if I may so adapt Girard's term, is gratuitous; yet it is arguably the narrative equivalent of the "repression" of Elisa that takes place in the original triangle.

My general point is not of course that Stendhal's inclusion of this detail is arbitrary, but that the detail is revelatory precisely inasmuch as it is concealed by its inconspicuousness. Stendhal's text performs a fully conscious concealment that is superimposed on the jailor's arbitrary one—thus confirming, against his reading of the novel, Girard's own definition of the structure of sacrificial deception.

Masochist Induction (Literary Truth)

Whatever may be said for Girardian transcendence, his conception of the decidedly nontranscendental "truth" of masochistic and sacrificial reasoning—which emphasizes the necessary relation between truth and deception—remains exemplary for this study. According to Girard, sacrificial masochism is an "advanced" form of mimetic desire consistent with a crucial insight into mimetic mechanisms, since it perceives the resemblance between master and slave: "The sadist cannot achieve the illusion of *being* the mediator [of desire] without transforming himself into a replica of his victim."[82] The more intelligent the sadist, in effect, the more he turns into a masochist, since the masochist's reasoning "is a model of scientific induction," and "may even be the archetype of inductive reasoning." For Girard, moreover, masochist induction is nothing less than a model of literary or novelistic truth: "We know that the future of mastery is slavery. True in theory, this principle is also true in the evolution of the novels. Slavery is the future of mastery; Proust and Dostoyevsky are therefore Stendhal's future; their novels are *the truth* of Stendhal's work. This movement toward slavery is one of the basic principles of novelistic structure."[83] Remarkably Stendhalian in its conception of the *predictive* character of "fictional" truth, Girard's masochist induction generalizes the principle of mimesis to science or logic as such, and accordingly returns us squarely to the theoretical landscape we encountered in chapter 2. Insofar as it hypothesizes mere mimesis of the past by the future, induction cannot escape arbitrariness—but nor (as Goodman showed) can we do without inductive law. For Girard, masochist induction—or fiction—is a model of sacrificial law conceived as an essentially arbitrary and deceptive, but nonetheless eminently *true* self-fulfilling prophecy. Its very deceptiveness, as we shall confirm in Beckett, is an index of its truth.

5

Fundaments and Accidents:

Mimesis and Mendacity

■ **in *Molloy***

Mimétique malgré lui, voilà Molloy ...
—SAMUEL BECKETT

Whereas Defoe provided an early-eighteenth-century approach to fiction that could not yet presume any stable conventional distinction
between fiction and lying (and exploited this to pass off his fictions as
histories), Stendhal showed us how the relation between fiction and
falsification remained just as urgent and even more complex during
the full flowering of nineteenth-century realism, when the truth-
value of novels was more readily taken for granted. However, the
problem of the relation between fiction and falsification can by no
means be limited to realism; and I turn now to Samuel Beckett because
his work demonstrates how this problem remains central even when
no attempt is made to keep up a realistic facade. Indeed, Beckett is
exemplary to this study both because he flatly condemned the very

idea of realistic art as a "grotesque fallacy"[1]—a falsification well suited, by implication, to the self-delusion of authors or the conscious deception of readers—and because he pursues the mutual entanglement of falsehood and truth well beyond its realist complications.

There seems to be little comparable in Beckett's life, unless one counts his work for the French Resistance, to the extrafictional deceptions practiced by Defoe or Stendhal. Moreover, though he was notorious for his public reticence and refusal to contribute to public discourse in any form other than his fictions, those fictions have often been regarded as a model of existential honesty. Yet Beckett repeatedly insisted on a principle of mendacity, in the fiction itself, that seems quite as general as Kafka's "universal principle" of lying. Take *Molloy*, for example: "I am merely complying with the convention that demands you either lie or hold your peace."[2] Or *The Unnamable*: "how can you not tell a lie, what an idea" (415). Indeed, the second part of *Molloy* is quite explicitly structured as a falsehood, and its closing avowal of this falsehood leads into the explicitly fictional territory of *Malone Dies*—as though fiction were a mode of truth predicated on the prior admission of mendacity, only to be embarked upon once the structure of this mendacity has been thoroughly acknowledged.

Like Stendhal, but in a still more explicit and advanced manner, Beckett is also exemplary for my project because he situates lying, concealment, and fiction in the context of a mimetic-sacrificial analysis of culture more generally. Though it takes a fictional form, this analysis is arguably at least as coherent and provocative as anything available on the current theoretical or culture-studies market, including the work of Girard. As noted in my introduction, my reading of Beckett is independent of Girard in the sense that the basic principles of sacrificial mimesis can be stated in Beckett's language without need for specifically Girardian interpolation, and indeed in a way that is challenging to orthodox Girardianism (not least because it extends these principles to Christianity).[3] *Malone Dies*, for example, both thematizes and enacts a *coincidence of fiction and religion mutually conceived as sacrificial systems* that anticipates Girard's theory, while extending its provenance into territory largely untouched by Girard himself (including the incorporation of "deconstructive" modes more commonly associated with Beckett's achievement). What clinches Girard's relevance, however, is not simply Beckett's relentless generalization of the sacrificial principle to cover almost every mode of experience and cultural production, but his definition of the basic sacrificial mechanism in explicitly mimetic terms. In *Molloy*, for example, the simplest model of differentiation is that of a violent encounter between un-differentiated antagonist-twins whose very resemblance generates their violent act of differentiation—a model which might almost be regarded as textbook Girard. Similarly, the anus, in *Molloy*, plays a comically *fundamental* role that conforms to the logic of mimetic exclusion; indeed, the first important scatological passage of the novel is preceded in the French version by the sentence: "*Mimétique malgré lui, voilà Molloy, vu sous un certain angle.*"[4] This, as we shall see, is also the mimetic-sacrificial logic that underlies Molloy's general epistemological pun that "when it comes to neglecting fundamentals, I think I have nothing to learn, and indeed I confuse them with accidentals" (80). The fundamental exclusion of "fundaments" is here a model for all "fundamentals" (laws, differences, etc.) constructed on an arbitrary and exclusionary basis. Beckettian epistemology does not just demystify sacrificial logic; it too has a sacrificial dimension that has much in common with Girard's "masochist induction." Indeed, the confusion between induction and deduction is mentioned in *Molloy* just prior to Molloy's joke about fundamentals.[5]

I shall not attempt here to adjudicate Leo Bersani's and Ulysse Dutoit's seemingly exaggerated claim as to the "irrelevance characteristic of almost everything that has been written about [Beckett],"[6] though the vast quantity of Beckett criticism makes one sympathize with Stanley Cavell's position, in his essay on *Endgame*, that "I did not want to get talked out of [my own methodological route] by arguing with others."[7] Nevertheless, without any claim to exhaustiveness, it will be helpful to note some parallels and contrasts with other interpreters in order to clarify what is at stake, and perhaps unique, in my mimetic-sacrificial approach. Above all, lest I be accused of too glib an attribution of logic and system—not to speak of "meaning"—to Beckett, it is important to discredit the common prejudice that his work "defies all attempts at interpretation."[8] On the contrary, as Bersani and Dutoit ironically put it, "perhaps the most serious reproach we can make against Samuel Beckett is that he failed to fail . . . to become as inexpressive, as devoid of meaning, as possible."[9] Thus we should not forget, as Bersani and Dutoit also remind us,[10] that Beckett's famous declaration, in the *Three Dialogues with Georges Duthuit*, of the impossibility as well as undesirability of artistic "expression" is accompanied by a declaration of the "obligation to express." This is tautological as well as ethical: expression and interpretation are inevitable. The same goes for method or system, and no apology need therefore be made for aiming at a systematic approach: in *The Unnamable* an initial anathema against "the spirit of system" (294) accordingly gives way to "let us proceed with method . . . since I cannot do otherwise" (352). Similarly, far from signaling an escape from logical determinacy, the Beckettian idea of expressing "nothing" in the *Three Dialogues*—later echoed in the only italicized sentence of the trilogy *"nothing is more real than nothing"* (193) (an allusion to Democritus that Beckett himself recommended as critical guide)—is explicitly said to presuppose "an exquisitely logical attitude. In any case, it is hardly to be confused with the void."[11] Moreover, Beckett's famous remark that he was interested not in ideas per se but in the shape of ideas accords very well with our emphasis here on mimetic law, which is by definition, like logic itself, a law of form. Molloy, "mimetic in spite of himself," makes the point that "it is certain I saw [the world] in a way inordinately formal, though I was far from being an aesthete, or an artist" (50). Beckett also claimed, in a way that hardly confirms the skeptical stereotypes usually associated with him, that "Being has a form. Someone will find it someday."[12]

We find claims like "understanding *Endgame* can only mean understanding its unintelligibility" even in such evidently meaningful and intelligent commentators as Adorno.[13] But while it may or may not be true that "Beckett shrugs his shoulders [ironically or not] at the possibility of philosophy today, at the very possibility of theory," we may agree with Adorno that it may well be "the criterion of a philosophy whose hour has struck that it prove equal" to Beckett interpretation.[14] I am also close to Adorno in finding something like "philosophical anthropology"[15] in Beckett. Similarly, Bersani and Dutoit claim that in "representing the unrelated subject"—for whom the coherence of all subject-object relations seems to have broken down—Beckett is inevitably led "to the representation of the *genesis of relations*."[16] Indeed Bersani's and Dutoit's insistence on "the word Beckett uses to characterize the tormentor-victim relationship: *justice*"[17] and on his definition of communication in terms of torture, in *Comment c'est*, has an analogy with Girard's conception of the genesis of human societies: "To be tortured is the precondition for being humanized . . . a coercion that is, however, psychologically unmotivated"[18]—or, in Girard's terms, a sacrificial violence that is essentially arbitrary in principle. Bersani and Dutoit even stress, to a certain extent, the mimetic element implicit in "the reciprocity of the terroristic process that we name justice."[19] Thus, while their lack of reference to Girard is perhaps by no means neutral, their work is certainly relevant to the mimetic-sacrificial or "Girardian" principle that we can independently isolate in

Beckett.[20] Similarly, their claim that "expressiveness appears to be inherent in narrativity," entailing "techniques of exclusion,"[21] is consistent with Beckett's extension of the mimetic-sacrificial principle of exclusion to all communication, including the putative goal of nonexpression itself. The attempt "to say nothing" is inevitably ironic and sacrificial: "you always overlook something, a little yes, a little no, *enough to exterminate a regiment of dragoons*" (*The Unnamable*, 303, my emphasis).[22] Hence it makes sense for my purposes to take the trilogy—where Beckett at least quantitatively says *most*—as primary example of his sacrificial understanding and deployment of relations between fiction, lying, and concealment. As in Stendhal and Defoe, the theme or motif of clothing provides a significant instance, among others, of the latter.

Epistemological Fundaments

Molloy is divided into two parts: Molloy's autobiographical account, his "diary" (62), and Moran's account of his assignment to file a biographical "report" on Molloy. This narrative division, though hardly stable, entails others: between generally male-female (mother/son) and generally male-male (father/son) relations, between sexual and family matters treated in relative abstraction from religion (despite a number of religious references) and increasingly explicit religious mediation,[23] and between seemingly relatively undifferentiated experience (reflected by the absence of paragraph structure of part 1) and relatively analytic accounting—to name a few of the more obvious distinctions. I will argue that the second part provides, in general, a more explicitly *mediated* extension of the first, in which analysis of the mimetic-sacrificial principle becomes increasingly naked.[24]

First, however, we should attend to the carefully plotted epistemology of the text, an epistemology *in which the logical principle of negation mirrors the sacrificial principle of exclusion*—a sacrificial identity epigrammatically summed up in the phrase "No's knife."[25] The overall structure of *Molloy* illustrates this well, since just as the second part is structured as a circle (a journey from Turdy back to Turdy) in which the formal point of departure and return coincides with a falsehood, so the first part (a journey back to the mother) is structured as a circle in which there is an apparently arbitrary discontinuity or *hole* (also the name of a town in part 2): Molloy doesn't explain how he got from the ditch at the end of part 1 to his mother's room at the beginning. Formally, then, the principle of negation occurs first as "unconscious" arbitrariness (Molloy says he was unconscious) and second, consciously, as mendacity or self-contradiction. This precisely represents the kind of epistemological movement from arbitrariness to falsehood I have stressed throughout this study.

Significantly, given the general epistemological skepticism usually attributed to Beckett,[26] Molloy explicitly opens on the other side of skeptical disbelief: "I've disbelieved only too much in my long life"(13). Admittedly, his solution, *to negate the negation*—"my only chance, I believe all I'm told . . . now I swallow everything, greedily"(13)—seems hardly less sacrificial.[27] Nevertheless, Molloy's initial impulse toward truth and truthfulness is striking: "No, I will not lie, I can easily conceive it [the landscape and situation]"(15). These are not the words of a generalized epistemological skeptic.

Epistemological scrutiny actually intensifies as the text seemingly throws conventional epistemology to the wind. When we hear, to give a paradigmatic example, that Molloy was born from his mother's arse, "if my memory is correct" (16), it is obvious that we are not dealing with what Beckett called "the grotesque fallacy of a realistic art." However, the deep entrenchment of such a figure in the comic tradition from Aristophanes onward (not to speak of psychoanalysis or myth) hardly leaves us short on models of interpretation; indeed, the problem, as demonstrated by the mass of Beckett criticism, is rather the reverse. The text accordingly pursues its own distinctive trajectory through the minefields of conventional epistemology in which predictable complications for truth quickly set in ("the lie, the lie, to lying thought" [28]), beginning with the nominalist doctrine that "there could be no things but nameless things, no names but thingless names"(31). This exclusionary generalization is illustrated by a more specific exclusion borrowed from physics: light considered as "waves and particles"(31).[28]

Nominalism, though seemingly epistemologically bleak, may nevertheless hold out possible comfort in the "invented" (and thus potentially controllable) character of language.[29] But in Beckett invention is always compromised by mimesis: "Saying is inventing. Wrong, very rightly wrong. You invent nothing, you think you are inventing, you think you are escaping, and all you do is stammer out your lesson, the remnants of a pensum one day got by heart and long forgotten, life without tears, as it is wept" (32). Jean Toyami claims that invention is replaced by discovery in this context, but fails to observe that the discovery is here merely a "stammered" mimesis of what has been invented (which is why "saying is inventing" is "very rightly wrong") and forgotten.[30] Moreover, it is significant that the pertinent "rightly wrong" invention here—"life without tears, as it is wept"—is not merely a contradictory statement of the noncoincidence of signs and things, but implicitly draws attention to the fact that the seemingly barren epistemological paradoxes of nominalism become more interesting and less paradoxical as soon as we focus on the *maximum coincidence* of sign and thing—above all in bodily states that are simultaneously signs for a state ("of mind") and constitutive of that state itself, as in crying/pain (or laughing and blushing). The referential relation in such cases (where blushing, for instance, may generate as well as signify embarrassment) is constituted by a kind of a specular *feedback* generated by the simultaneous coincidence and noncoincidence of sign and thing.[31] Invention is thus the "right" as well as the "wrong" word, and Molloy appeals to the proverbial resemblance of laughter and tears in this connection, to the possibility of "crying, with the noise of laughter" (37). The mimetic-sacrificial and *pharmacological* dimension of both these states will later be a focus in *The Unnamable*, and such a mimetic doubling of sign and thing (of "mind" and "body") is also crucial to Malone's investigation of the relation between violence and symbolic violence, where the sign/thing "pain" appears successively as cause and effect (along the general lines of "masochist induction" outlined in the previous chapter).[32]

The referential inadequation of signs and things is thus not denied, but nor is it inconsistent with Molloy's believing all he hears, since such inadequation, *continually reproduced*, constitutes the "coincidence" of mimetic law.[33] Lousse's parrot, whose repertoire is "fuck the son of a bitch" and "putain de merde," is paradigmatic in this context, imitating human models, "unless he had hit on it alone, it wouldn't surprise me"(38).[34] Both arbitrary ("inventive") and mimetic in principle, these formulae comically summarize the novel's entire thematic topos from the Countess Caca of the opening (one of Molloy's names for his mother) to the Turdy Madonna of the conclusion. The parrot speaks the truth while understanding nothing, just as the "messenger" of part 2, Gaber, is said to understand nothing of the messages he relays, and as Moran finally claims to have learned to write in the same way—by pure mimesis. As Malone later puts it: "I simply believe I can say nothing that is not true, I mean that has not happened, it's not the same thing but no matter" (236).[35] The epistemological lesson, formulated as a double negation, is thus that fiction is a fiction, not because fiction is wholly "true" in the sense of lawful or truthful, but because it expresses "facts" or "happenings" generated by fundamental accidents, errors, and lies. This is why, for Beckett, realism is "a grotesque fallacy," since fiction does not merely represent history (and arbitrariness)—which would make of it a mere dissemblance of history; it *is* history (and arbitrariness). Thus Molloy's avid attempt to escape meaning in the accidents of realistic detail "that do not seem at first sight to signify anything in particular" (62), such as the size of his knees, is ironic, and will later be belied when Moran casually mentions, for example, that his knee resembles a clitoris (140). Arbitrariness in the trilogy, like mimesis, is sacrificial rather than "realistic."[36]

The facts of *Molloy* being notably "perverse," Molloy summarizes his relation to falsehood as follows: "And I for my part will never lend myself to such a perversion (of the truth), until such time as I am compelled or find it convenient to do so" (76). "Perversion" of the truth is compulsory in both senses, that of error and that of force; it is by turns voluntary and involuntary, the one entailing the other. Indeed, the very desire for truth and revelation (as Valéry noted in the context of Stendhalian eroticism) is one of the mechanisms of its perversion, as illustrated by Molloy's deceptive simile concerning incest: "to tell you the horrible truth, my mother's image sometimes mingles with theirs [his girlfriends'], which is literally unendurable, like being crucified, I don't know why, and I don't want to" (59). Though the Beckettian "horrible truth" is certainly that pseudosecular terms such as incest cannot be understood in isolation from religious-sacrificial ones, such as crucifixion, we note that the phrase "literally unendurable, like being crucified" is problematic. For if "literally" is taken literally, the claim that incest-fantasy and crucifixion are "literally unendurable" in similar ways is obviously false, unless indeed the former leads to suicide ("Is one to approve of the Italian cobbler Lovat who, having cut off his testicles, crucified himself?" [167–68].) On the other hand, we need hardly subscribe to Freud's particular theory of incest and its unendurability (source of repression) to be convinced that "*figuratively* unendurable" is equally unsatisfactory. Indeed, if experience can be structured as *an aberrant or arbitrary literalization of figure* (as we will see, most significantly, in Shakespeare's analysis of fashion), Molloy's formulation may again be "quite rightly wrong."[37] Since the operations of figuration in this sense are indifferent to truth and falsehood, but merely state a law of transformation, he is also shrewd, rather than merely repressed, in his petulant refusal "to know why," since knowledge can only repeat and elaborate the very figures that constituted the aberration in the first place.[38] Molloy's incest taboo is, if the phrase may be forgiven, a *crucifiction* that is all too real, whose remedy (insofar as possible, and contra Freud) is self-concealment.

I have said that the logical principle of negation mirrors the sacrificial principle of exclusion in the trilogy. What is epistemologically at stake in the relation between literature and the social sciences is analyzed in precisely these terms:

> The next pain in the balls was anthropology and the other disciplines, such as psychiatry, that are connected with it, disconnected, then connected again, according to the latest discoveries. What I liked in anthropology was its inexhaustible faculty of negation, its relentless definition of man, as though he were no better than God, in terms of what he is not. (39)

Whereas the putative identities of the social sciences here depend on arbitrary exclusions (definitions masquerading as empirical discoveries), literature has something in common with the all-inclusive negativities of theology, which in turn ironically resemble the unwitting negativity of anthropology. Molloy's liking for anthropology cannot be wholly ironic if his own privileging of falsehood is to stand: "I think that all that is false may more readily be reduced, to notions clear and distinct, distinct from all other notions. But I may be wrong" (82).[39]

Though Michael Mooney is doubtless right to pick up here an inversion of Descartes's and the Enlightenment notion of "clear and distinct ideas" as the basis of methodical reasoning, I cannot agree that this important passage simply "exposes the valuelessness of method."[40] On the contrary, providing a sly extension of the celebrated scientific principle of falsifiability (that the only "clear" or scientific theories are those capable of falsification)—which opts, despite Molloy's "mania for symmetry"(85), for an asymmetry between truth and falsehood—this assertion of the relative clarity of falsehood only reinforces Mooney's own emphasis on the novel's negative methodology more generally. There is, to be sure, a Cretan twist in Molloy's formula inasmuch as, if clear, it is likely to be false, while if true, its clarity may be deceptive ("But I may be wrong"). Nevertheless, Mooney's interpretation of both this and Molloy's immediately following remark, as simply affirming ignorance as opposed to method, seems to miss the main point. Speaking, in the above passage, of the difference between the clarity of true and false "presentiments" or predictions, Molloy adds:

> For I knew in advance, which made all presentiment superfluous. I will even go further (what can I lose?), I knew only in advance,

for when the time came I knew no longer, you may have noticed it, or only when I made a superhuman effort, and when the time was past I no longer knew either, I regained my ignorance. And all that taken together, if that is possible, *should serve to explain many things*. (82, my emphasis)

While Mooney is surely correct that "Beckett has Molloy condemn the self-satisfying Cartesian process of validating what one has already projected as true"—a definition of the self-fulfilling prophecy ("I knew in advance")—his summary that "as we might expect, when Molloy continues this process of reasoning from 'false' clear and distinct notions, he regains his ignorance"[41] is less satisfactory. For if false notions are more often clearer than true ones, this is no less a mode of knowledge (albeit negative) than its Cartesian contrary. Moreover, the ignorance regained by Molloy is not an escape from method, but precisely a blindness to the mechanism of the self-fulfilling prophecy—a blindness limited appropriately (since we are dealing in prophecies) by his "superhuman" efforts—which ensures its repetition. Far from claiming a superior ignorance as against methodological pretensions to knowledge, he claims that his own methodical insights into his methodical blindness should serve *to explain many things*. Thus, while Mooney is perfectly correct to cite in this connection the painstakingly (and even exaggeratedly) methodical way in which Molloy later kills the charcoal burner (84), we should conclude not that method and knowledge are "valueless," but rather that Molloy's own method yields a systematic insight into what Girard calls sacrificial or (sado)masochist induction. Method, through recurring blindness to its own operation, is ironically a sadomasochistically *reliable* guide to prediction (thus a "positive" mode of truth); while this insight itself is a negative mode.

Fiction conceived as falsification, as we shall see more extensively in *Malone Dies*, accordingly claims the epistemological rigor or clarity attributed to falsity more generally: "For where Molloy could not be, nor Moran either for that matter, there Moran could bend over Molloy. . . . *For the falsity of the terms does not necessarily imply that of the relation, so far as I know*" (112, my emphasis). Just as the quotient a/c can give a correct answer when both a and c are false, provided the error in both terms is systematic, so Beckett's fiction redefines the problem of truth in terms of the relation between falsehoods (and between necessary and contingent falsehoods): "a kind of connexion . . . not necessarily false" (112). This is a world in which falsehoods, like accidentals, serve as fundamentals. Indeed, the crucial relation between arbitrariness and falsehood, as I have said, is confirmed in the relation between the faux-circular narratives of parts 1 and 2 which mark a passage from arbitrariness to mendacity or self-contradiction. By his "system of going in a [false] circle" (85), Molloy—and Beckett—explicitly aims to avoid circularity and falsehood.[42]

The fundament/anus—which is the comic center of *Molloy* and image of its faux-circularity (the arse-hole's "centrality" is explicit [79])—is the first of several central figures in the trilogy of false transcendence generated by mimetic-sacrificial exclusion. Most obviously, as in the comic tradition more generally, it is an image that undercuts falsely transcendent (notably patriarchal) reifications of gender, emblem of the concealed undifferentiation of the sexes—something made fully explicit by Malone: "there is so little difference between a man and a woman, between mine I mean" (181).[43] I have said that Molloy is called "mimetic in spite of himself" just before the first extended passage concerning the anus. In fact, not only is the anus a figure of (concealed) mimesis between the sexes, but it leads us to the "undifferentiating" mimetic principle more generally. Adorno states this perfectly, though without making an explicit connection with mimesis: "Excretions become the substance of a life that is death . . . an image of indifference, that is, a state prior to differentiation."[44]

We shall shortly see how Beckett defines the general emergence of differentiation from indifference in explicitly mimetic terms. For the present it is enough to note that erotic relations, more specifically, are covertly defined by the principle of mimetic desire made explicit in the story "Enough": "Whenever he desired something so did I."[45] Molloy's pun on the fundamental confusion of "fundamentals" and "accidentals" demonstrates, moreover, how the anal-mimetic figure is epistemologically general in implication.

Beckett's anal jokes are both classic and novel, serious and comic, and they are wholly and explicitly central to the structure of *Molloy*. Molloy, dressed in the *Times Literary Supplement*, first defends his frequent recourse to the anus in pseudorealistic terms, calculating his number of farts per minute to demonstrate why the habitually excluded and taboo should be included in his "realistic" narrative (a comic summary of relations between literature and mathematics that recalls his treatment of the social sciences). Besides resulting in the comic conclusion—and recommendation to concealment—"Damn it, I hardly fart at all, I should never have mentioned it," this positivistic procedure is also said more obscurely to be "like one dying of cancer obliged to consult his dentist" (30). The point, as the appearance of Mr.

Py the dentist in part 2 confirms, is that no mere finite calculation of positive frequency (what is *included* in a sequence) can determine what is "fundamentally" *excluded*, since while π can be defined in terms of the infinite repetition (or mimesis) of an algorithm, its sequence is (at least to date) indistinguishable from an arbitrary sequence: a coincidence par excellence of fundamentals and accidentals that appears to characterize all transcendental and irrational numbers.[46] Thus the logic of exclusion appears more general, as previously mentioned, than that of identity;[47] and such a logic also underlies Molloy's famous cyclical problem of how to arrange his stones in his pockets so as not to suck the same stone twice in a given cycle. The solution is to leave one pocket *empty*, though Molloy still worries, having introduced a provisional order, that "in the cycles taken together utter confusion was bound to reign" (73).[48] His second defense of his recourse to the arse-*hole* is accordingly no longer pseudorealistic, but openly appeals to the principle of sacrificial exclusion, complete with reference to Jesus Christ and (for the only time in the trilogy) to "my muse": the anus as "a symbol of those passed over in silence" (79).[49]

We are now in a position to generalize that the trilogy's celebrated "nothing" appears successively in *Molloy* shaped *as anus, as zero, and as circular π*. The fact that π is treated in part 2, as we shall see, in openly sacrificial terms may serve as proof that Beckett conceived even mathematical epistemology and transcendence (in the mathematical sense) in such terms. Moreover, while critical descriptions of the text as moving from the rational to the irrational are accurate in the mathematical sense, they generally fail to register that the mathematical irrational is itself treated by Beckett as belonging to the exclusive logic of reason. The moral is thus not, as Mooney says of Molloy's fart calculations, merely to reject that "philosophical position which holds that intelligible reality may be explained by recourse to mathematical reasoning,"[50] or to provide a "counterpart of the irrational number [in] the irrational word."[51] Rather, Beckett's cal*cula*tions invoke mathematical rigor in service of what Adorno calls "philosophical anthropology," linking the exclusions of reason to those of human relations.

Mimetic Violence and Representation

I have mentioned that part 2 of *Molloy* provides a quite explicit model of mimetic violence in which differentiation is sacrificially generated. But since parts 1 and 2 contain parallel episodes of violence toward their conclusions which entail different degrees of mediation, it will be helpful to approach them together, alongside an account of representational mimesis—since interpersonal mimesis and representational mimesis are here, as in Stendhal, sacrificially conjoined.

Toward the conclusion of his wanderings in part 1, Molloy meets a charcoal burner, a "dirty old brute" who seems to want him for company:

> I might have loved him. . . . I never had much love to spare, but all the same I had my little quota, when I was small, and it went to the old men, when it could. And I even think I had time to love one or two, oh not with the true love, no, nothing like the old woman, I've lost her name again. (83)

The charcoal burner is thus associated with a powerful masculine alternative or rival to the original model of female or maternal "true love" (as posited, of course, by various psychologies including Freud's), and this is doubtless the most inevitable reason why he must be murdered by Molloy en route to his mother. But the pertinence of gender opposition (which sustains the maternal quest) also gives way here very pointedly to age difference: "I might have loved him . . . if I had been seventy years younger. . . . For then he too would have been younger by as much, *oh no quite as much*, but younger" (83, my emphasis).

The age gap given by this peculiar mathematics seems as hallucinatory and false as the gender gap.[52] Certainly homosexual *possibilities* are in play here (as when Lemuel, in *Malone Dies*, holds Macmann "perhaps lovingly"), but "tenderness" (83) is specified as the *mot juste* in this inter-male alternative—an alternative that is swiftly sacrificed (rather than merely repressed). At first Molloy is content to give this potential "lover" a blow on the head, resembling the knocks on the head he uses to communicate with his mother. Only, as it were on second thoughts, does he return to perform a violence at once more extreme and more phantasmagoric. Having described the attack in methodical detail, he specifies that he has "delayed over an incident of no interest in itself, like all that has a moral," to show how the weak "have a good chance of showing what stuff you are made of . . . given favourable conditions, a feeble and awkward assailant, *in your own class what* . . ." (84–85, my emphasis). This seeming aside about class is a crucial link to the murderous episode of part 2 which occurs between mimetic doubles, members of the same class with a vengeance.

In part 2, the confrontation between Moran and his double closely follows his meeting with another man (Molloy?), whose hat is "like none I had ever seen" (146). Moran stretches out his hand to hold this first stranger's stick without ill consequence (the stranger ambles off), but the similar gesture of a second stranger (mirroring the double-take of Molloy's reactions to the charcoal burner in part 1) leads immediately to violence. This second stranger is in search of the first, just as Moran is in search of Molloy; and when asked whether he has seen the first stranger, Moran lies. Thus Moran and the second stranger not only resemble each other physically, but their mimetic similarity is ironically founded on their mutual claim to, and search for, *difference* (the stranger with the unique hat). They are, so to speak, "postmodernists"—mimetic, like Molloy, in spite of themselves—in that their contentious likeness is founded on their mutual affirmation of difference, of "irreducible otherness."[53]

Between the two encounters, immediately after wondering about the "unknowns" concerning Molloy, Moran sees a kind of vision: "a crumbling, a frenzied collapsing of all that had always protected me from all I was always condemned to be" (148), which takes the form of a face: "with holes for the eyes and the mouth and other wounds, and nothing to show if it was a man's face or a woman's face, a young face or an old face, or if its calm was not an effect of the water trembling between it and the light" (149). By contrast to this picture of sacrificial undifferentiation (sacrificial because of the reduction of all orifices to wounds), Moran forms a very definite "idea of the type of individual" represented by the second stranger—in short, his *class* in every sense of the word. The epistemological thrust is clear: the second stranger and mimetic double is not merely a particular contingent type, but *the very definition of type*: "And indeed there reigned between his various parts great harmony and concord, and it could be truly said that his face was worthy of his body, and vice versa. And if I could have seen his arse, I do not doubt that I should have found it on a par with the whole" (150).

It is important to register that the predictable equation *hole = whole* expresses not merely Derridean *différance* or epistemological indeterminacy of the kind commonly eulogized (or elegized) in Beckett criticism, but, more strikingly, emphasizes to the maximum extent the sacrificial constitution of identity, both of the arse-hole and of the class-whole. As in Kafka's "Josephine the Singer,"[54] precisely mimetic "harmony and concord" here are the condition of discord and violence. "Sorry" that he cannot indicate more clearly how he reduces the stranger's face to a pulp, Moran adds: "it would have been something worth reading. But it is not at this late stage of my relation that I intend to give way to literature" (152). By implication, "literature" here would reduce quite generalized mimetic violence to titillating specificity, whereas Moran states that *to describe the victim is against his principles* (151). The aesthetic-sacrificial lure of a *differentiated victim* cedes to a general ("nonliterary") definition of the mimetic-sacrificial principle.[55] Having reduced the stranger's head to a pulp, Moran finds simply that "my leg was bending normally. *He no longer resembled me*" (152, my emphasis).[56] *The function of mimetic violence is differentiation as such.* "Living souls, you will see how alike they are."[57]

Despite its momentary curative effects on Moran's too obviously Oedipal leg, this generative violence is not Oedipal nor even particularly psychoanalytic. Rather, such general sacrificial production of difference from mimetic indifference reduces the specifically Oedipal mimetic model, at best, to a secondary phenomenon. Comically, Moran does actually condescend, despite his principles, to describe his victim in terms of the Freudian "artificial fly" in his hat which "produced a highly sporting effect" (151); but this is a mere "literary" excrescence on the essentially formal-mimetic model.[58] By contrast, when the theme of mimetic relations between Jacques Moran and his son Jacques is broached directly, representation and mendacity, as well as theft of money—essentially symbolic modes—occupy the foreground rather than literal violence (the Oedipal death wish). Symbolicity (including Oedipal symbolicity), the principle of differentiation, is thus consequence rather than cause—as we shall see even more clearly in *Malone Dies*—of mimetic violence.

One of the most obvious allegories in the novel of the relation between original and copy, father and son, old and new, concerns Jacques's duplicate stamp collection, whose originals Moran sternly forbids his son to take on their journey. Before they leave, Moran accuses him ("Silence, you little liar!") of transferring valuable originals into the duplicate album while claiming simply to be looking at them. To look at them on the journey, "he would have had to hide from his father. And when he had lost them, as he inevitably would, he would have been driven to lie, to account for their disappearance" (110). The quasi-postmodern and deconstructionist moral here is that Jacques is not *simply* lying about his looking at the originals: merely to look at an original (or a father) is "to transfer it to the duplicate album." This mimetic deconstruction of representation also recalls Moran's definition of "messengers" like Gaber (bearer of Youdi's commands to report on Molloy), whose amnesia is such that he remembers his written text only while actually looking at it, and who, despite using "a code incomprehensible to all but himself," understands nothing of his messages while believing he understands everything (106). Contrary to "agents" like Moran, who "never took anything in writing" (106), Gaber is a function of the duplicatory mediation of writing in relation to speech. In fact, both Gaber and Jacques, in his capacity as collector of duplicates and atheist provocateur of fathers, might well recall Jacques Derrida, whose views of writing and speech are here closely anticipated.[59] Nota bene, however, that this "postmodern" loss of origins and representational stability heralds an *intensification* of sacrificial psychology rather than the reverse, as might perhaps have been hoped.[60] I contend that it is because this crisis of "originality" is a matter of representation as such, and thus a *wholly abstract and generalized version of mimetic crisis*, that shortly after the episode of the stamp collection, Moran also takes time off from his narrative to generalize the sacrificial principle:

> From their places masses move, stark as laws. Masses of what? One does not ask. There somewhere man is too, vast conglomerate of all of nature's kingdoms, as lonely and as bound. And in that block the prey is lodged and thinks himself a being apart. Anyone would serve. But I am paid to seek. I arrive, he comes away. His life has been nothing but a waiting for this, to see himself preferred, to fancy himself damned,blessed, to fancy himself everyman, above all others. (111)

A "postmodern" undoing of essentialism ("masses of what? One does not ask") runs parallel here to an ever-increasing, indeed ideal arbitrariness of the victim ("anyone would serve") in an acme of oxymoronic undifferentiation where blessing and damnation coincide, alongside equality and superiority, and on which "a being apart . . . everyman, above all others" is sacrificially constructed.[61]

Shepherd's π: The Geography of Mediation

We move now to Beckett's sacrificial treatment of the opposition between science and religion, and to a "literal" geography of mediation which defines the exclusive principle. We previously observed that Molloy's avowed aim, having "probably read somewhere" that trying to go in a straight line generally means going in a circle, is to try to go in a circle in order (by exclusion) *not* to. Considering the "hypothetical imperatives" (87) that have given him the urge to leave the forest in search of his mother in the first place, he concludes first with longing to abandon the circular maternal quest, and finally, in a ditch between forest and open fields, with studied indifference to it (91).[62] The desire to break out of the circle, Freudian or otherwise, also accords well with Moran's sacrificial conception of π in part 2. If we believe Moran, who tries to conceal his physical weaknesses (his "clitoral" knee injury) while continually suspecting his son of exaggerating his own, the Oedipal paradigm of (rebellious) castrated son and potent father is generated *out of mutual mendacity*. Py the dentist, on the other hand, does not belong to a specifically psychoanalytic or phallic pattern of *pharmakon*, but rather to a pattern of sacrificial eating disorders, of which Jacques suffers from at least two: toothache and stomachache. (The sacrificial character of toothache is perhaps most economically suggested by Flann O'Brien's dictum that "nearly every sickness is from the teeth," prototype of the transition from natural to human violence.)[63] Moran accuses his son of lying in this connection, claiming that while he has really *had* toothache, "in a *bicuspid*[64] I believe" (my emphasis), there cannot be any more pain since the tooth was "dressed" by Mr. Py:

> He has naturally very bad teeth, said Py. Naturally, I said, what do you mean, naturally? What are you insinuating? He was born with bad teeth, said Py, and all his life he will have bad teeth. Naturally I shall do what I can. Meaning, I was born with the disposition to do all I can, all my life I shall do as I can, necessarily. (103)

"Doing everything possible necessarily" defines an infinite arbitrary sequence which *excludes the exclusion* of any possible finite sequence. Now we see more clearly why transcendental π appears as model of a possible cure for the general tension between "fundamentals" and "accidentals," and thus also for the arbitrarily exclusive mechanism of sacrificial law. However, if Jacques is telling the truth about his continued pain—as he is said to be telling the truth on the following page about the rain—this confirms Py's conclusion that Jacques will always have "bad" teeth. Moran nevertheless cruelly compels him to sacrifice his appointment, asserting that "Mr. Py is not the unique dentist in the northern hemisphere" (104). And to Jacques's response that Py is nevertheless "a very good dentist" (appropriate for the atheist scientist that Jacques is): "All dentists are alike, I said. I could have told him to get the hell out of that with his dentist, but no, I reasoned gently with him, I spoke with him as an equal" (104). This quasi-Kantian equation of reason and equality is pointed, since it is precisely in the context of the "likeness" of dentists—of *transcen-dental-ists*—that Moran feels able to reason with his son as an equal. However, the scope of Beckett's sacrificial joke only becomes fully explicit in the fundamental equation of π, as transcendental *pharmakon* of the "northern" hemisphere, with shepherd's *pie*, the Christian lamb-sacrifice. (Thus the resemblance of Py and Father Ambrose's pyx which holds the communion.)[65]

On the eve of their departure their servant, Martha, cooks shepherd's pie, rejected by Jacques on the grounds he has stomachache and subsequently condemned by Moran on the grounds that the shepherd's dog "wouldn't touch it" (118). Admitting to us "he had a temperature. There's nothing wrong with you, I said" (118), Moran gives him an enema (a strictly fundamental purgative, of course) associated with the patriarchal cigar that father Moran has received from Father Ambrose (118). The enema reveals according to Moran that Jacques hasn't eaten, despite his claims to have eaten lunch. The stomachache is thus a sacrificial disease for which the Christian sacrificial meal—did not Jacques the botanist find it "revolting"—might have promised relief, just as Py promises to "dress" his tooth. The equation between lamb-sacrifice and transcendentistry is made explicit in *Malone Dies* where Moll's tooth is drilled into the shape of a crucifix.

We may thus conclude that the sacrificial equation π = pie bears upon the transcendental "equality" and specularity common to both terms, the transcendental irrational in both religious and scientific senses. The circle, of course, is a classical emblem of perfect symmetry; while in Christian terms the transcendental "equality" of all men in the sight of God is sustained by the trinitarian mediation of Christ and the trinitarian equations: god = man, god $\neq$ man, and (in Beckettian terms) god = paraclete/parrot. Note also that sheep function more generally in Beckett as the mimetic-sacrificial animal par excellence (as in the films of Peter Greenaway).[66] They too are strictly fundamental to the Beckettian text: just as Molloy invokes Christ with his finger up his anus, so, in "First Love," the narrator parts his cheeks on the toilet before a picture of Christ among his sheep.[67] Even the faux-narrative circle of part 1 is defined by sheep: "I saw the sheep again. Or so I say now" (91).

All this illustrates our earlier description of part 2 as a more explicitly *mediated* version or extension of part 1, since here the mediators are generalized and exteriorized to such an extent as to take the blatant form of religious and mathematical law.[68] In general, where part 1 opens with a famous encounter (or lack of such) of A and C, part 2 everywhere develops the mediatory triangle A,B,C.[69] Fathers, à la Freud, are added to mothers and sons; religious fathers are conjoined with secular ones; Gaber mediates the relation between Moran and Youdi; Moran meets two strangers in the forest in place of Molloy's one; speech is mediated by writing; experience is mediated by an ironic two-in-one version of the Freudian drives, the "fatal pleasure principle" (99),[70] and so on.

The key to Beckett's deployment of the exclusionary principle of mediation, however, is clearest in the literal geography of part 2, where towns like Turdy, Moran's hometown, are defined in relation to their districts: Turdyba and Turdybaba. "Turdyba" is defined as the environs of Turdy including Turdy, while "Turdybaba" means the environs excluding Turdy, that is, the area *mediated by Turdy exclusive of the mediator*. (The same goes for Bally, Ballyba, etc.) We see again the extraordinary extent to which Beckett insists on a logic of exclusion.[71] Note especially that the exclusion of Turdy allows the opposition of the sexes to become "biologically" legible in Turdybaba (and that the turd-baby reciprocity is at one level certainly compatible with psychoanalytic theory). But the real key to this geography lies in the relatively illegible "Turdyba" (where the principle of mediation is *included*)—emblem, if I am not mistaken, of the baa-ing of sheep. I am thus arguing that the *mimetic-sacrificial sheep*, to put it bluntly, *is hidden behind the psychoanalytic turdy-baby*.

Ballyba, specified as "Molloy country," where Moran sees the man with the unique hat and annihilates his double, predictably turns out to be a land not of cows and horses (to which its grass is said to be fatal) but of "the ass, the goat and the black sheep": "What then was the source of Ballyba's prosperity? I'll tell you. No, I'll tell you nothing. Nothing" (134). This narrative uncooperativeness probably admits of two interpretations. First, insofar as Ballyba is associated with the *strictly* unique or singular hat, "nothing" (no law) can indeed explain it. But we should also emphasize that just as Molloy's pretensions to singularity/difference are compromised by his disarmingly confessed mimetism, so Moran's pretensions to grasp the economy of singularity entail not only his mendacity and mimetic violence against an innocent passer-by, but also, here, a symbolic equivalent of this violence directed against the reader, a provocative gesture of concealment. *Concealment also produces cognitive asymmetry between subjects*, and thus difference, the goal of mimetic violence—and we shall shortly see how concealment and violence are linked in the novel's sartorial figures.

Despite Moran's gesture of concealment, however, it is important to observe that the "nothing" here is in effect still quite legible in terms of transformation from the economy of the cow to that of the black sheep, and from the ass (arse) of *Molloy* to the ass (donkey) of *Malone Dies*. In the comic tradition, Shakespeare's "law of the ass" in *A Midsummer Night's Dream* and *Much Ado about Nothing* may serve as an excellent point of reference for understanding these Beckettian metamorphoses.[72] In each case, the law of the ass, of "Bottoms," turns out to be mimetic-sacrificial law founded on precisely "nothing"—Shakespeare's word, not only for the vagina, but for *fashion*: mimesis.[73]

Mirror-Freud: Lies Concerning Midnight and the Turdy Madonna

We come now to Moran's definitive structural mendacity about midnight and the rain as well as to several related lies. Analysis of these will clarify the general relation between sacred and secular in the novel, including its Freudian terminology, and also something of its temporal dimension.

Moran's quasi-circular return home from Ballyba to Turdy is triggered by the sudden reappearance of Gaber, reminder of his connection with Youdi. At first Gaber "can see nothing" in his notebook, but then he reads the tenseless imperative: "Moran, Jacques, home, instanter" (163). Asking whether Youdi has changed, Moran is told: "no, he hasn't changed, why would he have changed, he's getting old, that's all, like the world" (164). And later: "life is a thing of beauty and a joy forever" (165). The return to Turdy is tenseless because in a sense they have never left Turdy. The situation is akin to the joke implicit in Moran's present-tense instructions to Jacques about what to do in Hole: "Don't worry about the miles, I said. [Imagine] *You're in Hole*" (143, my emphasis). Since no one ever definitively leaves "Hole" in this novel, we are provided with this constant "fundament" against which change can be measured.

What does seem to have occurred in the course of part 2, as is fairly well recognized, is a movement toward atheism. While Moran is initially a Christian and sees plants as evidence of the glory of God, Jacques is a botanist and apparently represents a postreligious development (100). In order "to keep nothing from [us]" (108), Moran admits that he too has doubted the existence of Youdi at times, and even of his messenger Gaber, and by the end he tells Father Ambrose not "to count on him" anymore. Two kinds of father can thus no longer count on two kinds of son, and *Malone Dies* will subsequently investigate the "son of man" as a term poised ambiguously between Christianity and humanism.[74]

Though Youdi—the quasi-divine figure who lives, however, in London—is apparently far from dead but merely "getting old," one of the main questions raised by *Molloy* in its comic confrontation with Freudian geography is certainly what it might mean to adopt a genuinely postreligious terminology, rigorously freed of the sacred. Looking to the lights of Bally, Moran famously invokes Freud's libido, literally, *in the mirror*: "And with regard to the Obidil, of whom I have refrained from speaking, until now, and whom I so longed to see face to face, all I can say with regard to him is this, that I never saw him, either face to face or darkly, perhaps there is no such person" (162). The libido survives, in effect, only *as a principle of mirroring*, transformed from "it" to "he" and described in pointedly religious language. Similarly, when the text predictably serves up a scene of exaggerated Freudian castration anxiety—Jacques rides in front on their tandem while his father's testicles risk entanglement with the back wheel—there follows a "happy" displacement of Oedipal violence which may also be regarded as pointedly counterpsychoanalytic (158).[75] The upshot of this ultra-Oedipal ride is significantly indifferent with regard to Moran's Oedipal knee injury, which is said to feel neither better nor worse (whereas the later *purely mimetic* violence, as we have seen, has an immediate effect). Thus, though the text shares much of its basic territory with psychoanalysis, we may conclude that it is in strong tension with any libidinal or Oedipal theory.

Admittedly, in the same context in which Moran speaks of the possible truth of relations between false terms, he also invokes his "investment" of Molloy "with the air of a fabulous being" in quasi-masturbatory terms, opening his trousers and slipping "in between the sheets with an easy conscience, knowing only too well what I was doing" (112). The point, however, is that this eroticized definition of the "fabulous" *is* all too easy, and that the epistemological structure that really interests Moran is a general *epistemology of concealment* rather than merely of sexual repression. Accordingly, shortly after this tongue-in-cheek evocation, he moves on more seriously to discuss nonsexual mediations, bearing on the exclusionary relation between "colleagues" and everyone else:

> Molloy, or Mollose, was not a stranger to me. If I had colleagues, I might have suspected I had spoken of him to them, as of one destined to occupy us, sooner or later. But I had no colleagues. . . . Among colleagues one says things which in any other company one keeps to oneself. (112)

Having established that concealment from noncolleagues—here *everyone*—is a determining structure in Moran's very definition of

Molloy, we may now turn to the most important of the novel's concluding mendacities. The first of these concerns the Turdy Madonna, to whom Moran claims to be on a pilgrimage when stopped by a Turdy farmer on his lands. The farmer knows no such Madonna in Turdy: "But where is the place in which there is no Madonna? The black one? he said, to try me. She is not black that I know of, I said" (174). The Turdy Madonna is a religious transformation of the Countess Caca of part 1, an oxymoronic virgin who whitens black, "Madonna of pregnant, married women," in whom the secular language of aristocracy has been replaced by the language of the sacred, ironically, at the very moment that Moran is losing his faith.[76] He confesses to lying about her:

> It's thanks to her I lost my infant boy, I said, and kept his mamma. Such sentiments could not fail to please a cattle breeder. Had he but known! I told him more fully what alas had never happened. (173)

This claim about both boy and mother is mendacious since precisely "the mamma" is conspicuous by her exclusion from part 2—a sacrificial exclusion, moreover, which defines her paradoxical omnipresence in the quasi-transcendental forms of the Madonna, Martha with her pie, Moran's hens, and so on. The point here is not to restore in place of Moran's mendacity an orthodox psychoanalytic tale of the infant's mother-losing, but to note the exclusion of the mother/wife ("Mollose") which is of a patriarchal piece with the transcendent-excluded status of woman as such in part 2.

Similarly, heterosexuality is allegorized earlier in part 2, where Moran quite gratuitously deceives a young man into believing "quite a well known actress" wants to meet him. It is not too much to say that *heterosexual love is defined here as gratuitous mendacity*, substituting *tout court* for a relation between males (since the youth is disappointed at Moran's departure: "I fancy he would have liked me for a friend" [137]). Moran also makes explicit the exclusionary principle at stake: "I have never had to deal with a woman. I regret it. I don't think Youdi had much interest in them" (137). "Have women a soul? Answer. Yes. . . . In order that they may be damned" (137).[77]

The essentially sacred,[78] rather than merely gendered, terms in which sexuality is defined at the end of *Molloy* are directly connected, I believe, to its famous concluding lines—much discussed but never to my knowledge very plausibly interpreted: "Then I went back into the house and wrote, It is midnight. The rain is beating on the windows. It was not midnight. It was not raining" (176). The lie about the rain will be clarified, as we will see, by the later transformation of Moran's patriarchal umbrella into the parasol or "pa-sol" of *Malone Dies*—it is the father/sun rather than the rain that Malone's creatures need protection against. The lie about midnight which concerns us here, on the other hand, concerns not the cyclical temporality of the seasons (winter/summer/sun/rain) but a putative turning point between one era and the next. Midnight actually strikes during part 2, "from the steeple of my beloved church," at the moment that Jacques is silent in answer to his father's question: "Are you capable of following me?" Moran "seized his [son's] thoughts as clearly as if he had spoken them, namely, And you, are you capable of leading me?" (130). Midnight thus proclaims, I think, not merely a predictable Oedipal shift of power from father to son, but also a more general confrontation between the botanist and the believer, the secular and the sacred.[79] While at a purely formal level, as has been widely noted, "it was not midnight" makes Moran's fiction a model of avowed mendacity or self-contradiction, these substantive associations of "midnight" are also crucial. Thus despite Moran's own avowed turning away from Christianity, "it was not midnight" implies that he is *not* located at any historic turning point, still less on the verge of the abolition of the sacred. After all, the Turdy Madonna and other sacred mediations still loom large in the text (in fact she has only just arrived), and Moran's concluding avowal of mendacity constitutes in effect the threshold of *Malone Dies*, in which sacred and sacrificial logic, far from disappearing with Moran's faith, becomes all-encompassing.

Clothing and Sacrificial Concealment

Before leaving *Molloy*, we must glance at its sartorial figures in which the sacrificial character of concealment is directly thematized, as for instance in Moran's winter coat, which "leaves great freedom of movement to the arms and at the same time conceals them" (125). I earlier suggested that concealment (directed at the reader) and violence (directed at Moran's double) should be regarded as belonging to the same sacrificial system. That Beckett conceived the relation between clothes and body in terms of violence is unmistakably proved by Moran's reference to "clothes that cleave so close to the body and are so to speak inseparable from it, *in time of peace*" (171, my emphasis). Sight of the body through a gap in his clothing is compared, moreover, to the "blow I had fetched [my son], so avid is the mind of the flimsiest analogy"

(171). This rather extraordinary equation of *dress-framed* nakedness and violence, far from being itself "flimsy," only wittily reemphasizes the flimsiness or arbitrariness of the analogies that form the basis of sacrificial operations. Moreover, the fact that literal violence is directed here against the head rather than the body reflects a passage *from literal to symbolic violence* entirely appropriate to (mental) pain caused by the sight of nakedness. Dress-concealment—a *sacrifice of truth*—may thus be conceived as functioning as antidote to violence, both literal and symbolic, to the *truth of sacrifice*. Malone's opening image of the violence of fiction is of the *pharmakos*: the scapegoat image of a hunchback compelled to undress.

6

The Violence of Fiction:

Concealment and Sacrifice

in _Malone Dies_ and

■ **_The Unnamable_**

How can you not tell a lie, what an idea . . .
—SAMUEL BECKETT

Malone Dies is an important work for my argument because it treats fiction as an explicit theme whose central model is symbolic violence, and because the general relation between violence and symbolicity is the focus of the novel's deceptions and analysis of deception. While we have seen that lying has often been regarded as the act of symbolic violence par excellence, *Malone Dies* extends Moran's aggressive concern in *Molloy* with concealment and mendacity into a concern with *appearances* more generally. Malone claims to have "pinned [his] faith to appearances, believing them to be vain"[1]—a caveat anticipated by the "inseparability" of body and clothing-appearance, in *Molloy*, only in "times of peace." *Malone Dies* explores the relation of the truth of sacrifice to the *sacrifice of truth*, thus understood as an affirmation of appearance, where *symbolic sacrifice* is surrogate for its literal counterpart. What is ultimately at stake in Malone's fiction, as his conclusion makes explicit, is a pseudo-Christian project to renounce sacrificial violence via a purely symbolic substitute, fiction itself. The ultra-violent appearance of the fiction is accordingly deceptive insofar as it operates as a *pharmakon* in a project to renounce violence—Christianity providing Beckett with an orthodox model of substitution of symbolic sacrifice for literal sacrifice in the quasi-cannibalistic symbolism of the mass.[2] Extending the sacred eating disorders of *Molloy*, Malone adopts the motif of "eating" his creation as a basic metaphor for fiction-making itself (226), and *Malone Dies* raises the curtain on a world in which the primary modes of pain are symbolic, where violence has been largely "internalized"—a metaphor more than once grotesquely literalized here.[3]

Fiction as Appearance

Malone Dies develops explicitly what was concealed behind Moran's lie about midnight and the rain—the putative passing, as I have argued, from a sacred to a secular era—by launching into a full-scale reconstruction of a religious-sacrificial model of fiction at the very moment in the development of the trilogy that religious faith is explicitly repudiated. Malone's opening lines measure his possible longevity in terms of Christian feast days, with the fourteenth of July ("festival of freedom") thrown in for good measure as though revolutionary atheism represented no significant deviation from the religious calendar, and *Malone Dies* brings to fulfillment the sacred mediations which increasingly dominate *Molloy* despite its movement toward atheism. Far from being dismissed as *mere* fiction, religious-sacrificial modes therefore become an increasingly general model of symbolic experience at the very moment their fictionality is made clear. We may recall Baudelaire: "Quand même Dieu n'existerait pas, la Religion serait encore Sainte et Divine." Or again: "Si la religion disparaissait du monde, c'est dans le coeur d'un athée qu'on la retrouverait."[4]

Malone begins by defining his fictions, apparently in line with orthodox post-Enlightenment aesthetics, as "play" (180). He himself claims that in the text's oscillation between play and earnest (between his fictions and his accounts of his present state and the project of an inventory of his possessions) "a certain kind of aesthetics" (182) is on his side. But this secular opposition threatens to be even less reliable than its religious counterpart, the distinction between Sundays and work days under threat at the end of *Molloy*.[5] Just as Malone's "inventory" of possessions is ironically named for things supposedly *not* invented, so the opposition between fiction and nonfiction, work and play, is increasingly undermined, concluding with the comic sacrifice of a "colossus" called Ernest near the end of the novel. It is well recognized in Beckett criticism that the most obvious form of this movement entails Malone's recognition that his main character (Saposcat/Macmann) is like himself despite every effort to make him different. Much less well recognized, however, is that the opposition between fiction and nonfiction, play and earnest, should accordingly be conceived in terms of the kind of sacrificial production of identity outlined in connection with Moran's murder of his double, and here reformulated via Malone's cannibalistic definition of fiction as eating one's fictional surrogate. We conclude that *the "freer" the play in appearance, the more striking its sacrificial dynamics, since "fictional" arbitrariness is precisely the cornerstone of sacrificial law.*

Malone's initial pretext for "playtime" is escapist, though he fears that even in his fictions he may be "incapable of lying on any other subject" than himself. The descriptive detail of the opening narrative concerning Saposcat is indeed suspiciously arbitrary in appearance, recalling Molloy's solace in reporting details that seem to mean nothing. It is in connection with Saposcat's blue eyes, however, that Malone warns us of "these little phrases that seem so innocuous and, once you let them in, pollute the whole of speech. *Nothing is more real than nothing*" (192).[6] The appearance of fictional arbitrariness thus only barely masks the fact that Malone's fiction turns out to be the most grandiose truth-project possible, and that his ambition to tell three stories—about humans, animals, and things—covers the three categories which conventionally exhaust the secular universe. If Malone succeeds in escaping from himself, in short, it is with the goal of telling the story not merely of a particular contingent man but of Macmann—both the Son of Man (the divine figure ironically omitted from the three secular categories), and man in general.

Conspicuously in relation to *Molloy*, divided into two parts, *Malone Dies* has the appearance of being undivided; but in fact it is divided internally, a division marked by Malone's (re)christening of Saposcat as Macmann. "Christening" is the *mot juste* here, since Sapo has no Christian name—"He will not need one" (187)—until he is renamed as the Son of Man. One may even read the second part of *Malone Dies* as a kind of "report" on the first, as in *Molloy*, involving both the introduction of explicitly sacred mediations and the recognition that

Saposcat/Macmann is after all like Malone, that fiction and fact (like god and man) stand in a *reciprocal relation*.[7] We may thus profitably return to Malone's dictum cited in the previous chapter: "I simply believe I can say nothing that is not true, I mean that has not happened, it's not the same thing but no matter" (236).[8] And in apparent contrast: "Decidedly this evening I shall say nothing that is not false, I mean nothing that is not calculated to leave me in doubt as to my real intentions" (207). Note especially that the logical opposition between fiction regarded as "nothing that is not true" and fiction regarded as "nothing that is not false" is discarded in favor of a relation between contingency ("what happened") and *calculated concealment*. Unlike *Molloy*, whose model is Moran's outright mendacity about midnight and the rain, *Malone Dies* conceives fiction in terms of concealment—or, more generally, appearance—by no means necessarily simply *opposed* to truth. Both body and clothes (to develop the sartorial motif) are equally "true" appearances. Indeed, Malone's "faith" in appearances (despite "belief" in their vanity) follows from the observation that certain important aspects of reality are constituted *only* as appearances: the sky, as his mother points out, is "precisely as far away as it appears to be. She was right" (270). This faith in appearances, associated with femininity as well as "vanity," has a positive moral dimension, illustrated in the goodness of the old woman who looks after him: "I don't know why she is good to me. Yes, let us call it goodness, without quibbling. For her it is certainly goodness" (185).

The most compressed image of fiction-as-appearance, however, is given in Malone's ironic self-portrait:

> My photograph. It is not a photograph of me, but I am perhaps at hand. It is an ass, taken from in front and close up, at the edge of the ocean, it is not the ocean, but for me it is the ocean. They naturally tried to make it raise its head, so that its beautiful eyes might be impressed on the celluloid, but it holds it lowered. You can tell by its ears that it is not pleased. . . . The outline is blurred, that's the operator's giggle shaking the camera. The ocean looks so unnatural that you'd think you were in a studio, but is it not rather the reverse I should say? No trace left of any clothes for example, apart from the boot, the hat and three socks, I counted them. Where have my clothes disappeared, my greatcoat, my trousers . . . ? (252)

Here the ass/arse that dominates *Molloy* is transformed into the ass/ Malone. Whereas Moran uses his coat as a classic figure of irony that conceals—but thus also draws attention to—his arse and in general the reality *behind* appearances, the equally classic ironic figure of the ass is now associated with the reality *of* appearances.[9] Unlike Moran, Malone here has no clothes (coat, trousers) that might conceal his ass, but his nudity does not preclude concealment of a different order, as denoted by the ass's modestly lowered eyes. The very shift from eyes to ears as means of signification, on the other hand, suggests the reality of Beckett's verbal, as opposed to visual, communication. This shift from the visual to the verbal is in fact a symptom, as we shall see, of a more general repudiation of vision as it figures in the novel's symbolic economy, the destruction of the "sol" as well as the "pa" in the *pa(ra)sol* mentioned in the previous chapter. The "operator's giggle" not only blurs the visual image, but underlines the ironic *doubling* of appearance and reality, play and earnest.

Fiction as Scapegoating

If *Molloy* can be said to be "Girardian" in providing a clearly mimetic model of sacrificial differentiation, *Malone Dies* is no less so in providing a narrative of scapegoat-expulsion as original or paradigm fiction. "Saposcat"—or perhaps *Homo scatologicus* (non-Christian forebear of Macmann)—has suggested to at least one critic the word "scapegoat";[10] and the definitive early event of Saposcat's story is an ironically recast version of the Fall. This recalls other Beckett stories, like "The Expelled" and "First Love," in which an expulsion initiates the action. In "The Expelled," for example, the opening fall (down steps) is explicitly said to be "not serious"[11] or (in Malone's language) "playful"—but this by no means prevents it from operating as a crucial structural marker.

In the case of Saposcat, this paradigm entails a scapegoat-expulsion performed by Malone himself—*qua* author/divinity[12]—organized around *the relation between violence and knowledge*. At school Sapo is threatened with a beating for asserting that he doesn't know the answer to the questions posed by his teachers—a kind of Socratic twist on the biblical sin of eating from the tree of knowledge, here replaced by the crime of claiming not to know. Refusing to be beaten, he snatches the cane from his master and throws it "out of the window, which was closed, for it was winter" (190). Claiming not to understand why he is not expelled from school "when he so richly deserved to be," Malone makes haste "to put a safe remove between him and this incomprehensible indulgence," by announcing he will "make him live as though he had been punished for his deserts" (190). In short, claiming to have lost control over the meaning of his fiction, which itself narrates Sapo's claim to ignorance, Malone reasserts control with a vengeance that is a parody of God's vengeance. Saposcat becomes scapegoat through his failure, as it were, to make his name legible as Sapiens.[13]

Not only is Malone's originary model of fiction, thus, that of a scapegoat-expulsion, but I suggest this model is itself intended to deceive. For while the phrase "out of the window, which was closed, for it was winter" certainly makes sense if one assumes that the cane breaks the window, such breakage is (it seems to me) pointedly not specified by the text, and the ghost of this inconsistency hovers over the entire proceedings as though Sapo's crime were a quasi-impossible act— indeed, as I have said, the very model of fiction.[14] Unlike Moran's blatant and avowed mendacities, however, Malone's equivocation is to say the least easily overlooked, and is a matter very much of *appearance*. In this connection we may recall that Moran's choice of his bold patriarchal umbrella over his concealing cloak, in *Molloy*, was made on account of the summer conditions (125), while here the action occurs in winter (both the season of Malone's writing and of Sapo's schooling). We might accordingly expect the narrative "cloaking" to be more evasive and ambivalent than hitherto.[15]

The *pharmakon*-ambivalence characteristic of sacrificial phenomena, illustrated by Sapo's simultaneous punishment and nonpunishment, extends in *Malone Dies* to every aspect of the narrative. The sacrificial principle itself frankly reverses life and death—"The end of a life is always vivifying" (212)[16]—and Malone's project of dying is a project to be born from "the great cunt of existence" (285), to become an "old foetus" (226) in a kind of parody of born-again enthusiasm.[17] Similarly sacrificial (recalling Girard's "masochist induction") is Macmann's confusion of "the ideas of guilt and punishment," as ideas of "cause and effect so often are [confused] in the mind of those who continue to think" (240). More generally, just as morning and evening are reversed (220), so every symbolic operation in the novel ultimately devolves on a sacrificial reversal and reciprocity which has sacrificial consequences for the symbolic (and epistemological) domain itself, since Malone's words thus tend to "annihilate all they purport to record" (261).[18] Above all, the text increasingly approaches an apparent (but, as we shall see, also deceptive) symbolic reciprocity, even *coincidence* of victim and victimizer, sacrifice and self-sacrifice—"the render rent" (285), as Malone puts it, just before launching into his murderous finale. Thus the quasi-Old Testament scapegoating of

Saposcat gives way to the quasi-New Testament model, as I have said, in which Malone "eats" Macmann, son of man, "a little creature in my image, no matter what I say" (226).

Since Sapo and Macmann are the same person (Sapiens or man), the first putatively unlike his author, the second like him, the Girardian claim that mimetic reciprocity is always implicit in the sacrificial process, however concealed, could hardly be more evident here. Indeed, the specifically mimetic aspect of the whole analysis is made quite explicit inasmuch as just as Molloy's arse becomes Malone's ass, so Molloy's parrot becomes Malone's paraclete (like Flaubert's Loulou in "Un Coeur Simple"), "psittaceously named," and the holy trinity turns out to be another mimetic triangle of father, son, and parrot—the psittaceous principle of mediation being mimesis as such. But whereas the world of Macmann is one in which violence is increasingly self-reflexive and self-sacrificial, Sapo's world depicts violence directed against victims whose sacrificial specificity or "difference" is defined by a matrix of interlocking hierarchies of gender, age, class, species, etc. Thus animals, to take the clearest example, are prominent victims in Sapo's narrative,[19] whereas in Macmann's the victims are all human. Indeed, the story of Sapo's neighbors, the Lamberts, further demonstrates the extent to which Beckett generalizes the sacrificial principle of differentiation as such. "Big Lambert," patriarch par excellence, is a "bleeder and disjointer" (199–200) whose existence is dominated by obsession with the pigs he slaughters, each "so unlike the other in every respect . . . yet at bottom the same," who die "in more or less the same way exactly, a way . . . that could never be imitated by a lamb, for example, or a kid" (201). While obsessed with the difference between his successive victims, Lambert's slaughter thus operates to enforce, and indeed *produce* (since it is in their death cries that the pigs are finally alike), *that sameness which defines species differentiation.*[20] (Similarly, the goal of unanimity or mimetic concord is said to be produced by the death of "someone even insignificant." The survivors "[try] to agree," though "agreement only comes a little later, with the forgetting" [218].)

As the violent climax of Macmann's tale predictably falls on Easter weekend, so the period of Lambert's slaughter falls around Christmas, specified more precisely as Christmas Eve (201). Though the Lamberts live "realistically" in a Christian world, and bear the name of the Lamb, the implication is that the bleeder's pre-Christmas activity is also "pre-Christian" in a certain sense—in exactly the same sense, in fact, that Sapo himself does not have a Christian name. Thus the passage from

Sapo's to Macmann's world, as we have seen, is linked to a passage from pre-Christian to Christian terminologies, and the apparent contradiction concerning Lambert, that he appears at once Christian and pre-Christian, is perfectly appropriate inasmuch as he represents an atavistic principle of animal sacrifice in a Christian context that has theoretically rejected it. Moreover, while violence against animals is legitimized by the disjunction between animal victim and human "disjoiner" (what is at stake here is indeed every kind of sacrificial "disjoining" and differentiation), Lambert's own name undermines this difference, offering us a model of violence which is a hairsbreadth from the comic reciprocity of Lambert killing lambs.[21] Malone's pointed differentiation between pigs and lambs or kids not only alludes to the general differentiation between sacrificial and nonsacrificial animals in the Judeo-Christian tradition, but more specifically recalls that the sacrifice of Christ is prefigured in the Old Testament by the kid sacrificed in place of Abraham's "kid" son (a narrative often interpreted as an allegory of the substitution of animal for human sacrifice). The ambivalence of such "progressive" attenuation of sacrificial violence is nicely imaged in the "terrible teeth" (201) of Lambert's son, which may equally suggest the teeth of a healthy carnivore or the kind of sacrificial tooth decay suffered by Moran's son in *Molloy*.

While the killing of animals may seem preferable to that of human beings, the world of the Lamberts predictably exhibits the kind of nasty fetishization of difference that patriarchy projects across the divide between male and female, age and youth, as well as animal and man. That "patriarchy" is the *mot juste* here is evidenced both by Saposcat, who (like Jacques Moran) has a name "like his father's" (201), and by Lambert's "respect and tenderness" (200) for his own father. Indeed, the passage from the world of the Lamberts to that of Macmann is evidently linked to the passage not only from pre-Christian to Christian, but also from patriarchy to its demise—the latter comically imaged, as I have mentioned, when a parasol, mispronounced "pasol" (father/sun), is broken in two at the end of the novel.

There is no mystery about one source of patriarchal power: Lambert simply beats his young wife into sexual submission rather than be brought "to heel, by means of her cunt, that trump card of young wives" (200). Note, however, that this quasi-legitimate (in patriarchal terms) symmetry of sex and violence has none of the self-reflexive and more properly sadomasochistic flavor and structure of the later part of the novel. It is doubtless a sign of the relative "success" of Lambert's patriarchal order, sustained by its total blindness to sacrificial symmetry, that violence and sexuality contrive to remain *exterior* to each other despite their evident reciprocity, in marked contrast to the erotic *internalization* of the sacrificial principle later allegorized in Moll's crucifix-tooth.[22]

While blindness to the sacrificial mechanism is necessary to its hygienic operation, Malone reveals how this mechanism inevitably undoes all such hygiene through the very principle of substitution by which it operates, revealing the "likeness" lurking behind every hyienic differentiation.[23] Not only is Lambert's wife his "third or fourth," but the marriage is also quasi-incestuous, she being his "young cousin" (199). Indeed, Malone develops the theme of incest to a sacrificial climax in the episode concerning Lambert and his daughter, where, however, the incestuous undifferentiation is still pointedly structured by age difference—the time had long gone, we are told, when Lambert would have liked to sleep with his sister (216).[24] One day when his young daughter is eating rabbit stew, he suddenly "sees" her "elsewhere and otherwise engaged than in bringing the spoon up from the pot into her mouth" (216). Not only does the unspoken incest fantasy—fiction in the double sense that it is imagined by Lambert and must be actively supplied by the reader—substitute for the image of eating flesh, but Lambert's response to his daughter's evident unhappiness is to promise her that she can hold the *female kid* Whitey ("Grisette" in the French)[25] while he kills it. *The sacrificial cure for incest is quite simply the animal victim which resembles the human one.*[26] That maximal undifferentiation is the focus of the narrative is further evidenced by Malone's interjection at this point: "What tedium. If I went onto the stone [to have been the subject of his third story]? No, *it would be the same thing*" (217, my emphasis). Such tedium may be compared to Stendhalian ennui and to Mathilde de la Mole's witticism that the only source of distinction in a boring world of copies is a death sentence.

Triangular Mediation

Much comes in threes in *Malone Dies,* including the number of Lambert's knives in the episode just discussed.[27] There are three putatively different stories (about humans, animals, and things), and the second of these, the story of a bird, turns out to refer to at least three birds in the text: first, the third member of the trinity, "the paraclete, psittaceously named" (250); second, the "gull's eyes" which son shares with father; and third, Saposcat's pen with the brand name Bird (211).

The latter suggests, of course, that language is an important mediating principle in this context, but Malone warns against a deconstructivist or postmodernist overemphasizing of the point: "There is no use indicting words, they are no shoddier than what they peddle" (195).[28] Over and above its "linguistic" abilities, the parrot-paraclete is simply a pseudotranscendental image of triangular mimesis that would be Girardian enough, as I have pointed out, were the sacrificial target not here Christian symbolism itself. It is the trinitarian version of what *The Unnamable* bluntly calls "the everlasting third party" (379), the general principle of mediation identified in that text, as we shall see, *as the most inevitable source of mendacity*. *The Unnamable*, moreover, makes it clear that even so far as language or "voices" are at stake, it is the mimetic *concord* of voices that matters: "often they all speak at once, they all say simultaneously the same thing exactly, but so perfectly together that one would take it for a single voice" (359).

Macmann's affair with Moll is also pointedly structured by a deceptive progression from two to three parties. The first comically grotesque love-making scene is given us, we are famously told, to explain the meaning of the proverb "two is company" (261). But, unrecognized to my knowledge in Beckett criticism, the unmentioned addendum to this proverb ("but three's a crowd") is implicitly *reversed* in a later description of their erotic practices, specifically, Macmann's tonguing of Moll's cruciform tooth: "But from these harmless aids what love is free? Sometimes it is an object, a garter I believe or a sweat-absorber for the armpit. And sometimes it is the simple image of a third party" (265). The several pages that separate "Two is Company" from this image conceal their combined moral: the third party, far from being *de trop*, is both necessary and "desirable"—either in the form of the symbolic object or fetish (exemplified here by various degrees of sartorial exteriority) or more frankly in the form of the external mimetic model as such. *The Unnamable* later generalizes this mediatory pattern to all forms of exteriority: "anything is preferable to the consciousness of third parties, and, *more generally speaking, of an outer world*" (393–94, my emphasis). Every exteriority, including the body, is constructed according to the principle of the sacred: "Organs, a without, it's easy to imagine, a god, it's unavoidable" (307).

The episode of Moll's loose cruciform tooth, a third crucifix between her Madonna-style earrings,[29] is an obvious comic allegory of the relation between external mediation and sacrificial internalization, extending the transcen-dental joke of *Molloy*.[30] Whether or not she will finally swallow or fully internalize the sacrificial mediator (her own patriarchal status as victim) seems to be resolved when the tooth drops out: she apparently cools in her affections for Macmann at this point (266)—though not without ambivalence—and the novel concludes, as I have said, with the allegoric destruction of patriarchy.[31] Nevertheless, though it becomes fully externalized, Moll keeps her sacrificial fetish about her "in a safe place" (267). Moreover, lest she escape her conventional role as victim, Malone stages a sacrificial parabasis, godlike, from the exterior: "Moll. I'm going to kill her" (267).

Once the "divine" Malone is said to have fallen mute in *The Unnamable*, such pseudotranscendent exteriority is generalized to such an extent that "I alone am man, and *all the rest divine*" (302, my emphasis). *The silencing of divinity merely leads to its ubiquity*—that is, to a potentially unlimited field of sacrificial substitution in which all forms of exteriority merge or become "alike." The sacred, in this sense, is defined (as my earlier reference to Baudelaire suggested) not by a set of beliefs but by this pattern of sacrificial substitution. Thus, for instance, the last "story" of *The Unnamable*, offered as a model of stories, is a purely substitutive, wholly secular tragicomedy about a woman who marries, thinks her husband dies in the war, and "yep, marries again" (410). The first husband, who has not died in the war, dies of emotion on the way to see her, while the second hangs himself at the thought of losing her. This narrative—confusing son and son-in-law, daughter and daughter-in-law, and mother and mother-in-law into the same bargain (411)—ultimately devolves into a single interpretive aporia concerning who bolted the door behind which the second husband committed suicide: the man himself "the better to hang himself, or the mother-in-law the better to take him down, or to prevent her daughter-in-law from re-entering the premises, there's a story for you" (411). The point here is thus simply the question of *who has been excluded by whom*; and the bolted door is a general figure for every sacrificial relation between "inside" and "outside," including the relation between the "I" and the door itself: "oh there's no danger, it's not I, it wasn't I, the door, it's the door that interests me" (411). The sacrificial relation between the unnamable "I" and the impenetrable door (the symbolic object) has the same exclusive structure as that between the "I" and "the everlasting third party."

Accordingly, while one should "probably not" (338) speak of the structures of symbolic mediation as "voices"—"the fact is all this business about voices requires to be revised, corrected and then abandoned" (338)—yet "no other image is appropriate" (350) to a mediation that is generated by other people as well as by symbolicity as such: "Hearing nothing I am none the less a prey to communications. And I speak of voices! After all, why not, *so long as one knows it's untrue*. But there are limits, it appears" (338, my emphasis).[32] Insofar as blame can be shifted onto the quasi-transcendent third party, the mendacious voices of mediation,[33] the Unnamable writes of "this innocence we have fallen to" (335). But there are pointed limits to such innocence: "Ah yes, all lies, God and man, nature and the light of day, the heart's outpourings and the means of understanding, all invented, basely, by me alone, with the help of no one" (306). Beckett's insistence on the centrality of lies to his project, far from disappearing as *The Unnamable* makes explicit the basic structure of the trilogy's third-party mediations, increasingly saturates the text.

Violence and Symbolicity

Malone Dies comically allegorizes the evolution of symbolicity via Malone's loss of his stick, a loss by which he is said to "ascend painfully, to an understanding of the Stick, shorn of all its accidents, such as [he] had never dreamt of," arriving at the process of ideation by which "man distinguishes himself from the ape and rises, from discovery to discovery, ever higher towards the light" (255). This pseudo-Platonic Stick is thus the very principle of symbolization—one of its obvious analogues is Malone's Venus pencil[34]—conceived in terms of the internalization of pain or loss. It appears in turn as an instrument of physical and mental violence which offers the "blessing in disguise" (255) characteristic of sacrificial phenomena: "How great is my debt to sticks! So great that I almost forget the blows they have transferred to me" (185).

Malone's analysis of the *ideation* of pain recalls Girard's provocative claim that "masochist induction" may "even be the archetype of inductive reasoning"—all the more so since the idea(liza)tion is surrounded, both here and in *Molloy*, by specifically mimetic mediations that Malone sums up in the phrase *"speculative* pain." So-called physical pain is generally considered by philosophers with toothache, of course, as an exemplar of epistemological indubitability in which subjective and objective, appearance and reality coincide; thus it particularly suits Malone's faith in appearances. However, what Beckett aptly calls "speculative pain" (pain that is not conceived merely *as a given* but as a mimetic and conceptual product)[35] also exhibits this coincidence inasmuch as it operates as a self-fulfilling prophecy, appearing successively as cause and effect—where "true" love seems to authenticate "true" pain and vice versa, for instance, or where ideas of cause and effect are reversed (to take Malone's own example) in punishment and guilt.[36] It is no wonder, then, that with all his faith in appearances, Malone still believes them "vain." On the other hand, we recall that just as this faith in appearances loyally follows his mother's dictum about the coincidence of appearance and reality, so Malone insists on a similar coincidence in the "goodness" of the woman who now looks after him: "It is she who got me this long stick," thanks to which "I can control the furthest recesses of my abode" (185). *Speculative* operations can of course be beneficial as well as masochistic.

Beckett further develops the masochistic theme in his treatment of Macmann's successive "keepers," Moll and Lemuel, in the asylum of St. John of God. Moll, despite her sacrificial tooth, refuses to smuggle oysters into the asylum (ultrasymbolic delicacies, presumably, because their pearls are produced by wounds): "when it came to the regulations Moll was inflexible and their voice was stronger than the voice of love, in her heart, whenever they made themselves heard simultaneously" (268). These regulations, like all sacrificial laws, thus protect against violence as well as enacting it ("stern measures were simply taken or not taken"), and Moll will later escape Macmann's "oyster-kisses" (263) around the same time that her sacrificial tooth is removed to "a safe place" (266). The regulations—"dictates," as Malone puts it, "of a peculiar logic" (277)—thus establish limits to sadomasochistic internalization and specularity.

But the contrary is true for Moll's successor, Lemuel, who "far from being a stickler for the statutes seemed to have little or no acquaintance with them" (268), and who accordingly expresses violence in all its unrestrained reversibility. His "probably" (267) Aryan background and Jewish-sounding name conform allegorically, of course, to a specifically twentieth-century coincidence of persecutor and persecuted, reinforced in turn by his particularly grotesque instantiation of a *pharmakon* identity of pain and cure:

> Flayed alive by memory, his mind crawling with cobras, not daring to dream or think and powerless not to, his cries were of two kinds, those having no other cause than moral anguish and those, *similar in every respect,* by which he hoped to forestall same. Physical pain, on the contrary, seemed to help him greatly. (269, my emphasis)[37]

It is the overt identity between the cries of moral pain and cure—the unconcealment of the *pharmakon* mechanism—that makes it ineffective; only physical pain can now reestablish the sacrificial exteriority required for curative efficacy. Lemuel solves the paradox of the *pharmakon*, in a manner of speaking, by becoming his own *pharmakos*. Grotesque index of modernity conceived in terms of the Holocaust, he exemplifies how decay of the sacred statutes of the House of St. John of God, the modern decay of the sacred as such, simultaneously reveals and reenacts their "ancient" (269) basis in sacrificial violence; how what Malone presents as the first metaphysical marker (the stick "shorn of all its accidents") might also be called "the last metaphysical marker"[38]—pain itself. Lemuel points both "backwards [into the past], or perhaps I should say forwards" (269) into the future.[39]

The metaphysical issue par excellence, of identity and equality, is at the center of Malone's analysis of Macmann's discomforts:

> [Macmann] stated . . . for he was artless, I have had enough, without pausing for a moment to reflect on what it was he had enough of or to compare it with what it had been he had had enough of, until he lost it, and would have enough of again, when he got it back again, and without suspecting that the thing so often felt to be excessive, and honored by such a variety of names, was perhaps in reality always one and the same. But there was one reflecting in his place and *setting down coldly the sign of equality where it was needed, as if that could make any difference.* (279–80, my emphasis)

This equal sign recalls *Molloy*, where Moran speaks to his son "as an equal" concerning Py the dentist, and where the "equalizing" circularity of the transcendental mathematical cure is linked to a transcendental reciprocity between god and man (and hence "equality" between men) signified by communion. Note that equality is also linked to the principle of substitution (the one, Malone or Beckett, "reflecting in his place"), and that it is accordingly this sacrificial principle—*in reality always one and the same*—that underlies all apparent differences. Again we must conclude that a "postmodern" affirmation of difference is scarcely to the point here (remaining, in effect, the butt of Beckett's joke about equality not making any difference) at least as long as it remains blind to the sacrificial principle that structures the text throughout, providing virtually total coherence and interpretability—contra so many conventional critical readings. In this context, perhaps, we must regrettably admit the justice of Bersani's and Dutoit's claim as to the "irrelevance" of so much Beckett criticism.

Similarly, recalling the circles of *Molloy*, it is significant that one of Malone's other representatives of modernity at the end of the novel, the so-called Saxon, is exhibited as "dislodged . . . imperceptibly from his coign of maximum vantage in the centre of the room" (284). A comically repellent image of Anglo-Saxon rationalism and imperialism, as well as of the more general secular ideologies of sex and money ("fucking" and "business"), and the world domination of the English language spoken "in a strong foreign accent"—which is why, though called Saxon, "he was far from being any such thing" (284)—he concludes by equalizing even "yes" and "no": "Good morning, good morning, good morning, he said, with a strong foreign accent and darting fearful glances all about him, fucking awful business this, no, yes?" (284).[40] Undifferentiation has here advanced to the point where the Saxon transfers his food, examining it drop by drop, to the chamber pot without internalization, establishing the final alimentary equation of the novel and its continuity with *Molloy*: food = excrement. It is to this threat of total *analytic* undifferentiation (hence the emphasis on examination)—the deconstruction, so to speak, of *all* statutes— that Lemuel's violence is a sacrificial response. Malone's cold "sign of equality," as I have said, is simply the sacrificial equation in all its analytic purity.

Violent Light (The End of Patriarchy)

The novel's final scene of slaughter, executed by Lemuel, may appear to be a more or less senseless bloodbath, an authorial massacre by fictive proxy that coincides with the author's own real death, whose cathartic efficacies nevertheless exhibit a pleasing "aesthetic" symmetry. I shall argue that this *appearance* of the symmetrical coincidence of authorial killing and dying, though not exactly mendacious on Malone's part (since he tells us clearly enough what to expect), is a deception of some importance and one of the points of departure for *The Unnamable*. For the present, however, it is sufficient to observe that the killing, far from being random, provides a comically constructed allegory of modernity in which the survivors—generic types called "the youth . . . the Saxon, the thin one and the giant" (284)—are as important as Lemuel's victims. Despite the appearance of generalized violence, there are in fact only two figures actually murdered at the conclusion, two hyperallegoric "colossi" (286) called Ernest and Maurice, and I suggest that both should be linked to the "sign of equality" established by Malone. For what permits this "equality" to appear ubiquitously in the novel, as we have seen, is Malone's relentless sacrificial doubling of various generalized oppositions—death and life, animal and human, persecutor and victim, pain and pleasure, play and earnest, and so on—which depends in turn on establishing the symbolic sign of equality, the *pharmakon* equation, that operates behind all such putative distinctions. In the case of Ernest, the implication is glaring enough. His murder by Lemuel allegorizes an abolition of the opposition between play and earnest, and thus also between literal and symbolic, that had been anticipated from the novel's opening pages. As for Maurice, I believe we must venture an even more ghastly pun in Franglais: *More Rice*. My contention, as I have said, is that *Malone Dies* raises the curtain on a world in which the primary modes of violence are symbolic, and thus in which the most determinedly literal or "earnest" causes of violent conflict, notably *rivalry over food*, have been eliminated.[41] In this light, we see again why so many of the text's dominant figures are alimentary and why so little of importance, including the definition of fiction itself, escapes alimentary formulation.

This is not to say that displacement of literal by figural foods (like Macmann's "oyster-kisses") is simply associated with first-world or wealthy modernity—though the modern history of eating disorders might certainly be considered in this connection. But of course the most ancient of sacred regulations also surround food, and history exhibits its own mode of reversibility in *Malone Dies*: "much water has passed beneath Butt Bridge, *in both directions*" (251, my emphasis). Once again the cannibalistic imagery of the communion is a paradigm case, since this imagery figuratively returns to cannibalism in the very ritual by which Christianity theoretically breaks with all forms of literal sacrifice. This imagery also provides a model for the Easter conclusion of the novel (though the man "with the Messiah beard" [286] is pointedly absent from the scene) inasmuch as its own violence is fictive or "merely" symbolic, and inasmuch as Malone is concerned with the possibility of a world in which earnest or wholly literal violence has entirely given way to symbolic or "internalized" equivalents. Just what is at stake in such equivalence, however, is the point of his obsessive concern with the sacrificial equality of Macmann's discomforts. The figure of Lemuel and his *pharmakon* equation of pain and cure suggest that the horizon of liberation from the inequalities of patriarchy in general—as well as from the "brothers-in-law" (288) Ernest and Maurice in particular—may be called sanguine in a less than purely metaphorical sense. The blood on his hatchet, the novel famously concludes, "will never dry" even if the hatchet "will not hit anyone any more" (289).

The undoing of patriarchy, as mentioned earlier, is imaged by the breaking of a parasol mispronounced "pasol," the father/sun. Malone's most compressed allegory of the relation between literal and symbolic pain also concerns sight:

> A needle stuck into two corks to prevent it from sticking into me, for if the point pricks less than the eye, no, that's wrong, for if the point pricks more than the eye, the eye pricks too, that's wrong too. Round the shank, between the two corks, a wisp of black thread clings. It is a pretty little object like a—no, it is like nothing. (248)

This needle is one of the mediating substitutive figures between Malone's Venus pencil and his stick (which he compares to "a little woman"). The general question of the relation between literal and symbolic pain devolves here into the more particular case of symbolic pain caused by vision and aesthetics (by "pretty little objects"), which in turn devolves into the still more particular (erotic) case of whether "pricks" or "eyes" (holes) hurt more. That Beckett conceived not only erotic but also *visual violence* as a limiting case of symbolic violence more generally is demonstrated by the conclusion of the novel, which gives preeminent, *doubled,* and final place to this form of "hitting with light," renounced by Malone after all other forms of hitting, literal and figurative: "with his hammer or with his stick or with his fist or in thought in dream I mean never he will never or with his pencil or with his stick or or light light I mean" (289).[42]

Malone's comic refusal to admit the eroticism of his "pricks" and "eyes," his claim that his needle is "like nothing," contains at the same time a serious point comparable to the "queer light"—"oh I insinuate *nothing*" (270, my emphasis)—which results from a blow on the head he gets from his male visitor shortly before the conclusion. For what is primarily at stake is not merely the eroticization of these figures of visual violence (however significant this may be) but the failure to discover any "likeness" between literal ("physical") and symbolic ("mental") pain upon which a reliable judgment of their relation could be founded. The "pretty little object" is sui generis partly because light/ sight is itself sui generis[43]—not only in the sense that vision and violence are linked in police manuals and animal behavior but because it appears as *ideal* mediator of relations between literal and symbolic as such.[44] Thus the "pricks" caused by narrowly sexual determinations (such as "queerness") give way in the trilogy to "light-effects" more generally, from the "lavatory lights" (60) of *Molloy,* and the "incandescent migraine" with which Malone prepares his sacrificial finale, to Worm's eye that cannot close in *The Unnamable* (364).

I earlier noted that Malone stresses a passage from eyes to ears in his self-portrait as ass. Similarly, when he fears his exercise book will be stolen by his aggressive male visitor, maneuvers of visual hide-and-seek are obsessively stressed; but the exercise book turns out to be "no longer . . . where he had seen me put it" (272).[45] Having eluded the aggressive strategies of vision with his (verbal) book, Malone now fears "willful murder" (by umbrella point, anticipating the "pasol") from his visitor, a return to quasi-literal violence. Failing this final recourse to brute force, however, "I think we gazed at each other *literally* for hours, without winking. He probably imagined he could stare me down" (272, my emphasis). Sight offers a special coincidence of literal and symbolic, of experience as *literalization of figure*, which I stressed in the previous chapter. In the next chapter, we will see how Shakespeare's mimetic-sacrificial analysis of fashion revolves around precisely this kind of aberrant literalization.[46]

As for the visual dimension of Malone's allegoric destruction of patriarchy, we recall that it entails the transformation of the patriarchal umbrella into parasol. More particularly, it is "the youth, tormented by the sun" who grasps "the thin one's" umbrella, "saying Pasol! Pasol!" (285), while it is the thin one who later breaks this patriarchal device against a rock, "a curious gesture" (288). Though father and sun are often regarded as twin stars of patriarchal epistemology, we should note that the youth regards the patriarchal device as defense *against* the sun—light operates, like all symbolic violence, as *pharmakon*—and that it is the thin one, "shivering, though in theory the Saxon is the shiverer" (287), rather than the youth who does the breaking with the Saxon's approbation: "Nice work, sir, nice work!" (288). It appears that "thinness" and Saxon rationality here collude against patriarchal virility—in each case a triumph of mental over physical strength (still represented in this scenario by "the giant," atavistic colossus like Ernest and Maurice).[47] But the irony of a narrative in which *thinness* triumphs over patriarchal light should be obvious to any casual observer of modern eating disorders or contemporary fashion, whose obsession with both youth and thinness is proverbial. An obsession with "pretty little objects," however putatively unique, can hardly be said to constitute liberation; and without his parasol the youth has nothing to protect him from the sun.

Moreover, the sadistic treatment reserved by Malone and Lemuel for an older woman at the conclusion (the do-gooder Lady Pedal), not to speak of Malone's own fantasies about little girls (274–95),[48] hardly indicate that the demise of patriarchy is favorable to all women. Admittedly Lady Pedal—read the "pedal" of Moran's patriarchal bicycle as well as "petal"—who sings of the sun and the flowers, the birds and the kingship of Christ, and who has a hat resembling the sun made of artificial daisies (286–87), is the patriarchal woman par excellence. But, unlike her patriarchal counterparts, the brothers-in-law Ernest and Maurice, she is *not* definitively killed off by Lemuel, but merely breaks her hip. Once again, we may note that the appearance of "Lemuel's mass homicide"[49] is belied by the fact that he kills *only* these two ultrasymbolic "colossi"—an appearance which we may connect to the deception or "vanity" of appearances in the novel as a whole. The others all survive, in my reading, as types that define the future. It is thus highly pointed that *Malone Dies* reserves a special scapegoat role, in the context of patriarchal decline, for both an old woman *and* a little girl.

Aesthetic Concealment

I come now to the central strategic concealment enacted by the novel at its sacrificial conclusion. Malone claims, as I have said, that "a certain kind of aesthetics" is on his side; but we have seen that aesthetics offer no alternative to the sacrificial mechanism—indeed, aesthetic catharsis (as Girard and others have argued against Aristotle) has all the hallmarks of attenuated sacrifice—and several varieties of "prettiness" are explicitly subject to sacrificial analysis in the text. Malone's grotesquely cathartic finale is no exception to this rule: it mimics the Christian sacrifice as interpreted by St. Paul, where the definitive sacrifice of the Word-made-flesh—here, also *the Flesh-made-word*[50]—will make possible the end of sacrifice. But Macmann, son of man, survives intact, and the "beautiful young man with the Messiah beard" (286) is also absent from the scene.[51] Moreover, although we are presented with a historical break described in terms of a gulf between two island-reefs "narrow at first, then wider and wider as the centuries slip by" (288), its consequence is that "it is difficult to speak of man, under such conditions" (288), rather than any definite horizon of liberation—from the "Druid remains" (288), for instance, associated with archaic sacrificial religion.

Nevertheless, the utopian and moral dimension of Malone's highly "aesthetic" finale (which includes haunting scenes of the Irish landscape alongside Lemuel's tragicomic slaughter of his victims) certainly seems to offer a liberational promise. In particular, since Malone *appears* to die while murdering his characters, his final renunciation of violence seems to follow from the total reciprocity (or equality) between self and other, victim and victimizer. But this utopian coincidence of "render" and "rent," of sacrifice and self-sacrifice, is indistinguishable in structure or form from its sadomasochistic parody—one may equally strike the other and desist from striking because one has "internalized" his pain.[52] This is not to say, however, that the pseudo-Christian finale offers no hope. In fact, contrary to the stereotype of hopelessness that Beckett himself often encouraged in his critics—and bearing in mind that Lemuel, in anticipation of the slaughter, holds Macmann by the waist "perhaps lovingly" (287)—we may be reminded of "The Calmative," where the narrator is held forcefully by the neck by a male stranger who at the same time speaks to him tenderly. The roweling of his neck and the caressing voice "merge *in a devastating hope, if I dare say so, and I dare.*"[53]

However, as Malone makes clear, the rub of the matter is that relations between render and rent are *not* quite symmetrical:

> All is ready. Except me. I am being given, if I may venture the expression, birth into death, such is my impression. The feet are clear already, of the great cunt of existence. Favourable presentation I trust. My head will be the last to die. Haul in your hands. I can't. The render rent. My story ended, I'll be living yet. Promising lag. That is the end of me. I shall say no more. (285)

Although the great majority of critics assume that Malone dies at the end of the novel—and it has even been rather foolishly argued that the blow on the head received by him is "a figurative representation of Malone's having suffered a stroke"[54]—a few have recognized that this is an appearance only.[55] No one to my knowledge, however, has connected this with the novel's more general stress on appearances as a model of fiction, or to the fact that Malone's sacrificial aesthetics are just as deceptive as Moran's claims about midnight and the rain.[56] The fundamental lie of *Malone Dies* is not in the text but the title: Malone does *not* die. For despite the poetic broken syntax of the text's final lines designed to seduce readers into believing that Malone's death coincides with the end of the story, this is explicitly denied ("My story ended, I'll be living yet"), if we are alert enough not to repress this denial in the cathartic violence of what follows. Malone's concealment—which is nevertheless clearly avowed, like Moran's mendacity—is one that all our aesthetic habits conspire to confirm, like the "favourable presentation" which similarly emphasizes an obscene symmetry between birth and death, rending and being rent. All renders are of course rent after a "promising lag," since they eventually die like those they have killed; but here "the end of me" simply refers to the cessation of the first-person narrative ("I shall say no more"). In *The Unnamable*, though "little trace" of Malone's "mortal liveliness" is said to remain; he survives as "god" and mute (302), in a kind of parody of the divine status habitually accorded to sacrificial victims. But he survives nonetheless—man having become god at the very moment that god should, in Christian terms, have become man, or, in post-Christian terms, should have been displaced by man.

The basic structural concealment of *Malone Dies* is therefore that its project to escape sacrifice by pursuing the reciprocal (and "playful") logic of sacrificial symmetry to the bitter end is intentionally deceptive. At the start of *The Unnamable*, the divine Malone is pitied for having two strands of beard *of unequal length* on either side of his chin (295), and his utopian goal of escaping sacrificial law by saying "nothing" meets a definitive objection: "you always overlook a little something, a little yes, a little no, enough to exterminate a brigade of dragoons" (305). Malone's faith in appearances therefore gives way to the Unnamable's "stupid obsession with depth" (295). "Once a certain degree of insight has been reached . . . all men talk . . . the same tripe."[57]

Sacrificial Mendacity in *The Unnamable*

That Beckett originally planned to write only *Molloy* and *Malone Dies* rather than a trilogy is evidence that sacred patterns lay at the heart of his original design. *The Unnamable* begins, as I have said, by identifying the entire external world including Malone as "divine," and can be regarded generally as an effort to translate sacrificial problems into properly secular terms. *The Unnamable* also confirms that mendacity and concealment are central elements in the structure of the trilogy taken as a whole. In parts of the novel, the words *lies*, *lying*, and so forth appear on almost every page, and in the last few pages they dominate the discourse, appearing no less than nine times in the final two long sentences.

I mentioned earlier that the secularization of the religious principle of mediation, redefining the divine in terms of "third parties," is identified as a necessary source of mendacity:

> All lies. I have nothing to do, that is to say *nothing in particular*. Having nothing to say, no words but the words of others, I have to speak. No one compels me to, there is no one, *it's an accident, a fact*. (316, my emphases)

Note that necessity and accident are again united here in "fact"— recalling both *Molloy* and Beckett's own claim, cited in the previous chapter, that history is "the result of a necessity that is not Fate, of a liberty that is not Chance. . . . Humanity is divine, but no man is divine." Thus while the compulsion to speak—or think (speak to oneself)—is defined in terms of the combination of accident and necessity, neither accident nor law fully determines what is said, which need be "nothing in particular." Bersani and Dutoit interestingly claim that "Beckettian behavior is true but implausible; it is never *like* the only behavior we can empirically know, which is contingency-determined behavior."[58] But we see here that Beckettian behavior *is* like all other behavior in being in part contingency determined, and moreover that its truth is in part determined by the compulsion to falsehood and mendacity insisted on by the Unnamable. Similarly, Richard Begam's precisely opposite claim that *"The Unnamable* delivers us . . . [into] a world not of transcendence but of contingency, a world not of truth but of fiction,"[59] is belied by the Unnamable's own principle that "unfortunately we must stick to the facts, *for what else is there. . . .* The facts are there, the facts are there" (366, my emphasis). *The Unnamable* operates in an area which transcends, in a manner of speaking, and renders conceptually inadequate the very opposition between necessity and arbitrariness, fact and fiction.

A similar logic also underlies the Unnamable's meditation on the relation of truth and error:

> Not to have been a dupe, that will have been my best possession, my best deed, to have been a dupe wishing I wasn't, knowing I was, *not being the dupe of not being a dupe. For any old thing, no, that doesn't work, that should work, but it doesn't.* (316, my emphasis)

Recalling Molloy's opening rejection of generalized epistemological skepticism, this epistemological *via negativa* once again proceeds by negation of error and arbitrariness. But the *double* negation also negates unlimited arbitrariness ("*any* old thing"—as opposed to "nothing in particular"—"doesn't work"), and thus resolves Molloy's initial dilemma of believing *all* he hears instead of believing nothing. The Unnamable's strategic immersion in error and mendacity is not merely a Kantian nightmare of gratuitousness and rational self-contradiction, of pure fiction or arbitrariness; rather, as in Moran's earlier consideration of true relations between false terms, he posits truth and "true interest" as his goal: "For it is difficult to speak, even any old rubbish, and at the same time focus one's attention on another point, where one's true interest lies" (310). *True interest lies,* whatever its difficulties, in establishing a relation to "even any old rubbish," and not in effecting a wholesale Kantian sacrifice of mendacity. "True interest," since it can only be deduced from the negation of arbitrary fiction and the mendacities of (self) interest that conceal it, is far from incompatible with an avid pursuit of falsehood. The "blessed pus of reason" (356) operates explicitly according to the *pharmakon* logic of "poison and antidote" (300).

Space compels us to pass over here the Unnamable's careful and complex distinction between three kinds of truths: those that have a beginning but no end, those that have no beginning but an end, and finally those that have neither beginning nor end. However, besides emphasizing that Beckett's concern with defining truth becomes ever more pointed as the trilogy progresses (rather than the reverse, as so much critical commentary seems to imply), we should observe that it is in connection with ends, and with the singular "encounters" associated with them, that we hear most particularly about "the concern with truth" and "hence the interest of possible deliverance by means of encounter" (302). The "encounter" in point—comically illustrated in the destruction of Mahood's family by sausage poisoning (320)—carries its traditional implication of the accidental interaction or encounter of otherwise law-bound entities.[60] We have seen how the family is defined in *Molloy* and *Malone Dies* in mimetic terms. Since, moreover, mimetic law evolves in part arbitrarily by definition, we now see why the delimitation of a given mimetic "truth" (or fact) can only be given retrospectively from a perspective that has come to the (rear) *end* of that truth's development, from a position that has already excluded or superseded it. The family (and its concept) accordingly dies self-sacrificially, so to speak, of its own principle of truth: the quasi-Freudian sausage—"not to mention the two cunts [Mahood's wife and mother] into the bargain" (325).

We must also pass over here the quasi-dialectical narratives associated with Mahood and Worm that parallel this abstract analysis of truth in terms of beginnings and ends, noting only that these are defined in terms of "two falsehoods" (337) to be negated, and that the secular principle of "mastery" (or power) associated with Mahood is said to provide no genuine explanatory alternative, not only to the erotic and procreative principle of the family (378), but also to that of the sacred: "we'd end up by needing god" (378). The sacred itself, as we have seen, is identified with a principle of exterior and pseudotranscendent mediation that ultimately governs, and gives the lie to, all bipolar relations of power or mastery/slavery conceived as such: "we've been told a lot of lies, he's been told a lot of lies, who he, the master, by whom, no one knows, the everlasting third party, he's the one to blame, for this state of affairs, the master's not to blame" (379). After the voices associated with Mahood ("the master's voice") and Worm (paradoxically speechless, associated with "a parting with truth") have run their course, however, the Unnamable finally reaffirms "this source in me, without specifying where exactly, no finicking, anything is preferable to the consciousness of third parties and, more generally speaking, of an outer world" (393–94). Crucially, moreover, this affirmation of singularity has both a mendacious-sacrificial and—at last—an explicitly nonsacrificial dimension. On the one hand, the text approaches singularity via the blatantly sacrificial metaphor of "killing" all such third-party voices (406). On the other hand, the "phrases that die for no reason" (406) without having to be killed, are endings linked to a more optimistic and nonsacrificial turn: "I believe in progress" (407).[61]

Consistent with its effort to approach singularity, the final pages of the text initially return strategically from the third-person plural to the third-person singular—"they who believe, no, in the singular, he who lived" (407)—and increasingly also to first- and second-person singular. This return is first heralded by a sacrificial prohibition of laughter in favor of tears: "it's screamingly sad, anything rather than laughter" (405). It is no accident that the phrasing here resembles "anything is preferable to consciousness of third parties," since comedy tends to accentuate consciousness of mimetic mediation and substitution.[62] But we already know from *Molloy* how laughter and tears resemble each other; so, after the trilogy's final "story" has been told, this prohibition is comically reversed:

> as I groan along, I'll laugh, that's how it will end, in a chuckle, chuck, chuck, ow, ha, pa, I'll practise, nyum, hoo, plop, psss, nothing but emotion, bing bang, that's blows, ugh, pooh, what else, ook, aah, that's love, enough, it's tiring, hee hee. (412)

This comic zenith of emotional undifferentiation pointedly follows on the heels of the final story, that of the closed door discussed earlier, which reduces tragedy to comedy by mere accumulation of third-party mediations and repetitions. Thus the text's "celebration" of laughter, if it can be called that, is less a modernist affirmation of aesthetic pleasure—and still less a postmodernist affirmation of "play" along the pseudo-Nietzschean lines so often cited by contemporary authors—than an enlistment of laughter and tears themselves into the realm of sacrificial catharsis. Laughter is "the ending end" (412) of the trilogy, connected with a desacralization of its "enormous prison, like a hundred thousand cathedrals, *never anything else any more* . . . how false this space is, what falseness instantly" (413, my emphasis). But laughter's pleasurable and sympathetic dimension, its "fun," is not to be separated from sacrificial law: "more lies, just for the fun of it, fun, what fun we've had, what fun of it, more lies, that's soon said, you must say soon, *it's the regulations*" (415, my emphasis). Just following this passage, accordingly, the text returns squarely to the sacrificial mechanism and its alternative:

> it's like a confession, a last confession . . . no it's something else, it's an indictment, a dying voice accusing, accusing me, you must accuse someone, a culprit is indispensable . . . a victim is essential . . . so that I may go, make my escape, come to the place where the axe falls. (415–16)

The opposition between confession and indictment, like the novel's concluding contrast between the silence "that lasts" and "the one that doesn't last" (418), concerns the opposition between nonsacrificial and sacrificial modes of *both* speech and silence. "Confession" and "indictment" both derive from words meaning "to speak," with the difference, however, that "to confess" means not to accuse, but to avow.[63] The Unnamable's unachieved goal of confession is aligned with the unachieved subsequent goal of permanent silence, while incomplete silence, aligned by implication with the structure of indictment, is a sacrificial cycle of concealments and exposures.

The last two "lies" of the trilogy, labeled as such, also belong to this opposition between speech (now identified simply as "murmurs" or distant piacular "cries")[64] and the two types of silence just mentioned, and both lies reflect, significantly, on the text's own sacrificial meta-discourse. We are told that to speak of a mere sacrificial alternation between cries and temporary silences is "more lies," and that the narrator's claim to have had only the temporary kind is mendacious: "I must have had the other, the one that lasts, but it didn't last, I don't understand, that it is to say it did" (418). This conceivably nonsacrificial affirmation of lasting silence, since it cannot be spoken, is *logically* condemned to appear like the paradox of the Cretan Liar—but this is no logical drawback if the goal is actually to stop writing or indicting. By contrast, sacrificial oscillations between speech and silence—the "strange pain, strange sin" (418) of writing and, by extension, of all other modes of sacrificial revelation and concealment—merely obscure or postpone the *pharmakon* paradox, *whose form presents the same double bind as the logical one*: "silence once broken will never again be whole" (369).

Beckett's text therefore suggests how difficult it might be "to sacrifice sacrifice" (in Slavoj Žižek's admonitory phrase),[65] since it would be necessary to leave behind not only sacrifice per se, but all sacrificial reciprocities between speech and silence, concealment and revelation, truth and falsehood, that I have assimilated to *the sacrifice of truth*. To sacrifice sacrifice, as Žižek's phrase itself suggests, would likely be as sacrificial a project as the philosopher's proverbial recommendation that we all become nudists.

PART THREE

FASHION THEORY

7

Fashion Theory

But seest thou not what a deformed thief this fashion is?
—WILLIAM SHAKESPEARE

I have argued that the traditional moral distinction between lying and concealment, the first generally proscribed and the second frequently prescribed, is suspect. The kind of violence (moral or physical) characteristically directed against the liar finds its quasi-symmetrical counterpart in the violence characteristically directed against those who display certain aspects of the truth. This latter violence is nowhere more obvious, as we have seen in Defoe and as remains quite clear in modern society, than in the case of the proscription of nudity, the prescription of modest concealment: dress.

The subject of fashion and dress-concealment is, for several reasons, a natural extension of our earlier literary and philosophical preoccupations. First, it provides an empirical instance of more or less legalized and conventionalized concealment that belongs, I argue, to the same general mimetic-sacrificial landscape associated with mendacity and fiction. Second, our literary examples—Defoe and Stendhal on modesty of dress on the one hand, and Beckett's sartorial metaphors on the other—have prepared us quite thoroughly for this topic. Third and perhaps most important, fashion itself is, beyond any particular theoretical premise, literally mimetic in operation, and thus provides a peculiarly appropriate testing ground for any mimetic theory.[1]

Beckett's sartorial metaphors belong not only to his mimetic logic but even more to his sacrificial logic. Beckett conceives dress-concealment as belonging to the system of sacrificial violence that governs all symbolic order. Specifically, he conceives clothing as a kind of *sacrifice of truth* that tenuously provides protection against sacrificial violence as such: "clothes are so to speak inseparable from the body, *in times of peace.*" His pointed description of the gap between clothes and body as "like" a blow on the head suggests a kind of mental violence as counterpart to the physical. Moran's excuse that this peculiar simile is the product of a mind "avid for the flimsiest analogy," far from emphasizing the merely metaphorical character of the analogy, merely underlines that psychological pain is essentially symbolic in character. Beckett's image, moreover, *literalizes* the symbol of violence in a manner that is comparable, as we shall see in a moment, to Shakespeare's treatment of fashion. In *Malone Dies*, we recall, the relation of literal and symbolic violence was organized above all around the sense of sight and the interplay between visible concealment and revelation.

The Law of the Ass in *Much Ado about Nothing*

In addition to Beckett, Shakespeare provides an excellent literary starting point in what is perhaps the most spectacular mimetic-sacrificial allegory of fashion in all of literature: act 3, scene 3 of *Much Ado about Nothing*. The "nothing" about which there is so much ado—aside from its traditional metaphorization of the vagina and love itself—relates directly to fashion as defined by one of the villains: "fashion is . . . nothing to man."[2] Fashion is "nothing," not only because it is (or should be) secondary to the essential man, but because its forms seem so arbitrary, mere "nothings," in their evolution—something that makes it notoriously difficult to explain. As Roland Barthes remarked, in fashion "*nothing* can signify *everything*," and "it is precisely this 'nothing' which is the radiant nucleus" of the structure of fashion.[3] The relation between arbitrariness and law is perhaps even more crucial to dress theory than to the materials hitherto treated. Shakespeare and Barthes both treat fashion, as we shall see, in terms of the relation between law and law-breaking in every sense.

Before coming to Shakespeare, it may be helpful to recall the general sartorial background of the Renaissance period. Though it is doubtless possible to exaggerate the relative sartorial stability of the first Christian millennium, most fashion historians stress it, alongside the absence of any extreme opposition between male and female dress. Geoffrey Squire, for example, describes the relatively sudden development of fashion (in the modern sense of perennial sartorial "revolution") in mimetic terms when he locates its origin in middle-to-late medieval urban "centres for display and competitive emulation."[4] By the Renaissance, fashion in this sense was clearly established (at least among the well-to-do) as a characteristic of modern society, and, by the Elizabethan period, mannerist exaggerations had led to an almost parodic emphasis on sexual opposition. This was exemplified not only, for instance, in masculine tight hose and codpieces (as tunics rose steadily higher in a manner reminiscent of modern skirts and tights), contrasted with enormous feminine bum-rolls, but in the quasi-abstract opposition whereby men were pictured as triangles standing on their vertices, as Squire puts it, while women approximated triangles standing on their bases. Such drastic differentiation did not necessarily reflect secure gender identity, of course, but rather perhaps the contrary.[5]

Beatrice, in *Much Ado*, claims to reject love not only because all men are her "brothers" (a comic reduction of the world to incestuous indifference à la Beckett), but because gender itself seems to have become what psychologists of dress call a "neurotic paradox": men with beards are too manly for her, she insists, while men without beards are too effeminate.[6] This mimetic double bind (her would-be lover must both imitate and not imitate the fashion, whichever it happens to be) points to the arbitrariness of the gender/fashion system as a whole, an arbitrariness also captured by her famous raillery that "I had rather hear my dog bark at a crow than a man swear he loves me." Love seems to operate for Beatrice, as Sonnet 147 puts it, "at random from the truth."

But it is Borachio, an accomplice of the villain Don John, who is given Shakespeare's most extraordinary passage on fashion:

> Seest thou not, I say, what a deformed thief this fashion is, how giddily a' turns about all the hot bloods between fourteen and five-and-thirty, sometimes fashioning them like Pharaoh's soldiers in the reechy painting, sometime like god Bel's priests in the old church window, sometime like the shaven Hercules in

the smirched worm-eaten tapestry, where his codpiece seems as massy as his club?[7]

Taking his departure from the Elizabethan codpiece, Shakespeare swiftly generalizes to history at large: the history, respectively, of war, sacrificial religion, and eroticism, each mediated by deformed, "worm-eaten" artistic mimesis. The imagery is spectacular in its compression. Fashion here originates with both secular and religious violence (Bel is condemned in the Bible specifically for his association with human sacrifice), before being transformed into the symbolic violence of the penis and its fashionable appendage, the codpiece. A more directly sacrificial depiction can hardly be imagined.

The name "Bel," related to "hairy one," as well as more directly to "lord" or "master,"[8] also fits nicely with the beard-and-shaving imagery of the play as a whole. Editors have puzzled over the shaven Hercules, wondering if Shakespeare had in mind the story of Hercules dressed as a woman, or even—since he is wearing a codpiece, hardly feminine attire—perhaps Samson, sometimes identified by Christian writers with Hercules, shorn of his virility.[9] Though no interpretation to my knowledge solves the problem (and the image may originate with Shakespeare), it seems to me the commentators are on the right track: the shaven Hercules provides a kind of oxymoronic image of virility/castration not unlike the "cowardly giant-like ox-beef" of *A Midsummer Night's Dream*.[10] Note that Borachio does not say that Hercules's penis is as "massy" as his club, but that his codpiece is—this is definitely an Elizabethan Hercules. The affirmation of virility signified by the codpiece is obviously ambivalent (large codpieces may or may not reflect large penises). Even more than the Renaissance phalli attached to pointed shoes, the codpiece seems from a modern perspective to be a rather ludicrous mimetic artifice, of a kind nowadays only rationalized for football players and the like. It provides a particularly splendid example of the "neurotic paradox" of modesty/display, since "modest" concealment of the penis here frankly *coincides* with symbolic display. Though codpieces may inhibit direct phallic competition, they nevertheless appear, *pharmakon*-like, as symptom of the emulous disease.[11] (Incidentally, Greek depictions of Hercules often show him with a small penis, the latter being far from incompatible with ancient Greek ideas of virility. Penis size is itself subject to *pharmakon*-ambivalence.)

Shakespeare's dramatic context for this extraordinary speech is still more pointed and ingenious than the text itself, revolving around a scapegoat called "Deformed." When the constabulary overhear Borachio's metaphor for fashion as a "deformed thief," they deludedly *literalize* it, charging that "one Deformed" is a known villain who "wears a [love] lock," and is engaged in "the most dangerous piece of lechery that was ever known in the commonwealth."[12] The police identify the *pharmakos*, so to speak, behind the fashionable *pharmakon*. Fashion in Shakespeare—like fiction in Paul de Man—has the structure of an arbitrary indictment. Moreover, "deformity" here appears as the aberrant literalization of figure (a violent literalization characteristic, as we have seen, of Beckett's sartorial metaphor).[13] These, I suggest, are the most essential characteristics of the "law" of fashion as Shakespeare conceives it, the law that Constable Dogberry famously calls an "ass" in both senses. Fashion law arbitrarily scapegoats a lawbreaker called "Deformed" because its law *is* form. The aberrant literalization of metaphor by the law is (like so many other Fools' "mistakes" in the plays) the Shakespearean truth. Fashion really does *fashion*, form and deform—from the shocking physical deformations that have marked "beauty" in so many cultures to the (seemingly) attenuated deformations of our own.[14] The fact that a "beauty spot" is a literal deformity makes its own point.

Shakespeare's fashion law of the ass—of "nothing"[15]—at once refers to literal buttocks and bum-rolls (the ass that is simultaneously an object of disgust and desire, modesty and display) and to a more general structure of mimetic reversibility which, as in Beckett's *Molloy*, undoes the opposition between male and female, beauty and ugliness, policeman and criminal. Bottom, in *A Midsummer Night's Dream*, is an actor—mimesis incarnate (he wants to play *every* part)—transformed into the ass idolized by Titania. Similarly, anal "wind-instruments," highlighted by the clown in *Othello*, are a Shakespearean metaphor for the contradictory music of social/sexual concord and discord more generally.[16] The ass in *Much Ado* is not only the name of the law, but also of the social "nothing"—Deformed, the *model scapegoat*—at the heart of the sacrificial system.

In *Système de la mode*, Roland Barthes had the following to say about contemporary fashion models: "[A] structural paradox defines the cover girl utterly: her essential function is not aesthetic, it is not a question of delivering a 'beautiful body,' subject to the canonic rules of plastic success, but a 'deformed' body with a view to achieving a certain formal generality, i.e., a structure; it follows that the cover girl's body is no one's body, it is a pure form . . . and by a sort of tautology, it refers to the garment itself."[17] This reciprocity between body and garment, form and deformation, can be linked directly to Shakespeare's rhetoric.[18] Fashion is "nothing" in *Much Ado*, not just because it is the product of mimetic whim, but because it operates on the oxymoronic principle of the model-scapegoat, *the form of deformation*. Because it is a mimetic law of form whose content is "empty," the "nothing" of fashion comes in oxymorons, but equally in tautologies:

> Borachio: Thou knowest that the fashion . . . is nothing to a man.
> Conrade: Yes, it is apparel.
> Bora.: I mean, the fashion.
> Con.: Yes, the fashion is the fashion.
> Bora: Tush! I may as well say the fool's the fool. But seest thou not what a deformed thief this fashion is?[19]

Besides concerning the world of eros, this passage introducing the deformed thief is directly preceded by economic imagery, specifically stressing the dependence of the rich on the poor,[20] that is, the potential reciprocity between them. Clearly fashion in the modern world is less a military or religious matter (a matter for Bel or the Pharaohs) than an erotic and economic one. Indeed, Shakespeare himself implicitly connects the general structure of modern fashion with the decline of religion and its principle of differentiation:

> Dogberry: . . . well, God's a good man, and two men ride of a horse, one must ride behind. An honest soul, i'faith, sir, by my troth he is, as ever broke bread; but God is to be worshipped, all men are not alike, alas, good neighbour![21]

The pious policeman's invocation of faith is ironic since he states not merely the reciprocity but the identity of God and man: "God's a good man" and "an honest soul." God twice seems to guarantee the differentiation and ordering of men—"all men are not alike" and "one must ride behind"—but in a context in which God's distinction from man is itself put in question. Shakespeare's mimetic-sacrificial law of the ass thus has a good deal more in common with the ass of Beckett's trilogy than might appear, for it essentially states the form and implies the survival of the sacrificial principle in a potentially postreligious context. Fashion (in both its restricted and wider sense) still has the form of sacred mimetism in a fashion world dominated by the putatively secular values of sex and economics.[22]

Modesty/Display: The "Neurotic Paradox"
We do not have to read deeply in the history and theory of dress to discover the mimetic double bind. John Carl Flugel, in his *Psychology of Clothes*, writes of the "neurotic paradox" of dress generated by its

twin function of modesty and display.[23] Barthes also speaks of the "neurosis" of fashion, its simultaneous appeal to "fidelity" and "infidelity."[24] A discussion of the modesty/display couple is thus in order to clarify its relation to the kind of mimetic-sacrificial ambivalence we have just seen in Shakespeare. Though Western explanations of the origin of dress, influenced by Genesis, had long been modesty oriented, and to a lesser extent utility oriented, modern dress theorists of otherwise various persuasions seem generally to agree with Thomas Carlyle that the origin of dress is not to be located in either modesty or utility, but in "display."[25] Unlike the biblical motive of sexual modesty, "display" in and of itself has both the strength and weakness, from a theoretical point of view, of remaining theory neutral as to the kinds of display at stake. Whatever we may think about the transition from animal to human societies, it has the advantage of adapting itself to any contingency—from primates who seemingly gain "prestige" by donning tin foil, say, to the sartorial trophies of our own day—and in principle to pure arbitrariness. "Display" therefore lends itself well to mimetic modeling. At the limit, just because a random feather was fought over by two rivals might endow it with sartorial prestige.[26]

It is beyond the scope of this analysis to deal with either the origins or preorigins of clothing (ornament, body painting, penis strings, anus stoppers, and so on), something obviously necessary to a general theory of modesty/display. But it is well worth noting, in the context of so-called primitive bodily ornamentation and deformation, that "display" and "modesty" cannot be so easily distinguished, not least since the meaning of the latter must be extended beyond sexuality and dress-concealment to many other kinds of inhibition. The word *chastity*, related to *chastisement* (to "chasten" originally meant to mortify or purify), suggests the possible coincidence of display and modesty in this extended sense. Hilaire Hiler, for instance, observed that piacular deformations and mutilations associated with ritual mourning and "penance" are frequently similar if not identical to marks of caste display, status, and beautification—to such an extent that experts have sometimes mistaken the "irregular cicatrization" consequent on frequent blood lettings, slashings, and self-mutilations with a medicinal-religious meaning, for decorative scarring as such.[27] The widespread extraction of teeth and amputation of fingers may also be an instance of the formal coincidence, in this sense, of piacular "chastity" and "beautification."[28] Modest beauty is characteristically, as *Much Ado* puts it, "printed in blood."[29]

Though the violent deformations of so-called primitive bodily decoration lie beyond the scope of this analysis, we should make the obvious point that such deformations are enforced more or less permanently, in contrast to the modesties and displays characteristic of dress. Like "modest" marking of the body itself, nota bene, dress modesty does not necessarily entail concealment of the body; indeed, the fact that sumptuary law prohibited dress display rather than display of the body is itself an indication of the basic ambivalence of the body/clothes opposition as it concerns modesty of dress. The displacement of naked by partially clothed athletes in ancient Greece, for example, was regarded in some quarters as an offense against modesty, a sign of an unhealthily "effeminate" subservience to fashion.[30] Nevertheless, the passage between piacular or sacrificial deformation (and its decorative equivalents) and the deformation/concealment produced by dress—a passage implicitly bridged by Shakespeare's "Deformed"—may conveniently be regarded in terms of a passage, once again, from *the truth of sacrifice* to *the sacrifice of truth*, from purifying chastisement to chaste concealment. This is illustrated by the general historical transition from genital mutilation to genital concealment, for example (notwithstanding that both may occur concurrently); and a relatively modern instance of the general opposition is provided by a comparison of Chinese and Victorian women's feet—the former modestly/modishly mutilated, the latter modestly/modishly concealed.

I know of no theory that claims to account in detail for the development of what we call sexual modesty in dress—marked often, but by no means necessarily, by concealment of the pubic area and/or other parts of the body.[31] The problem is complicated, as we have seen, by the fact that the modest or immodest meanings of the dress/nudity opposition are constituted not by any inherent meaning of the terms, but (as Lévi-Strauss and the structuralists recognized) by their structural opposition as such. For example, in some societies only married women are modestly covered, unappropriated girls being left unconcealed; in others only virgins wear "aprons."[32] Men, similarly, may either conceal less than usual of their bodies during display rituals, or don a larger than usual "apron" for such rituals.[33] In general, even within a single culture, the same sartorial signs very often appear in contexts with apparently opposed motives (mourning and marriage, penance and displays of caste, and so on). Hiler gives a suggestive example of such ambivalence in his discussion of the masks associated in certain societies with both law enforcers and lawbreakers (recalling the hidden identity of law and lawbreaking highlighted by Shakespeare).[34] In Western art criticism, the conventional opposition between "nude" and "naked" figures suggests a similar *pharmakon* pattern—as does Freud's rather amusing thesis, cited by Flugel, that to dream of clothing means to dream of nudity.[35]

The modesty/display opposition is further complicated by the formal observation that even where modesty is defined in terms of bodily concealment, accidental overlaps between the two functions are frequently to be expected. The most primitive prototype of the formal properties of modest pubic dress, for example, seems to have occurred in many cultures when the material hung from the girdle—originally, according to James Laver, Hiler, and others, to *highlight* the genital region—was enlarged to such an extent as to end by concealing it altogether. In general, as we have noted, *some* concealment of the body is necessarily produced by the "accidental" properties of all but totally transparent dress; in this sense, dress display almost always produces concealment—a contingency *legalized* in modesty. A certain physical as well as symbolic arbitrariness is accordingly endemic to the system, as for instance when material hung from the waist to highlight the genitals, say, conceals the stomach—with the accidental consequence, perhaps, that naked stomachs later acquire special effects. The arbitrariness of the sartorial cut is well illustrated by the magical power it conferred on the female Victorian ankle.

Though concealment is not necessarily incompatible with heightened display rivalry—on the contrary, skirts were and are often donned by both male and female with the evident purpose of exciting desire—it seems to be assumed by most experts that modest concealment emerged originally in order to regulate sexual activity, discouraging overt rivalry by establishing symbolic hierarchies and prohibitions. In short, modesty inhibits emulous display. However, the positivist notion that sexual desire is reduced by minimizing "direct stimulus" produced by the sight of the body (notably the genitals or the face), while doubtless in some respects adequate, and effective under certain contingent conditions, has no general validity. First, by concealing the genitals, for example, one may merely succeed in redirecting "direct stimulus" to other parts—parts which may be (or become) even more provocative. Since the Enlightenment, cultural relativists have never tired of reminding us that North African women have often been known to throw their skirts over their faces rather than reveal the latter. The only foolproof solution thus appears to be dress that, as in the case of certain Muslim women, is so sacklike that it not merely conceals the entire body (the face being covered by a veil), but makes its shape impossible to deduce. At this point, however, the "neurotic paradox" rears its head in its clearest form.

This "paradox" can be stated in terms of mimetic rivalry. Though a minimal necessity may govern the inhibitory function of dress modesty—both primitive penis sheaths and modern underwear, for instance, must be removed to conduct certain forms of sex—we need not presuppose its mechanism, but only that the beliefs, myths, rituals, and other circumstances of a given culture tend toward a given form of sexual inhibition *more or less* arbitrarily associated with certain sartorial signs and effects. In the case of dress-concealment, whatever the belief system in which it originated, developing reflection on the function of such concealment might naturally draw the conclusion, as contemporary theorists do, that bodies are modestly concealed because they are potentially attractive. It is only a short step from this to the inversion characteristic of Girard's "masochist induction"—that if attractive bodies are concealed, concealed bodies must be attractive. The "neurotic paradox" of dress in its twin function of modesty/display is a version, proverbial enough, of the mimetic double bind.[36]

Concealment also has a metalevel structure generated by the specular interplay of what I think you think I think, et cetera. Clothing, at the first level, is overt concealment of the body; it does not conceal its concealment. But even at this level, inasmuch as bodies are signs and clothes are signs about those signs, dress generates its own metalevel hierarchies. By modestly concealing a part of the body, dress effectively *replaces individual differentiation by class differentiation* (the masculine class of penis-codpieces, for instance), and by classes of classes (the transsexual class of codpieces/bum-rolls, for instance). Even the simplest girdle that conceals nothing divides the body formally into the classes of upper and lower. Moreover, metalevel concealment and metalevel class hierarchy clearly interpenetrate. Implied classes of body (and soul) may be generated by such combinations as immodest-unfashionable, modest-fashionable, modest-unfashionable, immodest-fashionable, and so on. Such "paradoxes" are the staple diet of moral poetry on fashion, and of such moral compromises as "the doctrine of fashionable virtue."[37] They also inform fashionable oscillations between dressing "up" and dressing "down," carefully or casually—and between dressing carefully carelessly and carelessly carelessly, and so on. The potentially unlimited metalevel interplay between accident and intention, detail and ensemble, renders clothing "by nature deceptive."[38]

James Laver and others divide display into two basic kinds, "hierarchical" and "seductive," social and sexual.[39] He illustrates the opposition by pointing out, for example, that where Christian men were required to bare their heads in church (removing clothes signifying social hierarchy), women were required to cover theirs (concealing seductive body parts such as hair). Essentially, the opposition is between dress that replaces differentiation between individual bodies by nonphysical/nonsexual classes such as rank, and dress that replaces individual differentiation by physical/sexual classes. Laver himself admits his alignment of the hierarchical and seductive with male and female, for "the greater part of human history," is simplistic. Without elaborating the various indefensible paradoxes deriving from this view of gender,[40] we may exploit the fact that while the hierarchy/seduction opposition is even more arbitrary in its principle than modesty/display, it has nevertheless been sufficiently codified in various historical contexts to be reified as a basic explanatory principle by a number of dress theorists and historians. What we can especially exploit about the opposition, moreover, is the fact that inasmuch as hierarchical dress *also* generates potentially seductive body classes, it is in contradiction with itself both as defined by theorists and as codified in actual fact.[41] I have spoken of "physical" classes, but of course no classes are strictly physical. What is characteristic of dress-concealment, particularly, is that the individual body falls out of the visible picture in favor of the symbolics of potentially *any* kind of class. The "neurotic paradoxes" of both modesty/display and hierarchy/seduction are the products of metalevel class systems *in formal contradiction with themselves*, which characteristically generate every kind of *pharmakon* effect we could desire.[42]

Jean Baudrillard, for example, has argued that the development of highly articulated social hierarchies tends to turn into seductive signs the very exclusions and inferiorities it has created; women, peasants, foreigners, prostitutes, and so on characteristically acquire, along with their sartorial habits, what might be called a *hetero-erotic* mystique.[43] The excluded *pharmakos*, as Girard argues, invariably becomes sacred in one form or another, along the lines suggested by Shakespeare's law of the ass and the scapegoating of Deformed. Indeed, Hunt's claim that dress codes are generally "constructed not of stipulative rules" or positive prescriptions but rather in terms of semiological *exclusions* ("clothing item X may be worn in combination with A, B, and C, but not with D") which "are always subject to the possibility of innovative transgression"[44] makes a similar point at the most general level of sartorial semiotics—with the difference, however, that Shakespeare's law of the ass suggests that such "innovative transgression" is more than a mere playful possibility, but rather the very form of mimetic-sacrificial law.

Metalevel sartorial mediation is also illustrated by the shaman "not-men" (either male or female) of Native American and Siberian tribes, who are frequently "transsexual" in dress. Such figures represent a kind of metasocial and metaerotic class which mediates between the sexes. Not only are their qualifications for the job often explicitly sacrificial in character,[45] but they are sometimes permitted to have sexual relations with both men and women, though not with each other. This might be called metaexogamy or *metaheterosexuality* (not inconsistent with homosexuality). In societies like our own, characterized by what Girard calls internal mediation (where no transcendental mediator or holy man is generally accepted), such mediatory patterns commonly take on an even more paradoxical appearance, often expressed by clothing. Angela Carter, among others, has argued that the garter-belted dominatrix-whore who came into her own in the Victorian period should be conceived as conjoining erotic dominance and social submission in an emphatic "paradox" of seduction/hierarchy.[46] As for the more baroque outreaches of the contemporary world, beyond transvesticism there is the transsexualism that seeks a cure in mutilatory surgery; and beyond "simple" transsexualism, there is the paradoxical kind that seeks a change of sex into order to become homosexual. At this point the old metaphor for the body as mere clothing of the soul seems disturbingly literalized. Dress itself, to extend this metaphor, would thus be mere clothing of clothing: metadress.

Seeing through Clothes

Anne Hollander's stylish *Seeing through Clothes* analyzes Western fashion since the Renaissance in terms very suited to a mimetic approach. Her major thesis is that fashions in both clothes and bodies are not only mutually interactive, but generated in part by artistic representation. "People inwardly model themselves on pictures and on other people, who also look like pictures because they are doing it, too."[47] Hollander's emphasis on the artistic mediation of relations between clothes and bodies recalls the mediation of the worm-eaten tapestry, the reechy painting, and the old church window in Shakespeare's fashion speech. Indeed, since her thesis about the swift co-development of mimetic art and fashion in Renaissance and post-Renaissance culture is set against an early medieval and premedieval backdrop of relative sartorial stability and relatively nonmimetic religious art, we may again take our cue from Shakespeare's imagery, which might suggest that contemporary fashion—the codpiece superimposed on classical artistic models—replaces the old-fashioned mediation of religion (the old church window) by the mediation of artistic mimesis as such. The Renaissance was a highly mimetic age in the sense both that it resurrected the mimetic forms of classical art and that it was characterized by a high degree of fashion. Even its major religious crisis, the Reformation, can be conceived in part as a kind of "mimetic crisis," inasmuch as both the role of art and the representational status of Communion were at stake.

Though the centrality of art should not be theoretically overemphasized—both clothes and bodies can also serve as the generative "origin" in the art-clothes-bodies triangle—Hollander argues that its practical importance after the Middle Ages can hardly be overestimated. Her basic argument can be illustrated as follows. A clothed portrait implies more or less overtly or deceptively the shape of the concealed body. That body can be a *fiction*, since artists often portray figures that, if undressed, would turn out to be in impossible positions. Thus an artist influenced by a clothed portrait might produce a nude modeled, within or even beyond the limits of possibility, on the hypothetical figure beneath the clothes. In a certain sense, as Hollander's title suggests, the body is always "seen through clothes" even when it is naked, and in art it may be shaped as though still subject to the constraints of invisible clothing (naked breasts, for example, in positions that they would usually achieve when clothed). Where actual nudity is generally prohibited, the importance of artistic representation and dress, either together or separately, is obviously especially important in generating the "ideal" nude. But the importance of such hypothetical, even fictional mimetic models is not diminished even where actual naked models are readily available, for actual bodies may be selected for their resemblance to hypothetical or even impossible ones.[48]

Another of Hollander's central points, following Kenneth Clark, stresses what we may regard as the *pharmakon* opposition between "nudity" and "nakedness" in the tradition of Western art, an opposition aligned with ideality and reality, purity and obscenity, and other loaded categories.[49] In this context, clothing appears not only an indication of what kind of body is at stake, but as a metalevel sign of the relation between nakedness and clothing. Whereas the Renaissance and post-Renaissance nude is characteristically accompanied by drapery recalling classical dress (indicating, among other things, the prestigious mediation of classical art), the so-called naked "non-nude" is characteristically accompanied by contemporary clothing, as it were recently discarded. This kind of metalevel interplay can be further complicated, as when "naked" clothing accompanies a nude, or where "nude" drapery accompanies nakedness, and so on.

Hollander claims that the Renaissance eroticization of the nude and naked body derived mainly on the one hand from medieval depictions of naked and usually suffering males (Christ on the cross, the martyrdom of Saint Sebastian, and so on), and on the other hand from classical models. She claims, in particular, that conventions of the *female* nude often derived from *masculine* models.[50] Kenneth Dover claims that this goes for classical models too, citing among other things a remark attributed to Kritias in the late fifth century B.C.: "In males, the most beautiful appearance (*eidos,* 'shape,' 'form,' 'type') is that which is female; but in females the opposite."[51] Art is also presented as a mediator between male and female: "It is arguable that whereas down to the mid-fifth century women were commonly assimilated to men in vase-painting, thereafter men were increasingly assimilated to women."[52] Dover suggests that a shift toward masculine "effeminacy" may have occurred as much as a century earlier than its reflection in vases,[53] and he makes much of an earlier Homeric stress on masculine beauty.[54] Just as in the case of Hollander's emphasis on the crucifixion and scenes of martyrdom, moreover, he emphasizes that young male beauty was considered to be enhanced by wounds (while "it is shameful to see an old man dying of wounds").[55] In both instances, the original model of beauty is violent, providing a sacrificial backdrop to the subsequent *pharmakon* doubling of male and female. The connection between beauty and violence is even more direct here than in the case of the piacular and ornamental scarrings mentioned earlier.[56]

Hollander's history of Western body fashions in their relations to clothes is too complex to summarize here. Her charting of a progression from eroticization of the female belly ("it was apparently impossible until the late seventeenth century for a woman to have too big a belly")[57] to focus on breasts and buttocks, to the twentieth-century attitude toward legs, for example, tells a convincing visual story, and warns against merely ideological explanations for either bodily or dress fashion: "It is obviously not for simple reasons that people copy the dress and manners of others they admire, but *the surface mechanism is purely visual.*"[58] Without denying the possible relevance of the idealization of pregnancy to the idealization of bellies, for instance, or of female emancipation to the idealization of legs, Hollander insists that we stick close to the physical facts—the relations between bodies, clothes, and their representations—which are always subject to contingency, generated by the arbitrariness of the sartorial cut. Though clothes may symbolize the grandest determinations, "knowledge and language, art and love, time and death . . . to do this, they (like language) are condemned to contingency, and consequently the idea of them is something of a thorn and a goad. As a concept, clothing resists clarity, even as fashion defies augury."[59]

We need not question the difficulty of theorizing fashion in its detailed or even its grander developments.[60] I have suggested, however, that the various *pharmakon* effects associated with the relation between bodies and clothes are a general consequence of a semiological system in "neurotic" contradiction with itself, which, in a quasi-dialectical fashion, generates both metalevel class categories and sartorial "solutions" of a sort. The equation male = female beauty, for instance, presupposes not only the body classes of "male males," "female males," "male females," and "female females," but also the possibility—if we dress the figures in male or female dress—of "male male males," "female male females," and so on. Similarly, since male and female clothes are potentially subject to the same metalevel doubling, we can extend the pattern to the fourth level, generating still more categorical possibilities, and so on. With this kind of generative mimetic model in mind, and for the purpose of illustration, we may propose the hypothesis that two extremely important modern sartorial developments—children's clothing and underwear—play the role of metalevel mediators between male and female on the one hand, and nakedness and clothing on the other; and, moreover, that these two developments are interlinked. The class of children's dress is an *external* mediator, in the sense that the category of childhood is not a dress category, while the class of underwear is a mediator *internal* to dress in both literal and metaphorical senses.

Just as class relations in general in the post-Renaissance period were increasingly mediated by the middle class, so Squire observes of late-eighteenth-century fashion in France and England that "the middle class no longer needed to race after their superiors [who] seemed to be running after them."[61] He also quotes Sir William Wraxall to the effect that classically inspired, more or less simple dress seemed to be "finally levelling or obliterating almost all external distinction of costume between the highest and the lowest of the sex."[62] Mutual imitation thus became increasingly reciprocal, along the lines that Girard defines in terms of "internal" and "double mediation," leading to what Roche calls a "scrambling of sartorial signs."[63] But while such scrambling seemingly makes it more and more difficult to locate "originary" models of imitation—in sharp contrast to the days in which society imitated the court, which in turn imitated the king—the role played by the development of children's dress in this period is all the more arresting. Laver claims that, inspired by a Rousseauesque idealization of childhood, "the dress of little girls [in the 1770s] . . . anticipate grown-up fashions by a whole generation"(133). Something similar seems to have been the case for male trousers: little boys "were undoubtedly wearing trousers long before the *sans-culottes* of the French Revolution had been heard of. If one cannot call this an eccentricity of children's dress, it is certainly an eccentricity in the history of costume."[64] Hollander is similarly startled by the eccentricity of children's dress, especially by what she calls the uniquely nineteenth-century "idea of associating a short skirt with female childhood," which she says is "all the more bizarre when one considers the impulse to superimpose the image of childhood on the traditional connotations of wantonness attached to short skirts."[65] Hollander does not resort to ad hoc explanations of this phenomenon (that short skirts allow more freedom, for example, for the legs of newly liberated children),[66] but rather stresses to the utmost the apparently paradoxical exchange between innocence-childhood and wantonness-femininity.

It is important to note, in this context, that relative erosion of differentiation between upper- and lower-class dress in the later eighteenth century was accompanied by a relative erosion of the opposition between male and female as regards dress modesties. For a short period after the French Revolution, for example, French women wore more or less diaphanous "classical" dresses that concealed very little beneath: either, occasionally, the naked body or, more often, pink or skin-colored body tights.[67] This relative undifferentiation between male and female modesty is in marked contrast to the extreme opposition of the Victorian period. Indeed, it is one of the most notable "paradoxes" of this transitional period that, while fashion seemingly played a role "less oppressive than liberating" for both social and sexual equality, "the principle of the equality of persons ceded to the inegalitarian celebration of female beauty"[68]—with consequences arguably both positive and extremely negative for women of the following century. Here we confront a particularly crucial example of the general mimetic double bind of fashion, where the new order "tries to efface, though it only multiplies, differences."[69]

The eighteenth-century "invention of childhood," we may suggest, played an important mediating role in a renewed differentiation of the sexes.[70] Laver's astonished observation that late-eighteenth-century children's dress was prophetic of adult dress confirms that children really *were* mimetic models for adults, at least in the sartorial domain.

Daniel Roche similarly observes that aristocratic children, put in trousers by their governesses, were "effective intermediaries" in the general adult transition from breeches to trousers.[71] Moreover, while it may at first seem arbitrary to talk of children in general as mediators between male and female—the triangle male-female-child should surely be a quadrilateral generated out of the four possible combinations of child/adult and female/male—the novel nineteenth-century habit of dressing male children in more or less female dress precisely illustrates both the mediatory unity and the ambivalence of the category of childhood vis-à-vis the opposition of the sexes. Dressing both males and females as females formally signified sexual undifferentiation among children, their sexual innocence, but it also projected this innocence specifically onto feminine dress. Moreover, if innocent children were sartorially female in the nineteenth century, so, conversely, women were increasingly supposed to be like innocent children (as illustrated by the notorious Victorian tendency to deny them sexual feeling altogether). The *pharmakon*-ambivalence of short skirts, which Hollander so stresses, is to be expected of such metalevel classes as children's dress. Stendhal, as we saw in chapter 4, linked the principle of mimetic undifferentiation to a sacrificial substitution of women and children. Barthes, too, stresses the "role, simultaneously maternal and childlike, that devolves upon the garment" in modern fashion.[72]

Corresponding to the "external" mediation of children's dress between male and female was the development of underwear as "internal" mediator, literally, *between* body and clothes. An empirical connection between underwear and children's dress is provided by Laver's observation that nineteenth-century children of both sexes often wore "pantalettes," which gave the impression of undergarments emerging ostentatiously from beneath their dresses.[73] Hollander also observes that while female performers had always worn drawers or pants, "in the early nineteenth century pre-pubescent little girls wore pantalets, but respectable women did not."[74] According to Laver, "the extremely scanty dresses of the [French] Empire period made some kind of divided [under] garment for women inevitable, although their introduction was fiercely resisted by moralists."[75] Underwear in the modern sense begins as *pharmakon*: an immodest supplement to counteract immodesty.

Prior to the nineteenth century, Hollander claims, underwear—to the extent that it existed, in the sense that undergarments existed—was generally simple, relatively unfetishized, and, where it was the object of artistic attention, often mediated by classical allusions to Greek *chitones* and *himatia*.[76] In the nineteenth century, however, artists began to repudiate the need to incorporate into modern images the antique methods for showing clothes coming off women's bodies. . . . Modern underwear itself became a subject of pictorial concern, for both aesthetic and erotic purposes.

During the nineteenth century female underwear lost all its simplicity, in fact and as an idea . . . the sexual imagination did not concern itself with the details of real underwear until the galloping advance of sexual repression in the nineteenth century.[77]

We may generalize that modern underwear is a metalevel mediator not only of the body/clothes and modesty/display "neurosis," but also of a new differentiation between male and female,[78] which in turn was anticipated by the mediation of children's clothes. Underwear's metalevel status is well illustrated by the "paradox," so often pointed out, that an underclothed person is in a state of "undressed dress." Victorian pornography, for instance, no longer relied on the traditional erotic tension between dress and nudity as such: the woman in underwear was "naked" and immodest even though her underwear appeared a veritable armory, concealing her body even more than overwear from earlier periods.[79] Clothed in underwear, she was even more "naked" than she would be naked. Nineteenth-century underwear was also surrounded with a considerable suggestion of violence. Aside from the dominatrix-whore's characteristic underwear-dress which makes this context of violence explicit, Hollander notes the oxymoronic combination of softest silk and hardest metal pressed against the female body, coercing its torso, thrusting out its behind, and generally connecting "female dishevelment . . . with prostitution and victimization, with physical awkwardness, ugliness, and sexual cruelty, with smut, and with farce."[80]

It is perhaps worth remarking that contemporary fashion has taken the structural possibilities of underwear a step further, since it is now sometimes oxymoronically worn as overwear—a reversal analogous to the vogue of wearing clothes inside-out.[81] Beckett's garments are, on occasion, said to be defined by this latter possibility, as are others in the comic tradition. Modern fashion may thus be said, in a manner of speaking, to have caught up with the schemas of sartorial inversion predicted by literature.

Système de la Mode: Investment
I turn, finally, to Roland Barthes's theory of fashion in *Système de la mode*. A critique of this theory will enable us to formulate the role of

concealment in—and beyond—clothing more precisely. In his 1967 foreword, Barthes admitted that the book's structuralist method was "already dated."[82] Our critique will attempt to dismantle two forms of essentialism: first, the structuralist essentialism that amounts to viewing fashion systems as autonomous in their semiological structure, as systems of "pure" signs; and second, the economic essentialism by which Barthes ambiguously supplements his formal analysis, acknowledging that the "autonomous" sign system must somehow be grounded. As we shall see, however, Barthes's sketchy grounding does not make it possible for him to conceive his fashion models in a genuinely historical manner, even in principle. On the contrary, he tries to make a virtue out of structuralist vice, claiming that "Fashion remains outside history."[83]

Yet much of what Barthes says is very useful for our purposes, especially where he transcends his structuralist methodology. Shorn of its twin essentialisms, I will argue, his theory formulates a *système de la mode* whose basic mechanism is *mimetic concealment of a sacrificial order, including, in principle, both economic and erotic dimensions.* Regarding money and sex, in Shakespearean fashion, as suborders of sacrificial mimetism, of *fashion in its most general sense,* we may hope to achieve—in a theoretical terminology which (despite Barthes's modesty) is still fairly "up to date" thirty years later—a provisional closure to the argument of this book.

I shall not try to make Barthes's arguments for him, but will cite some of his most important claims, fashioning them to our purpose. We may begin at the most abstract pole: "Like logic, Fashion is defined by the infinite variation of a single tautology; like logic, Fashion seeks equivalences, validities, not truths; and like logic, Fashion is stripped of content, but not of meaning."[84] This "stripping" fashion of content amounts to regarding it, as I have said, as an autonomous system of signs that have meaning only in relation to each other. To give Barthes his due, however, he does not push this shaky distinction between "content" and "meaning," the semiology and sociology of fashion, too far. Accordingly, he appeals to "the *sociologics* postulated by Durkheim and Mauss"[85]—the intersection between sociology and semiology, history and the logic of form. In particular, he situates fashion—as we have situated fiction, mendacity, and concealment—at the crossroads between law and arbitrariness:

> Fashion, we are told, abhors system. Once more, the myth inverts reality: Fashion is an order made into a disorder. . . . Fashion doubtless belongs to all the phenomena of *neomania* which prob-

ably appeared in our civilization with the birth of capitalism. . . . But . . . what is new in Fashion seems to have a well-defined anthropological function, one which derives from its ambiguity: simultaneously unpredictable and systematic, regular and unknown, aleatory and structured, it fantastically conjoins the intelligible without which men could not live and the unpredictability attached to the myth of life.[86]

A footnote to this passage confirms Anne Hollander's claim concerning the crucial mediatory importance of art: "In the Renaissance, as soon as one got a new costume, one had a new portrait done." Another note claims that fashion conjoins "the desire for community and the desire for isolation"—that it stands, as so many commentators have observed, at the intersection of difference and mimetic similarity, class and the individual, exclusivity and the herd.[87] Just as fashionable portraiture mediates between public and private (allowing a person to appear in public while remaining solitary), and between law and singularity, so fashion mediates in Barthes's analysis between a whole set of general oppositions: work/idleness, nobility/ignobility, seriousness/frivolity, adulthood/childhood, wealth/poverty, and self/other (to name only some of the most important).[88] Barthes's semiology thus recalls and confirms Shakespeare's fashion system as a system of oxymorons. His formula that fashion turns order into disorder, however, needs to be supplemented and corrected by the Shakespearean mimetic-sacrificial formula that founds order on arbitrariness, form on the deformed. Barthes himself claims that "Fashion's reality is essentially the arbitrariness which establishes it: here we cannot transform a law into a fact except metaphorically."[89] In *Much Ado about Nothing*, however, we saw that the *arbitrary literalization of metaphor* was organized not merely around what Barthes calls fashion's theoretical "nothings" (the arbitrariness of its factual details), but around a social nothing, the victim Deformed.

This kind of reversal of literal and figural is precisely what we need to turn Barthes's text to our advantage, since his metaphors and imaginative sallies give us everything we need to deduce the kind of mimetic-sacrificial pattern represented by Shakespeare. At the same time, many of his literal theoretical claims—that fashion "originates" in economics, that its formal autonomy places it "outside history," and so on (claims we will return to later)—are best read as deceptive metaphors. When Barthes imaginatively reflects on the mimetic double bind of fashion ("the woman of Fashion dreaming of being at once herself and another"), he provides all the central concerns we discovered in Shakespeare: concealment, doubleness, the gods, the police, thieves, and in general the sacred and duplicitous ancestry of fashion. *"You're demanding, and you're sweet, too; with the couturiers you discover you can be both, you can lead a double life*: herein lies the ancestral theme of disguise, the essential attribute of gods, police, and bandits."[90] And elsewhere: "The Fashion text represents as it were the authoritative voice . . . [that] constitutes a technique of opening the invisible, where one could almost rediscover, in secular form, the sacred halo of divinatory texts; especially since the knowledge of Fashion is not without its price: those who exclude themselves from it suffer a sanction: the stigma of being *unfashionable*."[91]

Shakespeare clarifies Barthes by removing the "almost" from this secular rediscovery of the sacred, the "as it were" from the authoritative voice—Shakespeare's asinine police—and by presenting the stigma of fashion, not in the context of mere self-exclusion, but of exclusion by others. Barthes himself sacrificially metaphorizes the discontinuity of fashion's "series of choices" as "amputations,"[92] its repudiation of the past as "murder," and its aggressiveness as having the rhythm of "vendettas."[93] He also writes of the strong passions of play, madness, and war, which "place Fashion outside humanity, as it were, and constitute it as a malign contingency . . . at the crossroads of chance and divine decree: its decision becomes an obvious fact."[94] Distinguishing between the semiology of fashion and of language by the greater arbitrariness and "externality" of the former's signs (whereas the signs of the latter are "transformed from within"), we are told that fashion's signs are "attached to each other by what might be called a public affinity: the sign is no longer mobile, but only dead and renascent, ephemeral and eternal, capricious and reasonable; by naming its signifieds, Fashion thus proceeds to a kind of immediate sacralization of the sign."[95]

This "immediate sacralization" of the "dead and renascent" sign, combined with the description of fashion experienced as occupying a quasi-transcendent position "outside humanity" (whose "decision is an obvious fact" or self-fulfilling prophecy), is precisely analogous to Girard's definition of sacrifice. That Barthes applies the term *deformation* to fashion models, as we saw earlier, nicely emphasizes their Shakespearean status and ambivalence as *pharmaka*. The double bind of the model, at once to be imitated and impossible to emulate, is also doubtless often experienced by models themselves as catastrophically literal (as feminists and experts on eating disorders attest). On the same page that he speaks of the "vengeful present which each year *sacrifices* the signs of the preceding year,"[96] Barthes elaborates what he, like Flugel, calls the "neurosis" of fashion: "We could almost speak of a Fashion neurosis, but . . . Fashion is unfaithful only insofar as it *acts out* meaning, *plays* meaning." And in a footnote: "Fashion is systematically unfaithful. Now fidelity (like paralysis within the past) and infidelity (like the destruction of this same past) are equally neurotic, once they assume a form, the former of a legal or religious duty (of the Erinys type), the latter of a natural right to 'life.' "[97] Barthes confirms our contention that the fidelity/infidelity, modesty/display, and audaciousness/discretion "neuroses" are a product of the *pharmakon*-ambivalence of form as such. But this formal ambivalence, nota bene, is also of "the Erinys type"—the type of reciprocal sacrificial violence.

Having shown how Barthes rather impressively confirms the mimetic-sacrificial logic of *Much Ado*, we may now return to his treatment of fashion history, as well as to the essential role of concealment in fashion. In explicitly extending the generative role of concealment from sartorial to economic relations, we will see how Barthes himself provides the basis for a critique of the primacy he attributes to the latter. He devotes only an appendix to "the history and diachrony of fashion," the latter term meant to "shock historians, [designating] a process both temporal and ahistorical,"[98] the quasi-repetitive cycles of fashion:

> History cannot act on forms analogically [e.g., there is no analogical relation between the Napoleonic period and high waist-lines],[99] but it can certainly act on the rhythm of forms, to disturb or to change it. It follows that, paradoxically, Fashion can know only a very long history or no history at all; for, as long as its rhythm remains regular, Fashion remains outside history; it changes but its changes are alternative, purely endogenous: it is no more than a question of simple diachrony; in order for history to intervene in Fashion, it must modify its rhythm, which seems possible only with a history of very long duration. For example, if Kroeber's calculations are correct, our society practices the same Fashion rhythm over several centuries: *it is only when this rhythm changes that a historical explanation may intervene.*[100]

This "paradox" of either sartorial "long history" or "no history" seems to me to belong rather to Barthes's defensive structuralism than to sartorial history. For while, as in the sciences, "paradigm shifts" of a major order may appear to occur relatively rarely, even "discontinuously . . . by distinct thresholds,"[101] and certain formal relations may appear relatively stable and independent of other developments over long periods, this is only a relative and contingent matter, justifying not at all the idealizing generalizations he derives from it. As for the empirical support claimed from Kroeber's analysis of the regularities of change in lengths of skirt, widths of waist, and so on, over the last three centuries, we need only adduce underwear and children's clothes to throw a wrench in the "ahistorical" works. Or, if these are to be attributed to a "threshold leap," we may add Hollander's charting of the development of body fashions, which, as she shows, cannot be separated from the history of clothes, and certainly have some "analogical" relation to history more generally. "Long" or "short," the rhythm changes of fashion must be governed *more or less* by contingent historical contributions of all kinds, which cannot be banished from the realm of sartorial law. Hunt's observation that Kroeber's view of the long-term trends of fashion implies that "it is a classically 'social' phenomenon . . . not amenable to explanation pitched at the level of individual choice"[102] applies equally to short-term oscillations to which Barthes attributes a similar structural "transcendence." Barthes's structuralist detachment of semiology from history fails to take account of his own insight that arbitrariness and law belong to the same (historical) system and are mutually self-generative.

However, his suggestion that "we could even speak, as do the Bloomfieldians, of a meta-chrony, to mark a discontinuous process"[103] comes closer to our analysis of the metalevel structure of sartorial development. The crucial question of sartorial predictability is treated as follows:

> The freedom to combine supports and variants [of dress] is so great that it makes all Fashion forecasting difficult. Actually, this matters little. What is interesting is that if Fashion forecasting is illusory, its structuration is not. . . . In other words, Fashion is structured at the level of its history: it is destructured at the only level at which it is perceived: actuality.
>
> Thus the confusion of Fashion does not stem from its status but from the limits of our memory; the number of fashion features is high, it is not infinite: we could very well conceive of a Fashion-making machine.[104]

Barthes's gross exaggeration of the opposition between forecasting and structure, history and semiological actuality here leads him to an obvious misconception: the fact that the number of English words and their meaningful combinations is finite, for example, is not especially germane to the predictive powers of a conceivable discourse-making machine. As Alisdair MacIntyre has argued, the logical limits to social prediction entail not only the roles of pure chance and "radical innovation," but also "the game-theoretic character of social life," one of whose elements is the "indefinite reflexivity,"[105] or metalevel structure of social laws. Thus "we need to remain to some degree *opaque and unpredictable*, particularly when threatened by the predictive practices of others."[106] This kind of unpredictability is not an argument against the scientific character of the social sciences, MacIntyre argues, because it is in itself systematic. The literal opacity of clothing is a fine illustration of his point. Precisely inasmuch as we continue to conceal certain parts of our bodies, thus making certain kinds of prediction about our bodily states relatively difficult, certain essential elements of our sartorial habit, however otherwise whimsical, remain relatively easy to forecast.[107]

Our concluding focus concerns, however, not the literal opacity of clothing, but the general role of concealment in both the semiology of fashion and its economic basis as Barthes portrays them. In his introduction, he proposes an economic "origin" for fashion—moreover a *transparent* one. Because fashion substitutes "for the slow time of wear [natural wearing-out] a sovereign time free to destroy itself by an act of annual potlatch" benefiting manufacturers, we are told: "The commercial origin of our collective image-system (always subject to fashion, not merely in the case of clothing) cannot be a mystery to anyone. Yet no sooner has it altered than this universe detaches itself from its origin (moreover, how could it *copy* that origin?): its structure obeys certain universal constraints, those of any system of signs."[108] In an appendix we learn that "the intense variability . . . [of] Fashion is sustained by certain producer groups," and that "there is no secret about the economic implications of this variability."[109] Note, however, that economic "implications" are very different from economic "origins" in the strong sense posited above, and that Barthes seems ambivalent on this matter despite his claim that there is no "mystery" and no "secret" in economic determinations. Elsewhere, for example, he claims that the plausibility of neither Marxism (for economic determination) nor psychoanalysis (for sexual determination) rests entirely on the effects predicted or explained by these theories, "which owe a decisive part of their 'probability' to their systematic coherence,"[110] that is, their purely formal (rather than true or false) properties. Thus psychoanalytic and Marxist explanations of fashion seem adequate inasmuch as—I translate only partly tongue-in-cheek—they are fashionlike or fashionable.

Barthes asks the rhetorical question "how could fashion *copy* its economic origin?" In some sense, it is obvious that fashion cannot generally "copy" economic relations as such—though imitation jewelry and industrial fabrics that mimic, say, silk or fur are examples in which fashion imitates materials of economic value directly. As Roche observes, "the organization of distribution and trade today allow a highly complex system of substitutions, which depends on making people believe that the false can be more real than the real, that nylon fur and plastic are more 'in' than real fur and leather."[111] It is also important to point out that economic value may itself be determined by mimetic or fashionable behavior. Gold, to take the most notorious example, was once the focus of all kinds of frankly mystical values, but its value nowadays is no less a result of collective unanimity among its purchasers, whether it is stored in Fort Knox or placed around the ankle of Madonna. As Keynes elegantly summarized the mimetic anticipations of the stock market, the investor's success depends on his picking "not those faces which he himself finds prettiest, but those which he thinks likeliest to catch the fancy of the other competitors, *all of whom are looking at the problem from the same point of view.* ... We have reached *the third degree . . . anticipating what the average opinion expects the average opinion to be.* And there are . . . fourth, fifth and higher degrees."[112] Moreover, in many societies, ornaments (for example, teeth and shells) were themselves the first prototypes for currency, including the ornament/currency gold: money literally *copied* ornament.[113] Not only is Barthes clearly wrong to exclude mimesis from relations between fashion and economics, above all at the origins of their intersection, but we need to question the causal primacy he attributes to the latter more generally. Roche, by contrast, claims both that "fashion was a motor of the urban economy and instrumental in an effective transformation of social relations," and, more generally in Enlightenment France, that "fashion precedes or announces the economic."[114] Observing that "it was perhaps still within the economic and moral theme of luxury that fashion, like its economy, was drawn by *the fashion of the economy*," he also pointedly draws attention to the fact that "Karl Marx, in Book I of *Capital*, resorts to a clothing metaphor to decipher the hieroglyph of value and analyse the qualitative appearances in its constitution."[115] The word *investment* itself has obvious sartorial connotations.

Despite his insistence on the transparency of fashion's economic basis, Barthes himself provides us with a model of concealment that applies equally to sartorial and economic domains. In the realm of fashion, he distinguishes between two types of garment/wearer: the first ("A ensembles") which conceal their fashionability, the second ("B ensembles") which "do not 'lie' [but] signify Fashion openly."[116] In the first case, he stresses the "semiological paradox" whereby "A ensembles" makes every effort to signify fashion systematically while displaying "an equal activity in masking their systematic nature."[117] In this "double process, simultaneously contradictory and complementary: of signification and of rationalization,"[118] we encounter a sumptuary illustration of the "neurotic paradox" in which the contradictory motives of modesty/display of the dressed *body* are transferred onto the modesty/display of the *dress* itself, and *where concealment masks itself as arbitrariness*. This "paradox" does not, according to Barthes, have "a universal bearing, of an anthropological order; certain archaic types of societies allow the intelligible they elaborate to keep the form of an ensemble of declared signs [without converting] nature and the supernatural into a reason."[119] He thus rather congenially imagines "defining human societies according to the degree of 'frankness' of their semantic systems."[120]

Such an imagined anthropological classification of concealment systems comes very close to making the final point I need for my general argument: that concealment cannot be regarded merely as a product of other systems and motives, but may be regarded as a generative and classificatory principle in its own right. It is accordingly of considerable importance that Barthes defines the supposedly economic "origin" of fashion in terms of concealment, applying a metaphor of sartorial veiling to economic relations themselves:

> Why does Fashion utter clothing so abundantly? Why does it interpose, between the object and its user . . . such a network of meaning? The reason is of course an economic one . . . if clothing's producers and consumers had the same consciousness, clothing would be bought (and produced) only at the very slow rate of its dilapidation; *Fashion, like all fashions, depends on a disparity of two consciousnesses, each foreign to the other.* In order to blunt the buyer's calculating consciousness, a *veil* must be drawn around the object.[121]

Barthes's claim that *all* fashions—all mimetic phenomena in this sense—depend on concealment confirms the larger argument of this chapter, and indeed this book. However, his application of the point specifically to modern producer and consumer needs to be modified and clarified. In the Renaissance, for example, it is arguable that producer and consumer of fashion really *were* significantly "foreign" to each other, inasmuch as class distinctions between artisan-producer and aristocratic or wealthy consumer were radical enough to produce a similarly radical disparity of consciousness, and inasmuch as producer was rarely or never a consumer of the same fashionable product. Originally, as Geoffrey Squire observes, there was no third party between the producer and consumer, no tailor (as opposed to weaver), let alone fashion designer in the modern sense. Only slowly did tailors assume "an importance equal to that of the weaver and wearer,"[122] and, more importantly, "internalise . . . the sense of their social activity" to such an extent that producers of clothes themselves became "models, to be imitated both in general and in particular."[123] It is precisely in this more modern context that Barthes's claim concerning the essential disparity of consciousness between producer and consumer seems unconvincing, since modern producers of fashion—whether designers, tailors, corporate executives, factory workers, or, for that matter, fashion journalists and pop stars—almost invariably double as consumers. Already in the late eighteenth century, as Roche observes, "customers and producers were . . . brought together in a new . . . three-way circulation" created by advertisements and models, such as fashion dolls.[124] It seems characteristic of the modern world, moreover, that since differentiation between the economic producer and the consumer of fashion has increasingly eroded, the fashionable demimonde has generated ever more prestigious fashion designers and supermodels who seem to dictate fashion from a pseudotranscendent position foreign to both. The fact that neither manufacturers, designers, nor models really control fashion—as illustrated by their notorious collaborative failure to control the length of skirts during the 1970s, as during the "hemline battle" of 1929–31[125]—is hardly surprising. The point is that in the absence of any genuine "foreignness" between producer and consumer, the *illusion* of foreignness may be generated by new patterns of structural mediation. Hollander's artist-mediator of early modern fashion has been transformed, in a manner of speaking, into the *inside outsider* of our own day: the *fashion artist*.[126]

Conclusion

A very pious man in Prague, a certain K., knew a great deal of the worldly sciences, he had studied them all in the toilet.
—FRANZ KAFKA

The results of this book could not of course "solve" the problems of lying and concealment either inside or outside fiction. From the moral point of view, I have not sought to be didactic or essentialist (even by being rigidly antididactic or anti-essentialist), though I have shown, I hope, at least that conventional approaches stand in urgent need of critique, and that neither fiction nor concealment, innocent as they may sometimes appear, can be arbitrarily detached from the problem of deception more generally. This much is hardly news in the context of Western thought broadly considered, from Plato's praise of the "noble lie" onward, though perhaps I have succeeded in putting some of the central issues at stake in a somewhat new and more comprehensive manner than is customary. In a nutshell, I have sought to show that the relation between fiction and deception ultimately raises the question of the value and structure of social and intellectual unanimity as such—a crucial topic in modern Western thought from Kant to, say, Habermas—a structure that is frequently, if not invariably, sacrificial in character. But it was only in the course of actually writing the book that I came to suspect just how comprehensive an approach would be necessary to illuminate these issues in a way that did them a modicum of justice, and to recognize that I accordingly needed to expand my original focus on literary fiction—the genesis of the book derived from my studies of Defoe, Stendhal, and Beckett—to include forays into moral and analytic philosophy, and even fashion theory. Given the prominence in my account of the mimetic-sacrificial theory of René Girard, which itself grew out of his literary studies into a putatively global anthropology, this need for a broad sweep is in retrospect hardly surprising—though I must second Girard's own wry admission that a background in literature is not generally regarded as the best qualification for the kind of interdisciplinary synthesis attempted here.

So, first, where does all this leave us with respect to Girardian, as well as de Manian, theory as such—the two protagonists of my introduction? I said there that the linchpin of Girard's anthropology, his hypothesis of mimetic-sacrificial "origins" as the key to the sociobiological development from primates to humans, lies beyond the scope and competence of this book. What I have tried to show, however, is that mimetic-sacrificial models of various kinds—both Girardian and trans-Girardian—can provide a remarkably coherent accounting for a number of texts and contexts that may not at first seem promising materials for such accounting. In this general sense I am akin to, say, Michel Serres in *Les Origines de la géométrie*, who offers a thoroughly mimetic-sacrificial account of the early history of Western geometry (though it mentions Girard only once), or to Paul Dumouchel, who has applied mimetic models to economic history. I am similarly sympathetic to Mihai Spariosu's claim that "Girard's theory offers not only a solid basis for a radical critique of modernity . . . restoring an important anthropological function to literature . . . [but] deals a considerable blow to modern 'aestheticism.' "[1] In this at least, Girard is akin to the later Paul de Man, whose last collection, *Aesthetic Ideology*, explicitly takes the whole category of aesthetics as its target. If my analysis of the trilogy is even partly correct, something analogous can also be said for Beckett, whose extraordinary extension of the sacrificial principle to almost every aspect of social, psychological, and symbolic life constitutes—along with Shakespeare on fashion (a focus, surely, of cultural aesthetics par excellence)—the climax of the literary part of the book. Beckett goes further than Girard, two decades earlier than Girard, along what is a thoroughly mimetic-sacrificial route. Moreover, unlike Girard and Derrida, whom, if we are to believe Spariosu, have remained too much (even if, as with Derrida and the postmodernist case, only negatively) "within a metaphysical problematic of mimesis and truth,"[2] Beckett's trilogy, like Shakespeare's work (which Girard has argued, in *A Theater of Envy*, closely anticipated mimetic-sacrificial theory nearly four centuries earlier) is not obviously open to such a charge. To accuse the work of Shakespeare and Beckett of adhering to a particular philosophical or metaphysical dogma concerning truth is to risk accusing a figment of one's own philosophical imagination. It is the *form*, not the doctrine, of their work which clinches the mimetic-sacrificial thesis argued here.

It is worth emphasizing again that mimesis is itself a matter of form, and to this extent ineluctably also material. Adorno in *Kierkegaard: The Construction of the Aesthetic* similarly stressed the mimetic materialism that deceptively underlies Kierkegaard's sacrificial conception of the sacred, and made it a basis for his own *Aesthetic Theory*, in which the relation between sacrifice and mimesis, including fashion, remains (as I have argued elsewhere) central.[3] It is also significant that the later Paul de Man increasingly stressed the "materialist" dimension of the classic idealist philosophers, such as Kant and Hegel, at the same time that the notion of the sacred took on a more definite profile in his analyses of "aesthetic ideology." The centrality of the problem of the sacred, both in Girard and in Beckett's trilogy, is of course a key element of my own analyses. Baldly put, the central implication is that the dynamic structure of the sacred has quite easily survived the "death of god" (whether murdered by Nietzsche or otherwise laid to rest), or to put the point Baudelaire's way, that the sacred can be found again most obviously in the hearts of atheists. The sacred, in this sense, has little or nothing to do with the contents of belief, but with the structure of actual practice and experience.

Though broader implications for contemporary literary and cultural theory are, in any detail, obviously beyond my scope here, it is worth indicating briefly how the issue of deception intersects with the late de Man's conception of the sacred. De Man was previously useful to us both because his definition of fiction as arbitrariness could be formulated analytically (via Goodman et al.) and because his illustrative model of fiction as an arbitrary indictment, like Shakespeare's model of fashion, could be grafted onto Girard's scapegoating model of the sacred. We noted that the de Man of *Allegories of Reading* took an ironic distance from "Deconstruction"; but there was as yet no insistence on the sacred as pointed as that to be found in Beckett or Girard, and still the category of language remained apparently sovereign. In later de Man, however, language is admitted to be a deceptive and unstable concept that converges at key moments precisely with the sacred. Thus we read in *Aesthetic Ideology*, for example: "The convergence of discourse and the sacred, which, in the choice of example and in Hegel's commentary on it, is not in question, occurs by way of phenomenal cognition."[4] This, nota bene, is an extraordinarily concentrated claim whose putative validity, it would be easy to show, is not limited by de Man to his reading of Hegel. The example of light, which is de Man's Hegelian example in this context, recalls Beckett's treatment of vision in *Malone Dies*: to extend the principle of the sacred to "phenomenal cognition" is thoroughly Beckettian. Girard has also made tentative efforts in this direction (for instance in his theory of laughter in *To Double Business Bound*), but these efforts have been largely overshadowed by the controversy surrounding his treatment of Christianity and his Catholicism (his apparent assertion of a moral or religious truth that transcends the duplicity of the sacred, of sacrifice, altogether).

In de Man's reading of Hegel, by contrast, the sacred necessarily converges with the positing power of language and spirit considered as deception:

> The spirit posits itself as that which is unable to posit, and this declaration is either meaningless or duplicitous. One can pretend to be weak when one is strong, but the power to pretend is decisive proof of one's strength. One can know oneself, as man does, as that which is unable to know, but by moving from knowledge to position, all is changed. Position is all of a piece, and, moreover, unlike thought, it actually occurs.[5]

As in Beckett, the sacred and the secular can no longer be coherently held apart: "The only thing the misleading metaphor of a two-sided world accomplishes is to radicalize the separation between the sacred and the human in a manner that no dialectic can surmount (*aufheben*)."[6] Nor can de Man's theoretical irony (which knows its ignorance) and his practical irony (which knows its duplicity) be arbitrarily sundered. To be sure, according to de Man, "rather than put it in terms that suggest deceit and duplicity, one could say that the poet, like the philosopher, must *forget* what he knows."[7] Nevertheless, it follows logically that superior knowledge, if not superior wisdom, lies on the side of fully conscious, if not wholly avoidable, deceit. (This indeed, mutatis mutandis, is pretty much also the upshot of the late Girard's understanding of Shakespearean irony, which deceives one audience while enlightening another.) Intellectual non-unanimity or *difference* is thus affirmed in a way that hardly resembles the edifying stereotypes—humanist or postmodernist, left or right—currently associated with this term. Deception here is necessary in both causal and volitional or moral senses—a Kafkan "universal principle."

All this provides a perspective in which to situate de Man's relation not only to Deconstruction but to political and moral philosophy. Especially in the context of defending him against charges of fascism, de Man's deconstructivist friends have naturally tended to stress the inevitable or structural rather than the intentional side of his conception of irony. J. Hillis Miller, for example, rather piously claims that de Man, Derrida, and he himself are all "committed to a rigorous truth-telling about language."[8] Perhaps. But when de Man cites Friedrich Schlegel on the subject of the incomparable benefits of "nonunderstanding" to the "welfare of nations and families,"[9] he is well aware that such nonunderstanding may be not merely inevitable, but conscious and intentional. And in his late essay on Mikhail Bakhtin, with its pointed allusions to the political philosopher Leo Strauss, de Man shows himself well aware of the politically controversial dimension of irony so conceived. Strauss's conception of irony as the dissimulation of the virtuous, wise, or "superior" person has been widely interpreted as inherently "rightist"—partly because of Strauss's other associations, but above all by its seeming inegalitarianism—despite the potentially "leftist" element in his treatment of irony as the kind of dissimulation typically practiced by the persecuted (the element also strategically stressed by de Man in his allusion to Strauss's *Persecution and the Art of Writing*). Assimilating Strauss to a discussion of the Marxist (but also Christian) Bakhtin—with his conception of dialogism and what de Man calls "double-talk"—de Man implicitly but nonetheless pointedly poses the question of the left-right politics of irony considered as deception.[10] The "leftist" implication here, as also in the case of de Man's essay on Hegel, is that the prosaic discourse of "aesthetics" (and of irony) is the discourse of the persecuted slave, "politically legitimate and effective as the undoing of usurped authority."[11]

De Man, Strauss, and Girard have all, to a greater or lesser degree, been accused of being "right-wing." I cannot pursue that charge here, except by citing "left-wing" names like Adorno, Kenneth Burke, and Bakhtin as equally relevant in this context, and by noting that they have "left-wing" defenders. What is more important, in terms of political implication as well as aesthetic theory, is the kind of prominence given to the sacred, mutatis mutandis, by all three authors. In the context of Plato and Socratic irony, in *The City and Man* Strauss defined "the literary question, properly understood" as the question of the relation between society and philosophy, or philosophy and politics.[12] But Strauss's last work, *Studies in Platonic Political Philosophy*, bluntly concerns the relation between philosophy and religion. Similarly, in his essay on Hegel, de Man first observes that "by dint of the structure of the Hegelian system, the consideration of aesthetics only makes sense in the context of the larger question of the relationship between the political and the order of philosophy." But he then restates this mediation of the aesthetic as that between "two alien political forces, law and religion."[13] I would argue that there is a sufficient—and sufficiently unconventional—parallel here for pause. Despite their differences, Strauss's and de Man's insistence on practical deception is matched by a striking analogy in their general theoretical landscapes. Of course, these are mere indications of how the concerns of the present book might be developed, particularly in the direction of political theory. It would clearly also be necessary, if the present perspective were to be maintained, to show in detail how not only de Man's literary theory, but also Strauss's political philosophy, intersects with Girardian sacrifice.

Girard's own work stands in an ambivalent relation to truth and truth-telling. Both early and late Girard insist that as the mechanisms of sacrifice are increasing revealed, so their "curative" efficacy is weakened. But where the earlier Girard tended to emphasize the triumph of reason over sacrifice to such an extent that contemporary modernity could no longer appeal to sacrificial ruses for salvation, but must now openly embrace the antisacrificial (Christian) truth, the later Girard seems to have a somewhat more sanguine, or at least resigned, view of the continuing transformation and internalization of sacrificial phenomena, and of the necessary deceptions that must be practiced in a sacrificial world. Whether or not Spariosu is correct that Girard offers a "more plausible explanation than psychoanalysis of the structure of the human psyche and its disturbances,"[14] Beckett's relentlessly sacrificial reinterpretation of the psychoanalytic eros would seem strong support for such a hypothesis, and Slavoj Žižek's Lacanian exhortation that we "sacrifice sacrifice," as noted earlier, neatly suggests how difficult that undertaking might be.[15] It is no accident, of course, that the sacrificial dilemma of truth-telling is very sharply posed in the domain of medicine. When Ian Hacking, for example, juxtaposes the therapeutic goals of Pierre Janet and Freud—the former successfully curing so-called multiple personality disorder by hypnotic lies, the latter aiming at curative truth—we may find ourselves at a loss to type either view, since an entire theory of the psyche, not to speak of politics or morality, is at stake.[16]

I have argued that concealment and deception, in their reciprocal relation to truth-telling (or showing), are not only practical accessories to sacrificial phenomena, but deserve, at least at a certain level of structural generality, to be regarded as sacrificial phenomena in their own right. I have also argued that concealment, whether sacrificially regarded or not, deserves to be regarded as a global structuring principle sui generis, and not merely as ancillary to other structuring principles. Barthes's notion of classifying societies (including their economic structures) according to their degree of transparency indicates this possibility somewhat quaintly, in a kind of parody of the structuralist mania for classification. More concretely, even if we do not wholly deny the myth of transparency by which concealment is typically conceived as originally contingent on other motives (for instance dress-concealment on sexual desire), it is nonetheless clear that this relation inevitably becomes reciprocal and reversible. The intersection of concealment and sacrifice, I have argued, can be conceived as occurring where sacrificial exclusions and behaviors of the most literal or physical sort—by death or banishment, for example, or mutilation— coincide with, or are partially replaced by, the symbolic or cognitive exclusion that defines concealment as such. But this understates the intimacy of the connection, since concealment (as in the case of dress) is often evidently also quite literal and physical, a kind of attenuated "banishment" that concerns not just cognition in the abstract but "phenomenal cognition." The passage from sacrifice to concealment may look relatively straightforward or linear when we consider, for example, a passage from bodily mutilation to dress-concealment as religiously sanctioned modes of adornment. But this linearity is disrupted when we consider that concealment is an integral part of even the most "primitive" or openly sacrificial culture, and not merely an attenuated substitute for it. To put it another way: though there is obviously a considerable distance from the ancient menstrual hut to the modern toilet, it is not clear that basic forms (as opposed to ideologies) of concealment have always much progressed. "The transformation of sacrifice into subjectivity," Horkheimer and Adorno remark, occurs when "the deceit posited in sacrifice becomes an element of the character."[17]

In "Investigations of a Dog," Kafka (who, as seen in the epigraph, had studied all the worldly sciences on the toilet) provides a generalized model of sacrificial concealment when his canine investigator, having observed how the reciprocal dedication to silence and concealment is universal in dogdom, then explains that knowledge is like a bone whose marrow could easily be extracted if only all dogs unanimously willed it; but that marrow would turn out to be poison.[18] Kafka's dog is the opposite of postmodernist in that he states that the relevant truth is readily available, at least in principle, to every dog: truth and transparency are not so much unattainable as undesirable. Needless to say, one would hardly expect any philosopher or writer to assert this clearly or without equivocation.

I conclude by observing that if the global political structure of concealment or irony (that is, concealment intellectually conceived) has a dominant "objective correlative" in contemporary Western society, it is surely in the fundamental legal and moral distinction between public and private.[19]

**Appendix:
On René Girard
and Paul de Man**

■

My appeal to Derrida and Girard may well be provocative enough, without a further rapprochement or "monstrous doubling" of Girard and de Man as potentially opposed to Derrida. Certainly one is aware of the unbridgeable theoretical abyss that is supposed to lie between Girard and Deconstruction. Derrida is supposed to be the great iconoclast of origins, Girard the pig-headed theorist of origins; Girard is an avowed Catholic, Derrida *the* deconstructivist; the earlier Derrida refers very dismissively to Girard; and so on. For a book-length demonstration of what they share in common nevertheless, I refer the reader to Andrew McKenna's informative *Violence and Difference*.[1] My concern is not to compare their programs as a whole, but to emphasize a local coincidence concerning mimesis in Plato acknowledged by Girard himself.

My more sustained coupling of de Man and Girard may seem to some readers even more questionable than the brief connection with Derrida, especially since there is to my knowledge no Andrew McKenna to cite as mediator between the two. This is not the place to attempt any overview of their work as a whole. But we do have a 1967 essay by de Man himself on Girard's *Mensonge romantique* (admittedly written well before the later phase of de Man's work I have been referring to and before Girard developed his full-blown sacrificial theory) to serve as preliminary guide.

In contrast to Derrida's dismissive attitude to Girard, cited by McKenna, it is striking just how much de Man's critique accepts in Girard's analysis of mimetic desire. Indeed, no specific criticism of the mimetic theory is made at all in the realm of "the empirical world" (to use the phenomenological vocabulary de Man maintained at this stage).[2] Rather, Girard's insights at this level—especially into the patterns of blindness and insight generated by mimetic interactions—are said to be compromised by his own blindness, his refusal to acknowledge the source of these insights in "his own intellectual origin, namely romanticism." According to de Man, Girard also fails to make the proper distinction between the "empirical" and "transcendent" dimensions of the self (the latter being identified with properly literary understanding) and offers a misleadingly "apocalyptic" account of a movement from error to truth in the novelists under discussion (Cervantes, Stendhal, Flaubert, Proust, and Dostoyevsky). In sum, it is Girard's conception of literature rather than of "empirical entities" such as "other people"[3] (including their treatment as such in literature) that is under attack. Mimetic theory applies to the intersubjectivity of empirical people, but not to the "transcendence" of the work of art.

Though de Man approvingly noted, in the 1967 essay, that Girard's later work was moving toward "a hermeneutic instead of an intersubjective conception of the work of art,"[4] we do not need to enter the details of the argument to observe that the later Girard and de Man both abandoned what they earlier called "transcendence."[5] Similarly, just as Girard abandoned the novelistic/romantic opposition of his early work (and his theory of specifically novelistic and literary revelation), so de Man later admitted that he had been forced to abandon his own original project of a historical inquiry into Romanticism[6]—the very historical question over which he had chided Girard—in favor of a more general theory of reading whose sacrificial model I describe. Abandoning the empirical/transcendent contrast on which his early critique of Girard (and definition of literature) rested, the later de Man defined textual truth, as I noted in the introduction, in terms of empirical necessity or predictability. We see in chapter 4 that Girard speaks comparably of the "truth" of the text of Stendhal being confirmed by the texts of Dostoyevsky and Proust precisely insofar as it predicts them.

What both early and late de Man and Girard share, in any case, is a strong claim about the systematicity of relations between truth and falsehood, blindness and insight, of the kind for which de Man praises Girard's mimetic insight: "The more one censors, the more one reveals what is being effaced. A paraphrase is always what we called an analytical reading, that is, it is always susceptible of being made to point out what it was trying to conceal."[7]

In summary, even if de Man had rejected Girard's theory of sacrificial origins outright (which as far as I know he did not)—and bearing in mind Girard's own criticisms of Deconstruction for an overemphasis on language—this would not diminish but rather highlight their points of coincidence. Aside from the scapegoating definition of fiction we have outlined, it should also be observed that the later de Man both admitted the instability of his concept of language as such, and, more importantly, increasingly emphasized its inseparability from the concept of the sacred. As I remark in my conclusion, language converges with the sacred in a very basic manner according to de Man: "by way of phenomenal cognition."[8]

Notes

Introduction

1 Franz Kafka, *The Trial*, trans. Willa and Edwin Muir (New York: Schocken Books, 1984), 220.

2 J. A. Barnes, *A Pack of Lies: Towards a Sociology of Lying* (New York: Cambridge University Press, 1994), 4. Charles V. Ford agrees: "Deceit is a prevalent—perhaps even central—part of life that has received, in relation to its importance, comparatively little scientific investigation." See Ford, *Lies! Lies!! Lies!!!: The Psychology of Deceit* (Washington: American Pyschiatric Press, 1996), 271.

3 Brodsky as cited in Barnes, *A Pack of Lies*, 8. Brodsky the poet is supported in this connection by a number of child psychologists who connect lying to the development of conscious autonomy (ibid., 6–8).

4 Eco ("with the contingency of the relation between sign and referent in mind") as cited by Barnes, ibid., 4.

5 Edward Jayne, *Negative Poetics* (Iowa City: University of Iowa Press, 1992), 1. However, it by no means follows from this that "fiction gives intention primacy over cognition" (ibid., 2), or that Jayne's psychologization of fiction is generally valid.

6 Ibid., 13–14. But, as will be seen in what follows, Graff's accusation that, e.g., Paul de Man (ibid., 48) ignores literature's truth-status seriously misses the mark.

7 Max Horkheimer and Theodor W. Adorno, *Dialectic of Enlightenment*, trans. John Cumming (New York: Continuum, 1999), 51, 56.

8 Girard has the following to say: "As far as Derrida is concerned, I still view his *Pharmacie de Platon* [in *La Dissemination*] as an important contribution to the deconstruction of sacrificial thought. In *La Double Séance*, there is a long footnote on the impossibility of a consistent theory of mimesis in Plato that is by far the best thing on the subject and it is of great importance to me." (René Girard, *"To Double Business Bound": Essays on Literature, Mimesis, and Anthropology* (Baltimore: Johns Hopkins University Press, 1978), 220.

9 I am thinking especially of the so-called New Historicism in literary and cultural studies, which, like postmodernism, is generally hostile to ambitious global claims or so-called metanarratives.

10 Charles Sanders Peirce, "Uniformity," in *Philosophical Writings of Peirce*, ed. Justus Buchler (New York: Dover Publications, 1955), 225.

11 From de Man's introduction to Carol Jacobs's *The Dissimulating Harmony*, cited by J. Hillis Miller in *Romanticism and Contemporary Criticism*, ed. Morris Eaves and Michael Fischer (Ithaca: Cornell University Press, 1986), 122.

12 Paul de Man, *Allegories of Reading: Figural Language in Proust, Nietzsche, Rilke, and Rousseau* (New Haven: Yale University Press, 1979), 292.

13 In "Subversive Mimesis: Theodor W. Adorno and the Modern Impasse of the Critique," for example, Michael Cahn notes the homeopathic "disappearance of the distinction between cure and disease" that attends Adorno's sacrificial treatment of mimesis—which, though Cahn mentions neither, recalls both Derrida's and Girard's notion of the *pharmakon*. See Cahn, in *Mimesis in Contemporary Theory: An Interdisciplinary Approach*, ed. Mihai Spariosu, vol. 1, *The Literary and Philosophical Debate* (Philadelphia: John Benjamins Publishing, 1984), 54–55. See also my "Sacrificial Materialism in Kierkegaard and Adorno," forthcoming in *Idealism without Absolutes: Philosophy at the Limits of Romanticism*, ed. Arkadi Plotnitsky (SUNY University Press).

14 Outside fiction and the Girardian tradition, Bataille's *Les Larmes d'Eros* (Paris: Pauvert, 1961) provides perhaps the bluntest claim I know for sacrifice as key to the global anthropology of religion: "La religion dans son ensemble se fonda sur le sacrifice" (261). Beckett's *Malone Dies* provides perhaps the most analytic and complex fictional exposition of the interconnection between fiction, religion, and the symbolisms of violence.

15 I summarize this argument in a different context in "A Glance at SunSet: Numerical Fundaments in Frege, Wittgenstein, Shakespeare, Beckett," in *Mathematics, Science, and Postclassical Theory*, ed. Barbara Herrnstein Smith and Arkady Plotnitsky (Durham: Duke University Press, 1997), 213–14. For an introduction to Girard's sacrificial theory, see his *Violence and the Sacred*, trans. Patrick Gregory (Baltimore: Johns Hopkins University Press, 1977).

16 De Man, *Allegories of Reading*, 155.

17 Ibid., 293.

18 Uncritical assimilation of de Man to Derrida and vice versa remains common ten years after Lindsay Waters's criticism of the tendency in his introduction to Paul de Man, *Critical Writings, 1953–1978* (Minneapolis: University of Minnesota Press, 1989), liii.

19 Jacques Derrida, *Writing and Difference*, trans. and intro. Alan Bass (Chicago: University of Chicago Press, 1978), 250.

20 De Man, *Allegories of Reading*, 300.

21 Ibid., 301. "Parabasis" means the interruption of the fiction by the real, as when the Greek poet intervenes in his own comedy. See also Reginald McGinnis and John Vignaux Smyth, "Irony," in the *Encyclopedia of Aesthetics*, vol. 2, ed. Michael Kelly (Oxford: Oxford University Press, 1998), for an overview of Western irony, including its mimetic-sacrificial dimension, which relates de Man's conception to others.

22 De Man, *Allegories of Reading*, 291–93.

23 Ibid., 299.

1 The Liar as Scapegoat

1 Charles V. Ford *Lies! Lies!! Lies!!! The Psychology of Deceit* (Washington: American Psychiatric Press, 1996), 282.

2 Robert C. Solomon, in "What a Tangled Web: Deception and Self-Deception in Philosophy," argues that "whether philosophy merely follows the Zeitgeist or actually has some hand in directing it, it would be safe to say that the philosophical championing of honesty is an accurate reflection of popular morality" (in *Lying and Deception in Everyday life*, ed. Michael Lewis and Carolyn Saarni [New York: Guilford Press, 1993], 32).

3 Solomon's contention that Bok "upholds a virtually blanket condemnation of lying that is in practice as strict as Kant's deontologically 'perfect duty' to tell the truth" ("What a Tangled Web," 37) is highly exaggerated from a practical point of view, though it captures the theoretical appeal to "generality" on which they both converge and diverge.

4 Sissela Bok, *Lying: Moral Choice in Public and Private Life* (New York: Pantheon, 1978), 207.

5 Ibid., 31–32.

6 Sir Francis Bacon, as cited in Ford, *Lies! Lies!! Lies!!!*, 281. Bacon's sartorial metaphor nicely illustrates the "habit" (in the double sense) of lying in relation to concealment.

7 Ford, *Lies! Lies!! Lies!!!*, 151, 157, 274. On the other hand, the relative ubiquity or social homogeneity of lying is suggested by the result that "socioeconomic status was not related to lying" (85); though some studies claim, for example, that contemporary girls and women tell more lies of omission than boys and men (76). The significance of such supposed results is difficult to evaluate.

8 Bok, *Lying*, 29. Cf. also "Lies as an Act of Aggression" (Ford, *Lies! Lies!! Lies!!!*, 89).

9 Bok, *Lying*, 18 (my emphasis).

10 *Othello*, 4.3.4–5.

11 Bok, *Lying*, 30.

12 Martin Buber, *Good and Evil: Two Interpretations* (New York: Scribner's, 1952), 7.

13 Natural deception, such as chameleon behavior, is of course often mimetic. For such creatures as the so-called mimic octopus and fireflies, among whom "a mimic may mimic a mimic," deception is "a way of life" (Ford, *Lies! Lies!! Lies!!!*, 49). Ford, among many others, cites such behaviors as "face-saving tactics" in chimpanzees (51). See also, for instance, Robert W. Mitchell, "Animals as Liars: The Human Face of Nonhuman Duplicity," in *Lying and Deception in Everyday Life*, ed. Lewis and Saarni (59–89).

14 "Of Liars," in *The Complete Essays of Montaigne,* trans. Donald M. Frame (Stanford: Stanford University Press, 1958), 23.

15 Montaigne, "Of Giving the Lie," ibid., 506 (my emphasis).

16 Bok, *Lying,* 40.

17 Ibid., 33.

18 Judith N. Shklar, *Ordinary Vices* (Cambridge: Harvard University Press, 1984), 7–86.

19 Michel Foucault emphasizes the "dark twins" of truth-telling and torture in his *History of Sexuality,* vol. 1, trans. Robert Hurley (Layton, Utah: Peregrine Smith Books, 1984), 59.

20 Bok, *Lying,* 20ff. and 29.

21 Kant, "On a Supposed Right to Lie from Altruistic Motives" (his reply to Benjamin Constant), as cited by Bok, *Lying,* 269.

22 I am being schematic in following Bok's sense of Nietzsche as the celebrator of lies, and do not wish these generalizations to pass for an adequate reading of Nietzsche, who also affirms the heroic truthfulness of the philosopher. In Nietzsche, indeed, the oppositions truth/lies, truth/fiction, philosophy/literature, cruelty/love, etc. enter, even before his madness, into an exchange bordering on the delirious.

23 Ford, *Lies! Lies!! Lies!!!,* 77.

24 Experiments reported by Gerald R. Miller and James B. Stiff in *Deceptive Communication* (Newbury Park, Calif.: Sage Publications, 1993), 105, reveal (for what they're worth) that more than 50 percent of a sample of American students were dishonest when given an opportunity to cheat.

25 *Lying* is undoubtedly also based on utilitarian premises, which Kant rejected. But R. F. Harrod's "Utilitarianism Revised" (cited in Bok's appendix) offers a "refined utilitarianism" which claims to embody the Kantian principle of the categorical imperative, interpreted in terms of the consequences of unanimous *action* (Bok, *Lying,* 275–82). Solomon similarly likens the Kantian and the utilitarian principles, so conceived, in the context of his discussion of Bok (Solomon, "What a Tangled Web," 37).

26 Bok, *Lying,* 130–31.

27 Kant, *Perpetual Peace,* ed. Lewis White Beck (Indianapolis, Ind.: Library of Liberal Arts, 1967), 14.

28 Bok, *Lying,* 101.

29 Ibid., 214 (my emphasis).

30 Solomon ("What a Tangled Web," 36–37) calls it "the perfect example of a so-called 'deontological' (duty-defining) principle in ethics."

31 Bok cites Kant as follows: "By a lie a man throws away and, as it were, annihilates his dignity as a man" (Bok, *Lying,* 46).

32 In the chapter titled "Imitative Rites," in *The Elementary Forms of Religious Life,* trans. Joseph Ward Swain (London: George Allen and Unwin, 1915), Durkheim connects the origins of ideas of force and causality to "imperative rule[s] of thought" (367) more generally, explaining that "the ritual precept is doubled by a logical precept which is only the intellectual aspect of the former" (368). The conclusion of the book returns to Kant in particular (445–46): "Impersonal reason is only another name given to collective thought" (446).

33 Cited from R. F. Harrod, "Utilitarianism Revised," *Mind* 45 (1936): 137–56, in Bok's appendix (*Lying,* 276).

34 Lewis White Beck, *A Commentary on Kant's Critique of Practical Reason* (Chicago: Chicago University Press, 1966), 159n, 160 (my emphasis).

35 Cf. Montaigne: "If, like truth, the lie had but one face, we would be on better terms. For we would accept as certain the opposite of what the liar would say. But the reverse of truth has a hundred thousand faces and an infinite field" (Bok, *Lying*, 3).

36 Miller and Stiff cite Bok and others in this connection (*Deceptive Communication*, 1).

37 For example: "American society harbors a somewhat schizophrenic attitude toward deceptive communication in the marketplace" (Miller and Stiff, *Deceptive Communication*, 7). A study cited by these authors also illustrates how putative exceptions can become the norm: of a sample of student couples, most believed (or said they believed) that "a modest amount" of deception occurred in couples in general, but "almost all respondents replied hardly any" in their own (14)!

38 Kant, "On a Supposed Right to Lie" (cited in Bok, *Lying*, 269).

39 See Flann O'Brien, *The Third Policeman* (New York: Plume Press, 1976), 98, 114–15.

40 Kant, "On a Supposed Right to Lie" (cited in Bok, *Lying*, 269).

41 See Durkheim, "Piacular Rites and the Ambiguity of the Notion of Sacredness," in *Elementary Forms*, 389–414.

42 Readers interested in relations between apogogic (*reductio*) proofs and mimetic-sacrificial exclusions might find relevant my "A Glance at SunSet," in *Mathematics, Science, and Postclassical Theory*, ed. B. H. Smith and Arkadi Plotnitsky (Durham: Duke University Press, 1997), 214–15, 227, in connection with the work of Michel Serres and Wittgenstein.

43 Durkheim, "Piacular Rites," 445.

44 Cf. Kant, *Critique of Judgment*, section 59. On violence and the sublime in Kant see, for example, "Parergon," the opening section of Derrida's *La Verité en peinture* (Paris: Flammarion, 1978).

45 Bok, *Lying*, 207.

46 Franz Kafka, *Gesammelte Schriften* (New York: Schocken Books, 1946), vol. 5.

47 André Breton, "Second manifest du surréalisme," in *Manifestes du surréalisme*, ed. Jean-Jacques Pauvert (Paris: Gallimard, 1975), 78.

48 I deal with this remarkable aspect of Shakespeare at the beginning of chapter 7. Since mimesis-as-fashion differs from mimesis-as-representation, it is also worth observing that (like Baudelaire's metaphor of the poet as "sacred prostitute" to the crowd) Breton's metaphor ignores mimesis-as-representation in favor of the implicit mimesis of the crowd (its "crowd behavior"), against which the surrealist poet is sacrificially positioned—a reversal of the sacrificial violence of the crowd against the individual. (For a mimetic-sacrificial discussion of Baudelaire's figure, see Reginald McGinnis, *La Prostitution sacrée: essai sur Baudelaire* [Paris: Belin, 1994]).

49 Bok, *Lying*, 18–19.

50 *Othello*, 5.2.305.

51 The last line of the play is "I'll devise thee brave punishments for him. Strike up, pipers!" The Arden edition, edited by A. R. Humphries (London: Routledge, 1981), cites F. P. Wilson's observation that these punishments "seemingly add to the gaiety of the wedding festivities"—though this hardly supports his contention

that "the spirit of comedy prevails" (218) in a correct understanding of this dark final detail. Don John is the equivalent of Iago inasmuch as *Othello* represents a tragic rewriting, to a very considerable degree, of the Hero-Claudio plot of *Much Ado* (a play to which I return in chapter 7).

2 The Analytics of Fiction

1 See, for instance, Thomas Pavel, *Fictional Worlds* (Cambridge: Harvard University Press, 1986), 11ff.

2 Allegory and representation are synonymous insofar as the latter term is understood merely as any kind of systematic projection, not as a re-*presentation* or imitation. (Thus a set of musical notes, say, could "represent" a set of colors.)

3 *Poetics*, 9.i.

4 Richard Routley as cited in Pavel, *Fictional Worlds*, 31.

5 These differ crucially, since the *Tractatus* lacks Russell's empiricist/positivist emphasis on "acquaintance with sense-data."

6 Pavel presents Russell's view as consistent on this subject, though without explicitly considering the various phases of his philosophy (*Fictional Worlds*, 11ff.).

7 This includes some fairly shocking volte faces for those who associate Russell with epistemological realism. See, for instance, James Feibleman, *Inside the Great Mirror: A Critical Examination of Russell, Wittgenstein, and Their Followers* (The Hague: M. Nijhoff, 1973), 27; and John Vignaux Smyth, "A Glance at SunSet," in *Mathematics, Science, and Postclassical Theory*, ed. B. H. Smith and A. Plotnitsky (Durham: Duke University Press, 1997), 238n4.

8 Nelson Goodman, *Fact, Fiction, and Forecast*, 4th ed. (Cambridge: Harvard University Press, 1983), 57.

9 G. E. M. Anscombe, *An Introduction to Wittgenstein's "Tractatus"* (London: Hutchinson Library, 1963), 60. Sense and reference resemble form and content: grammatically well-formed propositions may possess "sense"; but only when asserted as such do they achieve "reference" (and hence truth-value).

10 *Tractatus*, 4.064.

11 Pavel's account of Strawson (*Fictional Worlds*, 14–18) is limited, because "Strawson's papers do not primarily focus on fictional entities" (15). Anscombe provides a clearer explanation of Strawson's desire to make sense of statements of possibility.

12 Ibid., 14.

13 Ibid.

14 Ibid.

15 To understand Pavel's account of Russell and "segregationalism" it is helpful to quote at greater length:

> The segregationalist attitude can perhaps be better understood if it is remembered that Russell's theory of descriptions had been designed for specific philosophic needs, in a context in which a strong control over language was required. To maintain such control seems indispensable for areas and periods in which a sense of responsibility must be preserved, such as, according to a widespread view, was the case at the turn of the century in the philosophy of mathematics, logic, and the exact sciences. But the criteria and restrictions applicable in these situations do not necessarily fit all fields of inquiry; in particular, the require-

ments of aesthetics and poetics may well be less stringent than those of the philosophy of mathematics and science, and in studying fictional statements tolerance may be the most appropriate attitude. (Ibid., 15)

Why contemporary literary theory should be held up to standards any less "stringent" or "responsible" than any other discipline (or period)—let alone where it concerns "control over language"—is mystifying. The distinction between science and literature on this basis seems to be a kind of segregation practiced at the crucial moment by Pavel himself.

16 Pavel, *Fictional Worlds*, 1–72.

17 Ibid., 25–27.

18 Richard Rorty, "Is There a Problem about Fictional Discourse?" in *Consequences of Pragmatism (Essays: 1972–1980)* (Minneapolis: University of Minnesota Press, 1982), 119.

19 Mikhail Bakhtin's *Marxism and the Philosophy of Language* is one example of a causal theory influential in literary theory, as is Barbara Herrnstein Smith's *On the Margins of Discourse: The Relation of Literature to Language* (Chicago: University of Chicago Press, 1978). Smith adopts the term *fictive* (as opposed to *fictional*) to distinguish her causal emphasis. Nonfictive or "natural" discourse is considered primarily in terms of "meanings-as-causes, though the expansion to meanings-as-consequences should be understood as possible in all cases" (96). Fictive discourse is defined as "the *representation* of a ["natural"] verbal act" (31), not necessarily containing any reference to fictions; and "to recognize a poem as fictive is to recognize it as the product of a human design in accord with certain valued effects" (39).

20 Rorty, "Is There a Problem," 119–23.

21 Though Barbara Herrnstein Smith, for example, also considers "non-causal meanings" (*On the Margins of Discourse*, 141ff.), this leads to a consideration of fiction in terms of a "*fictive exemplification* of some set of propositions" such as "for example, events such as these could occur"(142). Thus fictive exemplification amounts to a nonfictive statement of possibility. Moreover, inasmuch as this non-causal aspect is stressed by Smith, so is the relative indeterminacy of poetic meaning, poetry's ability to form "parables for an infinite number of propositions" (144), and the fact that "we must supply meanings for it" (145). One of the characteristic effects of fictive discourse consists in its "obliging us" (145) to formulate noncausal meanings against a background of relative indeterminacy, *its forcing us to be relatively arbitrary*.

22 Pavel, *Fictional Worlds*, 27–28.

23 "That from a structural point of view proper names are rigid designators does not entail that historically their attachment to entities is always recovered through a backward chain of causal or historical links, at least in the sense of contemporary factually oriented theories" (ibid., 41).

24 Named after Alexis Meinong, one of Russell's targets.

25 Rorty, "Is There a Problem," 127, 135.

26 Ibid., 136.

27 Cited from Derrida's "No Apocalypse," in Andrew McKenna, *Violence and Difference: Girard, Derrida, and Deconstruction* (Urbana: Illinois University Press, 1992), 111.

28 This insistence on reference goes even more for Paul de Man, for whom the

referential structure of language can be neither "avoided, bracketed, or reduced to being just one contingent property among others" (*Allegories of Reading* [New Haven: Yale University Press, 1979], 207).

29 I discuss Wittgenstein's antiphilosophical turn, his *pharmacological* proposal to cure the "disease" of philosophy, in "A Glance at SunSet," 223–24.

30 Rorty, "Is There a Problem," 137.

31 Ibid. (my emphasis).

32 Ibid., 136 (my emphasis).

33 Ibid., 142 (my emphasis). "We don't *want* works of literature to be criticizable within a terminology we already know; we want both those works and criticism of them to give us *new* terminologies."

34 At the end of *Fact, Fiction, and Forecast*, Goodman likens the "almost as comforting assurance that nothing can be done," philosophically or epistemologically about fiction and related matters, to "the comforting assurance that all has been done" (124).

35 Rorty, "Is There a Problem," 110.

36 Anscombe, *Introduction to Wittgenstein's "Tractatus*," 60. Anscombe sees Russell and Wittgenstein as basically on the same side of the fence in this matter (58), though the matter is complex (as demonstrated, for instance, by Wittgenstein's rejection of the Frege-Russell assertion sign in symbolic logic [113ff.]).

37 Ibid., 59.

38 Ibid., 58–59.

39 Rorty, "Is There a Problem," 110.

40 Ibid., 130.

41 Anscombe, *Introduction to Wittgenstein's "Tractatus*," 69.

42 Ibid., 17.

43 Cf. ibid., 78: "Wittgenstein used to say that the *Tractatus* was not *all* wrong."

44 Ibid., 81.

45 Anscombe points out that "logic cannot be thought of as something quite independent of the world either" (165), but this is because of the "all-comprehending world-mirroring" (167) nature of logical form.

46 I discuss Wittgenstein in a mimetic-sacrificial light in "A Glance at SunSet," 220–28.

47 Pavel, *Fictional Worlds*, 10.

48 Ibid., 60.

49 Ibid., 42, 50.

50 Ibid., 49.

51 Ibid., 50.

52 Ibid., 43.

53 Pavel cites Robert Howell's objection that "[the modal analogy] would entail the implausible conclusion that the author, Dickens for instance, did not create Mr. Pickwick but rather 'identified' him by inspecting the possible world to which the gentle bachelor belongs" (48).

54 Ibid., 57.

55 Ibid., 60.

56 Ibid., 24.

57 The lover appears beside the mime in ibid., 24.

58 Ibid., 73.

59 Ibid., 107 (my emphasis).

60 Hilary Putnam in the "Foreword to the Fourth Edition," vii.

61 Goodman, *Fact, Fiction, and Forecast*, 3.

62 Ibid., 5.

63 Ibid., 35

64 Ibid., 51.

65 Ibid., 56–57.

66 "I shall use the term 'lawlike' for sentences that, whether or not they are true, satisfy the other requirements in the definition of law" (ibid., 22). A refinement: "A sentence is lawlike if its acceptance does not depend upon the determination of any given instance" (23).

67 Ibid., 83.

68 Ibid., 73, 77.

69 Ibid., 19.

70 Ibid., 82.

71 Ibid., 83.

72 Ibid., "Note to the Fourth Edition, 1983," xxiv.

73 Ibid., "Note to the Third Edition, 1973," xxi–xxii.

74 Kurt Hubner, *Critique of Scientific Reason*, trans. Paul R. Dixon and Hollis M. Dixon (Chicago: University of Chicago Press, 1983), 163–64.

75 Rorty, "Is There a Problem," 35–36.

76 Goodman, *Fact, Fiction, and Forecast*, 122–24.

77 Cf. Rorty, "Is There a Problem," xlvii: "I think that Goodman's trope of 'many [actual] worlds' is misleading. . . . But his point that there is no way to compare descriptions of the world in respect of adequacy seems to me crucial."

78 Goodman, *Ways of Worldmaking* (Indianapolis, Ind.: Hackett Publishing, 1978), 103–5. Abstract works "*refer* by exemplification and expression" (105).

79 Ibid., 104.

80 Goodman, *The Languages of Art: An Approach to a Theory of Symbols* (Indianapolis: Hackett Publishing, 1986), 241–44.

81 Rorty, "Is There a Problem," 137.

82 Goodman, *Ways of Worldmaking*, 140.

83 Masochist induction and the mimetic double bind have suggestive analogies in game theory, for example in versions of "prisoner's dilemma." I discuss some of these in "A Glance at SunSet," 235–36 (noting that game theory expresses the mimetic double bind mathematically in terms of a contradiction between the axioms of determinacy and of choice).

3 Lying for No Reason

1 Cited in Madeleine Kahn, *Narrative Tranvestism: Rhetoric and Gender in the Eighteenth-Century English Novel* (Ithaca: Cornell University Press, 1991), 64.

2 Michel Seidel, *Robinson Crusoe: Island Myths and the Novel* (Boston: Twayne Publishers, 1991), 23.

3 Lincoln Faller, *Crime and Defoe: A New Kind of Writing* (Cambridge: Cambridge University Press, 1993), 75.

4 Faller regards the "question of whether Defoe was a 'conscious' or 'accidental'

artist" as being "(to me) unprofitable" (ibid., 73). Be that as it may, we may stress the difficulty of deciding.

5   Michael Boardman, for example, claims that "Defoe wrote for readers who affirmed an absolute and perhaps unbridgeable chasm between fact and fiction, history and deception," in *Defoe and the Uses of Narrative* (New Brunswick: Rutgers University Press, 1983), 62.

6   Faller, *Crime and Defoe*, xii.

7   Seidel, *Robinson Crusoe*, 21.

8   Ibid.

9   See Laura A. Curtis, *The Elusive Daniel Defoe* (London: Vision and Barnes and Noble, 1984), 138–39, for a discussion of Watt, Booth, and (in opposition) Maximillian Novak.

10 Seidel, *Robinson Crusoe*, 21.

11 Novak and Starr as cited in Curtis, *The Elusive Daniel Defoe*, 136n6.

12 Seidel, *Robinson Crusoe*, 21.

13 Cf. P. N. Furbank and W. R. Owens, *The Canonization of Daniel Defoe* (New Haven: Yale University Press, 1988), 100ff.

14 Cf. ibid., 177.

15 Ibid., 167. I am thinking of studies like that by Katherine A. Armstrong, *Defoe: Writer as Agent* (Victoria, B.C.: University of Victoria, 1996), 9–29.

16 Curtis, *The Elusive Daniel Defoe*, 135.

17 Faller cites Bran Djikstra's "peculiarly simple-minded *Defoe and Economics: The Fortunes of Roxana in the History of Interpretation*" in this connection (*Crime and Defoe*, 119n).

18 For example, J. R. Hammond still "supports Ian Watt's contention that 'there is certainly nothing in *Moll Flanders* which clearly indicates that Defoe saw the story differently from his heroine'" (Hammond, *A Defoe Companion* [Lanham, Md.: Barnes & Noble, 1993], 99). Ian Bell, in *Defoe's Fiction* (London: Croom Helm, 1985), regards *Crusoe*, despite "rare signs of a move toward the ironic mode," as essentially mimetic, while *Moll* "is never simply ironic or mimetic, but flits between these two modes" (111, 117). For Seidel, "the irony to which [Defoe] is drawn helps place the action of [*Crusoe*] in the context of those contingencies that make up a texture for realism or psychological realism." However, contra Seidel, for whom the preface to the *Serious Reflections of Robinson Crusoe* provides "a potent theory of realism" (*Robinson Crusoe*, 31), Laura Curtis eschews discussion of Defoe's "general theory of fiction" as being suspiciously ex post facto (*The Elusive Daniel Defoe*, 103). Meanwhile, Michael Boardman regards the trajectory from *Crusoe* to *Roxana* as a development "from fact to fiction, from the illusion of truth to structured fantasy," suggesting that "Defoe never wrote a coherent traditional novel" (Boardman, *Defoe and the Uses of Narrative*, 23, 30), and that by attending to "what Defoe does *not* do" we may avoid "self-confirming theories of 'irony'" and recognize that commonly in Defoe "the [interpretive] 'circle' remains firmly closed and resistant to interpretation" (Boardman, *Defoe and the Uses of Narrative*, 37, 62, 36).

19 Seidel, *Robinson Crusoe*, 31.

20 Boardman, *Defoe and the Uses of Narrative*, 32–33.

21 Armstrong, *Defoe: Writer as Agent*, 101.

22 Ibid., 113, 129.

23   Ibid., 114.
24   Faller, *Crime and Defoe*, 138.
25   Ibid., 42.
26   Ibid., 132–36.
27   Ibid., 164.
28   Ibid., 195.
29   Ibid., 253.
30   Cited from Macherey in ibid., 198.
31   Ibid., 199.
32   Søren Kierkegaard, *Either/Or*, vol. 1, trans. David F. Swenson and Lillian Marvin Swenson, rev. Howard A. Johnson (Princeton: Princeton University Press, 1959), 295.
33   Faller, *Crime and Defoe*, 87.
34   Cf. ibid., 18ff., 141ff., 153ff., 186ff.
35   I consulted two 1724 editions, both attributed on the title pages to Captain Charles Johnson (presumably Daniel Defoe) with titles (considerably shortened here): *A General History of the Robberies and Murders Of the most notorious Pyrates* (London: Printed for Ch. Rivington at the Bible and Crown in St. Paul's Church-Yard, J. Lacy at the Ship near the Temple-Gate, and J. Stone next to the Crown Coffee-house the back of Greys-Inn), pp. A1–A5, and *A General History of the Pirates* (London: Printed for, and sold by T. Warner, at the Black Boy in Pater-Noster Row), pp. A1–A5.
36   *Memoirs Of A Cavalier: Or A Military Journal of the Wars in Germany And The Wars in England, From the Year 1632, to the Year 1648.* Written Threescore Years ago by an English Gentleman, who served first in the Army of Gustavus Adolphus, the glorious King of Sweden, till his Death; and after that, in the Royal Army of King Charles the First, from the Beginning of the Rebellion, to the End of that War (London: Printed for A. Bell at the Cross Keys in Cornhill, J. Osborn at the Oxford Arms in Lombard-Street, W. Taylor at the Ship and Swan, and T. Warner at the Black Boy in Pater-Noster-Row, 1720), pp. A1–A3.
37   Armstrong, *Defoe: Writer as Agent*, 30.
38   Ibid., 45.
39   Faller, *Crime and Defoe*, 78–79.
40   Faller generalizes this problem to the novels, which are said to "go too far or not far enough," providing a "seeming 'openness' and 'incoherence' . . . both dizzying and fascinating . . . both familiar and strange" (*Crime and Defoe*, 50).
41   Defoe, *The History of Colonel Jack*, Shakespeare Head edition reprinted (London: William Clowes and Sons, 1974).
42   Faller, *Crime and Defoe*, 90.
43   Ibid., 89.
44   Ibid., 81.
45   Ibid., 90.
46   Defoe, *Moll Flanders*, ed. Edward Kelly (New York: Norton Critical Edition, 1973), 3–6. Kelly glosses "garbl'd" as "sifted."
47   Faller, *Crime and Defoe*, 78.
48   Armstrong, *Defoe: Writer as Agent*, 78.
49   Ibid., 70–73.
50   By contrast, the unanimity of eighteenth-century abridgements of *Moll* in bring-

ing her to an "unambiguously penitent death" (Faller, *Crime and Defoe*, 105–6) is striking.

51 Ibid., 106.

52 Faller more generously claims that these possible sequels illustrate how "Defoe's criminal protagonists move through a swirl of other sensibilities" (*Crime and Defoe*, 99).

53 Ibid., 106.

54 An ingenious apologist might conceivably argue that since the later part of Moll's life exhibited diminished penitence, such tepid virtue was likely to be of less aesthetic interest than extremes of either crime or remorse. But neither the preface nor the novel offers much support for such a hypothesis.

55 Having destroyed part 2 of *Dead Souls* (modeled on Dante's tripartite *Divine Comedy*), Gogol left us only part 1: hell.

56 Furbank and Owens, *The Canonization of Daniel Defoe*, 146.

57 Furbank and Owens, however, speak of "retrospective form" (ibid., 133) as characteristic in Defoe.

58 *The Serious Reflections During the Life and Surprising Adventures of Robinson Crusoe* (London: B. Yeats and J. M. Dent, 1985), 99, my emphases. References hereafter in the text.

59 Ian Bell emphasizes the incompatibility of the critics: in contrast to the spiritual interpretations of Starr and Hunter, "John J. Richetti talks of Crusoe's religious experiences as symptoms of schizophrenia; and Pierre Macherey refers to providence in the book as 'a mere smoke screen' " (Bell, *Defoe's Fiction*, 76).

60 Seidel, *Robinson Crusoe*, 31.

61 Michael Shinagel in the Norton critical edition of volume 1 (New York: W. W. Norton, 1975), 3, glosses "dispatch'd" as "quickly thrown aside." The prefaces to vols. 1, 2, and 3 are reprinted on pages 3, 258–59, and 259–62, respectively.

62 Perhaps because of its obscurity, some early editions give "disputed" instead of "dispatch'd." But this, even if the correct reading, does not alter my point (since the reconciliation of fiction and history would now take place on the even more dubious grounds of "disputes" about their very relation).

63 Shakespeare's phrase in the Sonnets.

64 Pat Rogers, *Robinson Crusoe* (London: George Allen and Unwin, 1979), 67.

65 Seidel, *Robinson Crusoe*, 77.

66 Views cited in the Norton critical edition, 299, 295.

67 J. M. Coetzee, *Foe* (London: Penguin, 1987), 121–22.

68 In *Foe*, the spelling is "Cruso," like Defoe's school friend mentioned above.

69 Valéry, as we shall see in chapter 4, was well aware of the duplicitous character of Stendhal's "realism."

70 Interestingly, Piaget found that children as old as six "equate swearing (naughty words) with lying" (Ford, *Lies! Lies!! Lies!!!*, 78).

71 Hence the pertinence of Faller's observation, in connection with *Roxana*, that "shame not only follows sin, but—and this is most interesting—it prompts Roxana into further sin" (*Crime and Defoe*, 225).

4 Lies and Truth

1 Stendhal, "Sur *Le Rouge et le noir*" (1832), in *Le Rouge et le noir: Chronique du XIXe siècle*, ed. Henri Martineau (Paris: Garnier Freres, 1960), 526. My translation.

2 Gérard Genette, as cited by Stirling Haig in *Stendhal: The Red and the Black* (Cambridge: Cambridge University Press, 1989), 50.

3 *Henry Brulard,* as cited in ibid., 3.

4 Emile Talbot, *Stendhal Revisited* (New York: Twayne Publishers, 1993), 70.

5 Ann Jefferson, *Reading Realism in Stendhal* (Cambridge: Cambridge University Press, 1988), 35 (my emphasis).

6 I shall refer to the English translation by Yvonne Freccero, *Deceit, Desire, and the Novel* (Baltimore: Johns Hopkins University Press, 1965).

7 Jefferson, *Reading Realism,* 111.

8 Ibid., 26; Haig, *Stendhal,* 42.

9 For an acute discussion of the relation between history and fiction in a Stendhalian context, see Jefferson Humphries, *The Red and the Black: Mimetic Desire and the Myth of Celebrity* (Boston: Twayne Publishers, 1991), 82ff.

10 Talbot, *Stendhal Revisited,* 62, 61.

11 Jefferson, *Reading Realism,* 231.

12 Humphries, *The Red and the Black,* 32.

13 Ibid., 34.

14 Robert Adams, in his Norton edition of the novel, observes that the mirror formula "is less true of Stendhal's own novels than of most others." (See *Red and Black,* trans. Robert Adams [New York: W. W. Norton, 1969], 60n.) Subsequent references to this edition appear in the text.

15 Jefferson, *Reading Realism,* 33.

16 Ibid., 24.

17 Humphries, *The Red and the Black,* 77.

18 Ibid. (citing Felman), 77.

19 Humphries makes the Girardian point that "mimetic desire enforces conformity by championing the individual," that what Girard calls "negative mimesis" (self-definition in opposition to the mimetic other) is no less thoroughly mimetic than its "positive" variety.

20 Christopher Prendergast, *The Order of Mimesis: Balzac, Stendhal, Nerval, Flaubert* (Cambridge: Cambridge University Press, 1986), 140.

21 Ibid., 146, 141.

22 Prendergast invokes the Platonic *pharmakon:* "Mimesis is excommunicated not because it is a threat to truth, but because it is a threat to order" (10).

23 David F. Bell, *Circumstances: Chance in the Literary Text* (Lincoln: University of Nebraska Press, 1993), 1.

24 Prendergast, *The Order of Mimesis,* 229.

25 Humphries, *The Red and the Black,* 35.

26 Ibid., 93.

27 Haig, *Stendhal,* 45. Prendergast, *The Order of Mimesis,* 125–26.

28 Jefferson, *Reading Realism,* 123.

29 Humphries, *The Red and the Black,* 68–69.

30 Prendergast, *The Order of Mimesis,* 126. (Though Humphries might doubtless rejoin that "realism" is a highly historical category.)

31 Valéry, "Stendhal," as cited in the Norton edition, 561–62.

32 From Paul Valéry's "Stendhal" as translated by Adams in the Norton Critical Edition of *Red and Black,* 561.

33 Humphries, *The Red and the Black,* 79.

34 Jefferson, *Reading Realism,* 39–40.

35 Epigraph to part 1 of the novel.

36 The link between the medicinal glass ("verre") and realism is supported by Humphries (74), who links the town *Verrieres* to realist metaphor in *Le Rouge*.

37 *Lucien Leuwen*, ed. Henri Martineau (Paris: Gallimard, 1973), 54 (translation and emphasis mine). Prendergast comments in a different context: "Consensual politics entail the impoverishing prospect of consensual art" (*The Order of Mimesis*, 121).

38 Valéry, "Stendhal," 561–62.

39 "Although Girard does not spend much time discussing the realist aesthetic, his argument reinforces the similarity between desire and realist fiction that emerges from Stendhal's writing" (Jefferson, *Reading Realism*, 49). This Girardian inheritance is everywhere implicit in Humphries.

40 Jefferson, for instance, associates a "passion for the real" with "Saint-Beuve who speaks of 'ce besoin presque unanime de vérité' " of the epoque (30).

41 Girard, *Deceit, Desire, and the Novel*, 177–78.

42 Ibid., 155 (my emphasis). He gives as preliminary example the episode where Julien gratuitously hangs his arm in a sling for a week after his picture of Napoleon has been found.

43 Cf. Prendergast, *The Order of Mimesis*, 135–36.

44 Kierkegaard's "The Rotation Method," in *Either/Or*, develops a similar concept of boredom.

45 Humphries, *The Red and the Black*, 42–43.

46 Adams's translation, though plausible enough, obscures (by adding "feminine") the genderless symmetry of their respective "timidities."

47 Jefferson, to my knowledge, is one of the few critics to emphasize the global significance of this pattern, observing that Mme. de Rênal's harrowing interpretation of her child's sickness reveals "a kind of double bind, in which her ignorance and the degree of her suffering are mutually correlated guarantees of her authenticity," and that "right up to the end [she] remains a victim of the discourses which so unadvantageously structure her life" (Jefferson, *Reading Realism*, 85).

48 Jefferson confirms that Mathilde's joke applies even better to Julien than to Count Altimira, with whom it is originally associated.

49 Humphries, *The Red and the Black*, 91.

50 The resemblances are helpfully summarized by Haig (*Stendhal*, 13–17).

51 Humphries, *The Red and the Black*, 73.

52 Ibid., 71.

53 Humphries, for example, claims that "there is no askesis for Julien, as there should be in any proper tragedy" (72).

54 Talbot (*Stendhal Revisited*, 58–59), for example, treats this episode in term of the "play" of the text, citing Armond Hoog's observation that the two names are also anagrams of *Je lis un rôle* ("I play a part").

55 Humphries, *The Red and the Black*, 73.

56 Of the latter, perhaps Henri Martineau comes closest to truly Stendhalian bravado in his claim that Julien's state prior to the murder is one of somnabulism (a state induced by shock), and that "divining . . . by instinct" the future of medical knowledge on this subject, Stendhal succeeded in remaining "faithful to his ideal of imitating nature." Cf. Martineau's *L'oeuvre de Stendhal: histoire de ses livres et de sa pensée* (Paris: Michel, 1945), as cited by Adams in the Norton *Red and Black*, 151–52.

57 Jefferson, *Reading Realism*, 88. Regarding the violence of the mimetic *doxa*, she is referring specifically to the fact that Mme. de Rênal's letter of denunciation is dictated by her confessor.

58 Humphries, *The Red and the Black*, 73.

59 Haig, *Stendhal*, 32.

60 In a letter to Mathilde, Julien cites the words of Shakespeare's Iago I referred to in chapter 1—"From this time forth I will never speak word" (365)—as though participating in Frilair's scapegoating solution to his own willful unintelligibility. Stendhal revised Julien's immediately subsequent thought, "I am going to die," to "I *must* die" (365, my emphasis).

61 It is worth mentioning, perhaps, that the gothic mode is associated with both violence of theme and irregularity of form.

62 Girard, *Deceit, Desire, and the Novel*, 145–46.

63 Ibid., 19.

64 Ibid., 173.

65 Ibid., 139 (my emphasis), 22 (my emphasis).

66 Drawing attention to the double meaning of *lunette* (semicircular window/guillotine-aperture), he generalizes: "The guillotine would thus represent the central governing metaphor of mimetic realism (the transparent window or lens), and Julien gets caught in this metaphor . . . so that when closure comes, as it is bound (formally) to do, it must split him into two pieces, one on the side of naive mimeticism, and one on the side of an ironic skepticism with regard to mimetic conventions. . . . Julien's head is severed by the glass(es) he has finally broken through" (Humphries, *The Red and the Black*, 75–76).

67 Ibid., 75.

68 Ibid., 88–90.

69 Ibid., 57.

70 Jefferson regards Stendhal's treatment of both Julien and Mme. de Rênal as implying that neither should be models for us (91).

71 Girard, *Deceit, Desire, and the Novel*, 311. Certainly Stendhal provides us with his own "deviated" sacrificial versions of aesthetico-religious transcendence, as for instance when the king visits the *chapelle ardente* at Verrieres: "His majesty flung himself, rather than placing himself, on a low stool. Only then did Julien, drawn back against the gilded door, perceive, under the bare arm of a girl, the enchanting statue of St. Clement. He was concealed beneath the altar, wearing the costume of a young Roman soldier. A wide wound appeared on his neck, from which the blood seemed to flow. The artist had quite outdone himself; the Saint's dying eyes, still full of grace, were half closed. A budding moustache adorned that charming mouth, which, though half closed, still seemed to be praying. Seeing this, the girl beside Julien wept bitterly; one of her tears fell warm on Julien's hand" (87).

72 Girard, *Deceit, Desire, and the Novel*, 311. But the later Girard gives up claims to the "purely novelistic" or indeed "literary" (see my appendix).

73 See the appendix.

74 See the appendix for brief discussion of Girard's later relinquishing of the notion of nonsacrificial transcendence.

75 Humphries, *The Red and the Black*, 77.

76 Girard, *Deceit, Desire, and the Novel*, 22.

77 Ibid., 165.

78 "Julien's desire is structured in such a way that he must be destroyed by his own

success. . . . One cannot become a perfect object of desire except by being absent or, even better (because absolutely absent, unattainable, *lost*), dead. To quote Proust again, 'The only true paradises are the ones that have been lost' " (Humphries, *The Red and the Black*, 72–73).

79 Stendhal (D. Gruffot Papera), "Sur *Le Rouge et le noir*," 526. This is the same Papera who emphasizes, indeed exaggerates, the difference between the two women, who insists that the novel is an accurate reflection of contemporary life in Paris and the provinces, who seems particularly concerned with the feminine readers of the novel, and who falsifies the date and place of Berthet's execution.

80 Jefferson, *The Red and the Black*, 91.

81 Ibid., 84.

82 Girard, *Deceit, Desire, and the Novel*, 185.

83 Ibid., 170.

5 Fundaments and Accidents

1 Samuel Beckett, *Proust and Three Dialogues with Georges Duthuit* (London: John Calder, 1987), 76.

2 Samuel Beckett, *Molloy, Malone Dies, The Unnamable* (London: Calder Publications, 1994), 87–88. Subsequent references to page numbers of this edition appear in my text.

3 Contrast with Girard's antisacrificial Catholicism, however, should be modified by Girard's own contention that the history of Christianity has been in large part the history of falsely sacrificial interpretations.

4 *Molloy* (Paris: Editions de Minuit, 1951), 39. In Beckett's English version: "Chameleon in spite of himself, there you have Molloy, viewed from a certain angle" (30).

5 For a more extended mimetic-sacrificial epistemology in the context of science, see Michel Serres, *Les Origines de la géométrie* (Paris: Flammarion, 1993). I deal with Beckett's mathematical imagery later in this chapter, but also more directly in "A Glance at SunSet: Numerical Fundaments in Frege, Wittgenstein, Shakespeare, Beckett," in *Mathematics, Science, and Postclassical Theory*, ed. Barbara Herrnstein Smith and Arkady Plotnitsky (Durham: Duke University Press, 1997).

6 Leo Bersani and Ulysse Dutoit, *Arts of Impoverishment: Beckett, Rothko, Renais* (Cambridge: Harvard University Press, 1993), 12.

7 Stanley Cavell, *Must We Mean What We Say?* (Cambridge: Cambridge University Press, 1969), 115.

8 Martin Esslin, the well-known Beckett scholar, as cited on the back cover of *The Expelled and Other Novellas* (London: Penguin Books, 1980).

9 Bersani and Dutoit, *Arts of Impoverishment*, 11.

10 Ibid., 17.

11 Beckett, *Proust and Three Dialogues with Georges Duthuit*, 111.

12 Cited by David Read in "Artistic Theory in the Work of Samuel Beckett," *Journal of Beckett Studies* 8 (1982): 22.

13 Theodor W. Adorno, *Notes to Literature*, vol. 1, ed. Rolf Tiedernmann, trans. Shierry Weter Nicholson (New York: Columbia University Press, 1991), 243.

14 Ibid., 244.

15 Ibid., 241.

16 Bersani and Dutoit, *Arts of Impoverishment,* 26.

17 Ibid., 62.

18 Ibid., 62.

19 Ibid., 63.

20 Their omission of any reference to Girard's theory makes it difficult to provide any succinct hypothesis as to their relation to it, though this kind of omission is common in intellectual politics surrounding Girardian material. See, for example, my discussion of Michel Serres in "A Glance at SunSet," 238n. I will note my own disagreements with Bersani and Dutoit later.

21 Bersani and Dutoit, *Arts of Impoverishment,* 88–89.

22 Among others, Jean Yamasaki Toyami, in *Beckett's Game: Self and Language in the Trilogy* (Baltimore: Johns Hopkins University Press, 1991), also cites this passage, but omits the extermination clause (69)—despite his insistence that Molloy "associate[s] death with words" (24), that "writing is the act of mutilation" (58) in *Malone Dies,* and (in an explanation armed with a reference to Derrida) that language is associated with death because it replaces things (92). Toyami admits that to write without expressing is "an impossibility" (38), but his characterization of Malone's fictions as "a discontinuous rambling of stories left hanging . . . resisting reduction to a meaning" (48–49), as well as his emphasis on Beckett's supposed "free play" (19), suggests that his ostensibly Derridean understanding of the relation of language and violence blinds him (as I will try to show in chapter 6) to Malone's frighteningly single-minded sacrificial continuity and coherence.

23 This does not contradict the many critical commentaries that highlight religious references in part 1; rather I mean that in part 2, for instance, a priest is a character, the secular Countess Caca becomes the Turdy Madonna, discussion of the relation between belief and nonbelief is explicit, and so on.

24 Without submerging my text in a veritable sea of references, I cannot begin to take account of the many and often contradictory critical accounts of the relation of the two parts, but I will nevertheless note some parallels and contrasts immediately relevant to my own interpretation.

25 Cf. Beckett, *No's Knife: Collected Shorter Prose, 1945–1966* (London: Calder and Boyars, 1967). The title recalls "Texts for Nothing 8": "ah if no were content to cut yes's throat and never cut its own" (*Stories and Texts for Nothing* [New York: Grove Press, 1967], 113–14). I develop the sacrificial logic of negation in the context of philosophy of mathematics in "A Glance at SunSet," where I cite James Feibleman's claim that Boolean algebra demonstrates that the logical principle of difference, negation, or exclusion is more general than identity (238n). Among Beckett critics, Michael E. Mooney, for instance, has aptly noted "the negatives which form the novel's backbone," claiming even that "Beckett suggests a new method of reasoning" ("*Molloy,* Part I: Beckett's 'Discourse on Method,' " *Journal of Beckett Studies* 3 [summer 1979]: 48). But neither he nor anyone else, to my knowledge, has fully conjoined the principles of logical and sacrificial exclusion in this connection. In "A Glance at SunSet" (214–15), I discuss Michel Serres's Girardian conjunction of these principles in *Les Origines de la géométrie.*

26 Bersani and Dutoit cite as representative such critical formulae as "the breakdown, the disintegration of language" in a "meaningless universe" (*Arts of Impoverishment,* 13).

27 The skeptic sacrifices (the veracity of) others, while the dupe is sacrificed by them.

28 In "A Glance at SunSet" (230), I discuss Reichenbach's three-valued logic, specifically developed to describe quantum physics, in connection with Shakespeare's and Beckett's mimetic-sacrificial patterns.

29 John Locke, for instance, provides a classic instance of such comfort in his position that since "mixed-modes"—human categories like murder—are not in nature but purely nominalistic or invented, we cannot make mistakes about their meaning. (See *An Essay Concerning Human Understanding*, book 3, chapter 5).

30 Though Toyami calls "life without tears, as it is wept," "a false invention [that] lies in himself [Molloy], ready to be discovered" (*Beckett's Game*, 30), he fails to take account of the mimetic dimension of this "discovery."

31 Toyami claims that "Beckett asserts that words are not mere signs, that they stand for themselves" when "a word ceases to represent" (*Beckett's Game*, 38), whereas in representation "the word can be taken for the thing itself. Because it is exactly what it claims to represent, it engenders meaning" (86). I would argue precisely the contrary: a representational word is a "mere sign" that *cannot* "be taken for the thing itself," whereas signs that "stand for themselves" (if we accept such a locution) "engender" rather than merely represent meanings.

32 In Girard's masochist induction, "true" pain authenticates "true" love and vice versa.

33 Compare Beckett's dictum that "History, then, is . . . the result of a Necessity that is not Fate, of a liberty that is not Chance" (cited by David Read from Beckett's "Dante . . . Bruno, Vico . . . Joyce" [10]). We have seen that masochist induction, in Girard's sense, is a self-fulfilling prophecy; and I have used the word *arbitrariness* throughout this study to suggest liberty (*arbitrium*) as well as chance.

34 This parrot is reminiscent of Flaubert's Loulou in *Un Coeur Simple*, like whom it turns into the "paraclete, psittaceously named" (250) in *Malone Dies*.

35 Thus I cannot agree with Toyami's contention that invention is no longer associated with discovery in *Malone Dies* (*Beckett's Game*, 47), but rather with fictional "free play." His claim that Malone "makes no effort to impart a truth or a fact, much less to represent a reality" (46) wholly ignores the distinction between truth and fact made explicit here.

36 I note again a contrast with David F. Bell's realistic thesis concerning accident in *Circumstances: Chances in the Literary Text* (Lincoln: University of Nebraska Press, 1993), discussed in the previous chapter. Bersani and Dutoit attempt to avoid the realistic fallacy and emphasize the sacrificial element, but their attempt to resolve the mimetic problem, while suggestive, seems opaque: "Literature imitates something fundamental that does not depend on literature but that might never have taken place without the literary repetition of it" (*Arts of Impoverishment*, 61). Moreover, this formulation ("does not depend on" and "might") suggests precisely "contingency-determined behavior," which they explicitly contrast with the "truth" of "Beckettian behavior" (41). I return to this problem in chapter 6; here it must suffice to say that "literary" remains an ambiguous category.

37 Stanley Cavell attributes to Beckett a tendency toward literalization that "shares with positivism its wish to escape connotation, the noncognitive, the irrationality and awkward memories of ordinary language" (118). Here, however, such "awkward memories" are *enforced* by the literalization: "Only Beckett sees how infinitely difficult this escape will be. Positivism said that statements about God are meaningless; Beckett shows that they mean too damn much" (*Must We Mean What We Say?* 110).

38 Cf. the final line of Kafka's "A Country Doctor": "A false alarm on the night bell once answered—it cannot be made good, not ever." *Complete Stories* (New York: Schocken Books, 1971), 225.

39 I discuss this passage in somewhat different terms in "A Glance at SunSet," 234.

40 Mooney, "*Molloy*, Part I," 54.

41 Ibid.

42 My reading contrasts with Toyami's chapter "Describing the Circle," where the circle "serves as a metaphor for the self in *Molloy*," the "relationship between the center and the circumference is unknowable because both seem in continuous interplay, even free play" (19), and where "neither [Molloy nor Moran] will be boxed into a definition or representation; each will continue his journey, searching for what (?), finding naught" (*Beckett's Game*, 40). I am closer to David Read: "The fact that the absolute centre of a circle can never be identified does not prevent the geometrician from basing his calculations upon it" ("Artistic Theory," 13)— though Read's analogy with Molloy's view of anthropology's "inexhaustible faculty of negation" (13) seems to underestimate the exclusionary logic at issue.

43 Many comic writers from Aristophanes onward deploy the anus comparably, including Shakespeare, whose "law of the ass" I discuss in chapter 7, and in "A Glance at SunSet" (228–30).

44 Adorno, *Notes to Literature*, 274.

45 *First Love and Other Shorts* (New York: Grove Press, 1974), 53.

46 Though both are "real" (as opposed to "imaginary") numbers in mathematical terminology, "transcendentals" differ from "irrationals" in not being solutions to any rational equation. I discuss *Molloy* in a mathematical context in "A Glance at SunSet," where, among other things, I cite Wittgenstein's skepticism regarding any conceivable ("Russellian") proof concerning the existence of a given sequence in π by apogogic proof, *excluding its exclusion* ("A Glance at Sunset," 227), and his consequent "sacrifice" of the real numbers as such. We will return to Beckett's treatment of the relation of the transcendental and the arbitrary later.

47 This parallels the emphasis on "difference" made by such Derrida-influenced critics as Toyami and Richard Begam (cited in note 52). But the connection with specifically sacrificial exclusion is never, to my knowledge, adequately recognized.

48 Cf. "A Glance at SunSet," 232, for a slightly more elaborate discussion of this passage.

49 Christian Pringent remarks, in "A Descent from Clowns," *Journal of Beckett Studies* 3.1 (autumn 1993), that the anus is "not even the Freudian emblem of 'everything that is forbidden'" (8), but rather the emblem "of the negative, the pataphysical and unnamable traces, the parodic, obsessional manifestations of the irreducible other" (8). But, if Molloy's anus is sign of the "irreducible otherness" critics like to see in Beckett, he is nevertheless, as I have emphasized, "mimetic *in spite of himself*." Similarly, Beckett's use of the term *symbol* in this central passage belies critics' frequent invocation of the conclusion of *Watt*—"no symbols where none intended"—to deny symbolicity (and allegory) in general in favor of a "principle of uncertainty" (Andrew Kennedy, *Samuel Beckett* [Cambridge: Cambridge University Press, 1989], 124).

50 Mooney, "*Molloy*, Part I," 47. J. D. O'Hara also ignores the specificity of these "mathematical games" when he reduces them all to repression ("Jung and the 'Molloy' Narrative," in *The Beckett Studies Reader*, ed. S. E. Gontarski [Gainesville: University of Florida Press, 1993], 144).

51 Read, "Artistic Theory," 21.

52 Richard Begam, in *Samuel Beckett and the End of Modernity* (Stanford: Stanford University Press, 1996), cites the phrase that the charcoal burner "would have been younger by as much" as evidence that he is Molloy's "vestigial self" (117), though this is a matter of simple mathematics whoever he is! His note (210, n.24) acknowledges the departure from ordinary mathematics, but claims "there is nothing surprising in this; the game throughout has involved a play of identity *and* difference." Admittedly Begam's parallel with Moran and his double gives this generalization plausibility, but he seems to ignore the patent falsity of the calculation.

53 Cf. note 49, above.

54 Where musical concord is described as "a cup of peace in common before the battle" (*Complete Stories*, 367). In "Music-Theory in Late Kafka," *Angelaki* 3.2 (1997), I analyze Kafka's mimetic-sacrificial treatment of music.

55 We may recall Molloy's distinction between formal and aesthetic (or artistic) views cited earlier.

56 Once again Adorno, in the context of *Endgame*, obliquely hits the nail on the head: "Differentiatedness cannot absolutely and without reflection be entered on the positive side of the ledger" (*Notes to Literature*, 248). Sylvie Deberec Henning, citing Jung rather than *Molloy*, notes that one way to deal with doubles is "to remove or subjugate them in some way, to 'kill' them, as it were. The double thus becomes a kind of scapegoat" (*Beckett's Critical Complicity: Carnival, Contestation, and Tradition* [Lexington: University Press of Kentucky, 1988], 125). But, though more than pertinent here, she does not make Adorno's crucial generalization to the principle of differentiation as such. Similarly, James Acheson's appeal to Jung, however relevant, fails to recognize the general trans-Jungian sacrificial principle at stake (*Samuel Beckett's Artistic Theory and Practice* [New York: St. Martin's, 1997], 100ff.). Finally, Richard Begam's chapter on *Molloy*, "Beckett's Mirror-Writing" (*Samuel Beckett and the End of Modernity*, 98–119), pursues a Derridean trajectory, without, however, acknowledging that the "playful" metaphysics or antimetaphysics of *différance* must be reconceptualized in the sober light of the sacrificial *production* of difference. It is precisely mimetic identity, *not* difference, that is "repressed."

57 The final line of "The Expelled" (*Stories and Texts for Nothing*, 25).

58 For purposes of comparison and contrast with psychoanalytic accounts of gender-production, note also that the hole in Moran's hat turns into a "slit" only after the differential process has been inaugurated in this anonymous mimetic violence. Of course, Freudians, Jungians, etc. may always choose to read the abstract mimetic model as a "repression" of the relevant psychoanalytic specifics. Beckett's texts (like the virulently anti-Freudian Nabokov's) allow and even encourage this mirror-game, as in the "Obidil" of part 2. We will return to Freud later.

59 Cf. Begam, *Samuel Beckett and the End of Modernity*, and also Phil Baker's Freudian and Lacanian essay "The Stamp of the Father in *Molloy*," *Journal of Beckett Studies* 5.1–2 (1996): 143–55.

60 Cf. my discussion, in the introduction, of Derrida's linkage of violence to the closure of representation. Beyond Derrida, we may think of various postmodernist positions with a liberational dimension, including those that interpret Beckett's supposed refusal of representation in liberational terms.

61 Earlier in the novel Gaber is described as a "high mass" (94), further emphasizing the sacrificial dimension of all such "masses."

62 One irony here is that if "ditches" mean what they mean in Flann O'Brien ("the crotch of a ditch"), then Molloy, as O'Hara and others have noted, ends with a "final comic image of his mother's womb" ("Jung and the 'Molloy' Narrative," 144)—or at least crotch.

63 Flann O'Brien, *The Third Policeman* (New York: Plume Books, 1976), 54. Whether or not Beckett read O'Brien, he shares his sacrificial teeth, gammy legs, and mimetic bi-cycles with his compatriot. The bicycle connection is made, though in a comically literal manner, by Janet Menzies in "Beckett's Bicycles," *Journal of Beckett Studies* 6 (autumn 1980): 97–105.

64 The bi-cuspid is predictable. There is also a pun on *dressed* in the sense of acculturated (and hidden).

65 Phil Baker recognizes this ("The Stamp of the Father in *Molloy*," 151), but sees only evidence of abstract repetition, not of transcendentalism.

66 Notably in Greenaway's films *The Draughtsman's Contract* and *Drowning by Numbers* (in which sheep are also numerical). Steven Connor astonishingly and utterly wrongly claims, in "Beckett's Animals," *Journal of Beckett Studies* 8 (1982): 37, that "there seems to be only one conspicuous example in the whole of Beckett's fiction of the emblematic use of an animal"!

67 Beckett, *First Love and Other Shorts* (New York: Grove Press, 1974), 15.

68 Angela Moorjani's description of the novel's analysis of "a radical exteriority" in terms of a demystification of the sacred is much to the point here ("A Crypto-analysis of Beckett's *Molloy*," in *The World of Samuel Beckett*, ed. Joseph H. Smith [Baltimore: Johns Hopkins University Press, 1991], 64), especially in connection with "Molloy/Moran's lying texts detailing falsely circular journeys" (64) and the "dying god" motif of the Molloy "subtext" (63), notably the burial of Lousse's dog/god and her alternate name Loy (law).

69 A quasi-conspicuous part of Moran's joke: "Conspicuousness is the A B C of my profession" (125).

70 This principle is connected with Moran's mistaken decision to leave on his "auto-cycle" (99). The pleasure principle is "autonomous," whereas Moran will later ride on a bi-cycle/tandem. (The early Freud posited the pleasure principle alone, without the so-called death drive which he introduced to account for masochism.)

71 Once again Toyami seems blind to the principle, citing this passage only as an "expression of this sexual and excremental combination" ("Beckett's Game," 99). But I have no wish to scapegoat him, since I have not found the passage better interpreted by others.

72 Cf. Smyth, "A Glance at SunSet," 228ff.

73 Cf. "Fashion is . . . nothing to a man" (*Much Ado about Nothing*, 3.3.115–16).

74 Moorjani aptly writes that Moran finally speaks of a language that is neither divine nor human, "yet to be decrypted" ("A Cryptoanalysis of Beckett's *Molloy*," 64).

75 Cf. also: "Happily I had mended my hat [whose hole has earlier become a slit], or the wind would have blown it away" (158). The Freudian "slit," source of Oedipal rivalry, disappears. My reading may be contrasted with Menzies's claim that "in the trilogy the picture of a real man [*sic*] on a real bicycle [*sic*] provides Beckett with an image of the method by which he may come nearest to confronting his

problems of self expression" ("Beckett's Bicycles," 103), and that "Moran's sense of elation stems from a sense that the real may also be the ideal" (105).

76 Reginald McGinnis, in "Samuel Beckett: un pèlerinage au-delà du romanesque," *L'Atelier du roman* 16 (winter 1998–99): 111–22, notes that there is a madonna in a (French) town called Turdy in George Sand's *Mademoiselle La Quintinie*. The joke is hidden in the French version of *Molloy*, where the town is called Shit. I have no space here to follow up on this original connection.

77 In case the moral seem too bleak, however, this indictment of heterosexuality as mendacious is modified by the sole explicit parabasis at this point (138). In mentioning characters from his other fictions, Beckett formally signals that this staging of heterosexual love as *simply* a lie is itself invented.

78 Cf. the pun on "sacral ruins" and "sacrum" in "Enough" (*First Love and Other Shorts*, 57, 59). (The sacrum is attached to the pelvic bone.)

79 Here I disagree with Moorjani's view that Moran represses his godlessness and "projects it onto Jacques, whom he suspects of skipping mass to play behind the slaughterhouse" ("A Cryptoanalysis of Beckett's *Molloy*," 63). Jacques *is* a modern atheist, substituting a secular sacrificial game for the religious one.

6 The Violence of Fiction

1 *Molloy, Malone Dies, The Unnamable* (London: Calder, 1994), 210. Subsequent references inserted in the text.

2 The question of whether the Eucharist is "merely symbolic," of course, defines a central aspect of the Reformation.

3 Balzac's *Louis Lambert*, which serves as concealed reference for one of Malone's characters (Louis in the French version, Lambert in the English), provides a subtext here. Balzac's narrator notes "the prodigious activity of [Louis's] spirit feeding on itself," and his voracious appetite for reading is also metaphorized in gastronomic terms. See Balzac, *Louis Lambert*, in vol. 25 of *Honoré de Balzac in Twenty-Five Volumes* (New York: Peter Fenelon Collier, 1900), 238, 182.

4 I cite from Reginald McGinnis, *La Prostitution sacrée: essai sur Baudelaire* (Paris: Belin, 1994), 31, 38. "Even if God didn't exist, religion would still be holy and *divine*." "If religion disappeared from the world, one would find it again in the heart of an atheist."

5 Critics have noted the ambivalent and potentially reversible character of this "play," including for instance Toyami and Begam (cited in the previous chapter). But their Derridean-style affirmation of play is not conducive to the blunt equation, which I have not seen noted in the criticism, between play and Sundays, as the sacred and sacrificial space as such (recalling Moran's suspicion that Jacques is "playing" by the slaughterhouse instead of going to mass). Begam's elision of the sacrificial structure of the text is all the more remarkable in that he cites Foucault on the relation of writing and sacrifice (*Samuel Beckett and the End of Modernity*, 125).

6 Like Moran's "clitoral" knee (which reflects on Molloy's "meaningless" description of the size of his knees), the eyes *are* significant, of course. They resemble his father's (and Beckett's), and also anticipate the seascape of the novel's climax.

7 Louis Lambert is especially concerned "to ascertain the real relation that may exist between God and man" (Balzac, *Louis Lambert*, 262).

8   This may be contrasted with Jean Toyami's *Beckett's Game*, cited in the previous chapter: "Malone's speech is fiction, not communication. He makes no effort to impart a truth or a fact, much less to represent a reality" (46).

9   As noted in the previous chapter, Steven Connor astonishingly claims that the "one conspicuous example in the whole of Beckett's fiction of the emblematic use of an animal" ("Beckett's Animals," 37) is Sapo's birds. Such critics as Hugh Kenner and James Acheson cite this passage about the ass, commenting respectively that "these are cautious affections that Malone is indulging" (*A Reader's Guide to Samuel Beckett* [New York: Farrar, Straus, and Giroux, 1973], 107), and "Like the child Malone, the ass has been made subject to someone else's idea of fun" (*Samuel Beckett's Artistic Theory and Practice*, 123). No one seems to connect the "operator's giggle" to the classic emblem of the ass as ironic self-portrait.

10   The connection with Sapiens and *skatos* (dung) has been made by many critics. Balzac's *Louis Lambert* speaks of *Homo Duplex* (222). Unfortunately, I cannot locate the text or critic in which I read the hypothesis regarding "scapegoat."

11   *Stories and Texts for Nothing* (New York: Grove Press, 1967), 10.

12   At the beginning of *The Unnamable* Malone is explicitly called "the god" (302). Toyami, among others, observes that Malone is "like a god" (*Beckett's Game*, 47); but his claim that accordingly "no longer is 'inventing' associated with 'finding'" (47), but rather with "free" creation, is belied by Beckett's inventive recasting of this oldest of stories. Toyami mentions Balzac's *Louis Lambert* as a reference in the novel, but without elaborating (49). Acheson helpfully notes that "Louis has by the age of five read both the Old and New Testaments" (*Samuel Beckett's Artistic Theory and Practice*, 121), but without making the connection with the Sapo/Macmann opposition, or drawing our attention to the fact that Louis holds that "not a book could be written . . . of which the subject might not . . . be discerned in its germ" in the combined scriptures of India, Greece, and Israel (Balzac, *Louis Lambert*, 248). The Bible, specifically, is called "blood-stained" poetry (248). Meanwhile, Begam correctly notes the "lapsarian epistemology" linked to Sapo and Macmann, but mentions only the Saposcats' garden in this connection (*Samuel Beckett and the End of Modernity*, 136–37), ignoring the central lapsarian allegory of Sapo's (non)expulsion.

13   Louis Lambert is similarly accused by his schoolmaster: "Lambert, you are doing nothing!"—which loses him his "play-time" (Balzac, 204–5). While his friend, the narrator, is earlier said to be the "least emulous" of the schoolboys, and thus "most frequently punished" (198–99), the two friends later learn exclusively by imitation of the other boys, which still earns them frequent punishment (205–6). This nicely suggests a mimetic double bind, since the narrator is punished both when he imitates and when he does not. The "imitative instinct" (213) is frequently at issue in Balzac's novel, as it is in Beckett.

14   Begam provides an acute half-truth: "What we finally confront with Sapo is something like a lapsarian epistemology in suspension: all the necessary elements have been assembled, but, purged of their significance, they now fail to cohere" (*Samuel Beckett and the End of Modernity*, 137). However, the text's coherence and significance lies in the fact that while expulsion does not take place along the lines of the Fall, Malone substitutes his own (human) scapegoating for divine expulsion. A sacrificial "lapsarianism"—all *too* significant and coherent—thus overlays the incoherence of the story.

15 Though many critics cite this passage about the winter window, I have not found any interpretation that confirms mine.

16 The "great calm"—"Great calm is an exaggeration. He felt better" (212)—that results from Sapo's witnessing the Lamberts' burial of a mule recalls the calm that follows Moran's murder of his double—a sacrificial "peace." Balzac's Louis Lambert, incidentally, suffers from a catalepsy that can leave him motionless for fifty-nine hours at a time (*Louis Lambert*, 294).

17 Begam remarks: "But if the nexus is clear—womb, room, tomb—its significance is less so" (139). Accordingly he launches into a discussion of "the nineteenth-century novelist's *faire vivre*" whose characters "[project] a species or kind," whereas for Beckett "this Balzacian process . . . fixes characters in formaldehyde" (139). Though we will see that the sacrificial production of "species or kind" is very much to the point, Begam seems to miss the sacrificial significance of the equation death = life—a significance that extends far beyond novelistic theory or practice.

18 Kafka's "In the Penal Colony," like *Alice in Wonderland*, provides a comparable reversal of guilt and punishment. Flann O'Brien's *The Third Policeman* offers a comparable reversal of east and west.

19 Connor is on the mark in emphasizing animals as victims ("Beckett's Animals," 33), and even on the dangers of anthropomorphism (29), though he apparently misses the sacrificial reciprocity between animal and man governing so much of the text.

20 *Louis Lambert* is again highly relevant in this context, since Louis both observes that "the ancient mode of representing human ideas as embodied in animals . . . gave rise to the first signs in the East for writing down language" (183), and proposes that "animal type has hitherto been studied with reference only to its differences, not to its similitudes" (Balzac, 265).

21 This reciprocity might recall Kafka's "A Crossbreed," concerning an animal that is half lamb, half cat.

22 While Acheson's description of Lambert as "sadistic" is understandable (and doubtless nontechnical), my point is that Lambert does not beat his wife directly for sexual gratification, but rather to induce her to offer it in the "normal" way; whereas Macmann's licking of Moll's cruciform tooth is explicitly erotic. Acheson's claim that Malone "has greater sympathy for the sadistic Lambert than for the passive, acquiescent Saposcats" (*Samuel Beckett's Artistic Theory and Practice*, 124) seems deaf to Malone's irony and the reverse of the truth.

23 The supplemental "play" of substitutions to which critics like Begam and Toyami appeal in Derridean *différance* here defines the sacrificial mechanism instead of offering any "postmodern" alternative to it (though Derrida's own treatments of sacrifice lie beyond the scope of this analysis).

24 We may recall the substitution of age difference for gender difference discussed in the previous chapter.

25 "Grisette" ("little Grey"), substituting for orthodox sacrificial white, moves a further step in the direction of undifferentiation (and may also suggest promiscuity).

26 Toyami comments, with reference to Lévi-Strauss, that "to commit incest is to mix paradigm and syntagm, an action that muddles the origin" (*Beckett's Game*, 97). But this ignores the sacrificial pattern of substitution. In *Louis Lambert*, incidentally, the school dining hall—"worthy of an ancient religious Order"—is a scene of "gastronomical barter [which] was always one of the chief pleasures of

our college." "If several identical offers were made, they were taken in order, and the formula would be, 'Lentils number one for dessert number one'" (Balzac, *Louis Lambert*, 191–92).

27   Cf. *Louis Lambert*: "Three is the formula of created worlds. It is the Spiritual Sign of the creation, as it is the Material sign of dimension" (312).

28   Language-centered critics like Toyami, by contrast, naturally tend to cite *The Unnamable*: "It all boils down to a question of words" (338) (*Beckett's Game*, 90). Admittedly *The Unnamable*, as its title suggests, is concerned at least negatively with naming; but, as we shall see, the matter is more complicated: "The fact is all this business about voices requires to be revised, corrected and then abandoned" (338).

29   I am referring to the pop star who helped make such crucifix earrings fashionable in the 1980s, not the virgin.

30   Though this has apparently not been transparent to critics. Acheson's claim, for example, that "Malone presents us with this curious example of Christian piety for the sake of suggesting that Moll's faith is misplaced" (*Samuel Beckett's Artistic Theory and Practice*, 128) seems misguided.

31   I have avoided entering the critical fray concerning Beckett's supposedly anti-allegoric stance. But I subscribe generally to the position advanced by Marius Buning in "Allegory's Double Bookkeeping: The Case of Samuel Beckett," *Samuel Beckett Today/Aujourd'hui* 1 (1992): 69–77, which criticizes slavish adherence to Beckett's own criticisms of allegory (in the sense that makes allegory just another wooden correspondence like the "grotesque fallacy" of realism). The fact that his allegories, once recognized, approach the level of farce hardly lessens their overwhelming structural importance.

32   Thus, while Toyami is perfectly correct to cite "no other image is appropriate," this is not ultimately because of the overriding importance of linguistic structures as such, but rather, as Bersani and Dutoit put it, in the context of *Company*, because "*there is no way to escape company*" more generally (*Arts of Impoverishment*, 75), and the potentially unlimited substitutive patterns, however "fictional" (76), of third-party mediation, whether linguistic or not. Hence, though Toyami's claim that "these are really futile [third-party] fictions created to explain what is, but they succeed only in muddling the source" (*Beckett's Game*, 73) is doubtless true up to a point, it ignores the implication that such potentially translinguistic patterns of mediation *are* the relevant source of what the Unnamable here calls "communication." Cf. "Why then the human voice, rather than a hyena's howls or the clanging of a hammer? Answer, so that the shock may not be too great" (*The Unnamable*, 359). Cf. also Bersani and Dutoit: "*Company* gives us something much more primitive [than listening to stories/voices]: the awakening to differences of sound" (*Arts of Impoverishment*, 70).

33   This may recall the putative transcendence of Jacques Lacan's "symbolic" domain—the so-called Big Other—which I discuss in "A Glance at SunSet," 236–37.

34   Toyami confirms this (*Beckett's Game*, 100).

35   Louis Lambert discusses the "acute pain as if I had really cut myself" caused by ideas, as well as the power of "imagined suffering" in general, and his friend, the narrator, collaborates by "obeying the mimetic instinct" (Balzac, *Louis Lambert*, 213–14). Louis also links "*species*, sight; speculation . . . [and] *Speculum*" (308).

36 I discuss this kind of pattern in connection with Shakespeare as well as Beckett in "A Glance at SunSet," 231, where I refer to Wittgenstein's rather astonishing claim (in his *Remarks on the Foundations of Mathematics*) that pain "is not a form of behaviour" (as he also distinguishes, in the same breath, calculation and poetry from "experiments").

37 Lemuel is also an anagram of "Le mule," the mule buried earlier (212), underlining the potentially symmetrical reversibility of victim and victimizer along the lines of "Lambert." The anagram is confirmed by David Hesla in *The Shape of Chaos: An Interpretation of the Art of Samuel Beckett* (Minneapolis: University of Minnesota Press, 1971), 110. As Toyami (57) suggests an analogy between Lemuel's hatchet and Malone's pencil, so Leslie Hill, like Begam (*Samuel Beckett and the End of Modernity*, 146), points out that Lemuel recalls Samuel (Beckett) and means "devoted to God" ("The Name, the Body, 'The Unnamable,'" *Oxford Literary Review* 6.1 [1983]: 54–55). Hill aptly cites the words taught to King Lemuel by his mother in Proverbs 31:8: "Open thy mouth for the dumb in the cause of all such as are appointed for destruction"—suggesting Lemuel's role as not only destroyer but also victim-advocate.

38 The American poet Alvin Feinman described pain thus in his critical introduction to Richard Rorty's lecture on Nabokov and cruelty at Bennington College (published in the Bennington Chapbook series).

39 Louis Lambert is once again highly relevant, since while his movements are described as like those of Orientals and savages, Christ (the Word-made-Flesh) is said to be the "perfect type of his system." Moreover, "though naturally religious," his religiosity is said to resemble that of "certain Saints, who, in our day, would be regarded as heresiarchs or atheists" (Balzac, *Louis Lambert*, 245). He and his friend, having got hold a "a great Martyrology," attempt "to endure pain by thinking of something else," and make cataleptic "experiments not unlike those of the epileptic fanatics of the last century, a religious mania *which will some day be of service to the science of humanity*" (295–96, my emphasis). Self-mutilation, incidentally, is now a common practice among students.

40 Malone also comments on secular—sexual and political—ideology as follows: "Yes, that's what I like about me . . . that I can say, Up the Republic!, for example, or Sweetheart!, for example, without having to wonder if I should not rather have cut my tongue out" (236).

41 I cannot cite much support from the critics here. For instance, Acheson's view that "Lemuel's hatchet slaying of the two sailors reminds us that there are two sides to Malone's personality" (*Samuel Beckett's Artistic Theory and Practice*, 131), malevolent and harmlessly passive, ignores the specificity I am claiming. Toyami, for all his insistence on Beckettian-Derridean play, doesn't mention the death of Ernest; nor does another Derridean, Begam. Hesla seems to miss the pun: "The excursion ends *in dire earnestness* when, after Lemuel [attacks] two sailors . . ." (*The Shape of Chaos*, 110, my emphasis).

42 Among others, Acheson's interpretation that "in spite of his early efforts to avoid exploring the darkness of his mind, Malone has ultimately tried and failed to shed light on himself through writing" (132) seems to miss the point. Cf. *The Unnamable*, 369: "To see the light, they call that seeing, no objection, since it causes him suffering." And 365: "Let there then be light, it will not *necessarily* be disastrous" (my emphasis). Once again, *Louis Lambert* seems to provide a more reliable guide

than Beckett criticism. Louis's painful experience of ideas as like a cut from his penknife is later elaborated in terms of the "prick of the penknife" as image of "the reversion, in the heart of the Paris world, to the savage passion that regards woman as its savage prey, an effect of animal instinct combining with the almost luminous flashes of a soul crushed under the weight of thought" (Balzac, *Louis Lambert*, 253).

43 Cf. *The Unnamable*, 358: "But this question of lights deserves to be treated *in a section apart*" (my emphasis). Here again we see why critical overemphasis on language, even in *The Unnamable*, where it is evidently important, is misguided.

44 "Idea" derives from a Greek root meaning "see." *Louis Lambert* provides every subtext we could wish for here. Not only does Louis claim that "thinking is seeing" (Balzac, *Louis Lambert*, 214), but that the five senses "in fact, are but one—the faculty of Sight" (305). Emphasis on relation between sight, thought, and pain are ubiquitous in Balzac's novel, as in Beckett's. Louis is compared to the "seer" Moses (188), whose regime "bears the authority of terror" (247).

45 Louis Lambert's master also attempts to seize his papers (225).

46 While Stanley Cavell is shrewd to stress Beckett's play with literalization in *Endgame*, his liberational emphasis ("To undo curses is just one service of literalization; another is to unfix clichés and idioms" [*Must We Mean What We Say?* 120]) is hardly what is at stake here. Rather, the dark side of Louis Lambert's obsession with light considered as Word-made-Flesh provides a relevant counterpart.

47 Again I do not have much support from the criticism on all this, though I do not deny the relevance of Hesla's assimilation (*The Shape of Chaos*, 110), recently repeated by Begam (*Samuel Beckett and the End of Modernity*, 145–46), of the youth, "dead young," to Murphy, Watt to the Saxon, Moran to the thin one, and the giant to Molloy. If this is in part correct, the irony of Moran, the patriarch, breaking the patriarchal "pasol," further underlines the reversibility at stake in *Malone Dies*. But neither critic concerns himself with the generic significance of these figures, nor with the fact that Louis Lambert, incidentally, is himself successively described as a giant, a woman, and divine (Balzac, *Louis Lambert*, 199, 201, 202)—a progression that neatly sums up the Beckettian nexus in this context.

48 But these fantasies hardly support Acheson's claim, citing this passage, that "Malone's self-awareness is limited" (*Samuel Beckett's Artistic Theory and Practice*, 124). On the contrary, Malone's irony is obvious: "I am such a good man, *at bottom*, how is it nobody ever noticed it?" (275, my emphasis).

49 Begam, *Samuel Beckett and the End of Modernity*, 146.

50 Cf. *Louis Lambert*: "Hence, perhaps, some day the converse of 'Et Verbum caro factum est' will become the epitome of a new Gospel, which will proclaim that The Flesh shall be made the Word and become the utterance of God" (Balzac, *Louis Lambert*, 309).

51 Although we may initially be seduced in this context by the postmodern idea that "as Deleuze explains, instead of supporting these characters as representations of Christ, these simulacra mock the model" (Toyami, *Beckett's Game*, 56), we should recall *The Unnamable*: "Between me and that miscreant who mocked the gods . . . in a word obliged humanity . . . I trust there is nothing in common" (305). A more accurate—and subversive—view is represented by Mary Bryden: "The crucifixion-event may be apprehended as coterminous with the scope and variety of human malaise" ("Figures of Golgotha: Beckett's Pinioned People," in *The Ideal*

Core of the Onion: Reading Beckett Archives, ed. John Pilling and Mary Bryden [Reading, Eng.: Beckett International Foundation], 47). Though Beckett may be "skittishly blasphemous," he provides "a negotiable middle ground which belongs neither to the deconstructed cult nor to the re-mysticised banality" (52). Once again Louis Lambert provides a guide, since in him the appearances of religiosity and atheism merge.

52   We may recall the indefinitely close resemblance, discussed in chapter 4, between what Girard calls "vertical" and "deviated" transcendence.

53   "The Calmative," *Stories and Texts for Nothing,* 42 (my emphasis). Once again Adorno calls it just right in emphasizing that the undermining of differentiation in Beckett goes so far as to abolish the distinction "between [the hell of] absolute domination" and "the messianic state in which everything would be in the right place," between "the peacefulness of the void and the peacefulness of reconciliation" (*Notes to Literature,* 274). Cf. also Bersani and Dutoit: "There are hints that the reign of justice itself is somehow sustained by love, by a gratuitous attentiveness to others that has nothing to do with the right of each individual to inflict on others the pain inflicted on him" (*Arts of Impoverishment,* 64). "Most unexpectedly, sociality—from within the operations of torture but perhaps also in excess of them—generate sociability" (65). However, their "has *nothing* to do with" (my emphasis) is ambivalent: the gratuitousness of love, in this context, *should be compared rather than contrasted* to the gratuitousness of the sacrificial principle. The "devastating hope" concerns the possibility that quasi-sadomasochistic behavior takes a step in the direction of abolishing "earnest" violence.

54   Acheson, *Samuel Beckett's Artistic Theory and Practice,* 129. Acheson cites Malone's remark that his aggressive visitor looks like "the undertaker's man, annoyed at having called prematurely," without seeming to be aware of the meaning of this prematurity.

55   Hill, for instance, astutely notes that "the ending of *Malone Dies* falls short of its own fantasmic closure" ("The Name," 290), and thus leads to *The Unnamable.* Begam also accurately reads "My story ended, I'll be living yet"—though he somewhat confuses matters, like Malone himself, by raising the possibility that Malone is already dead while still narrating (*Samuel Beckett and the End of Modernity,* 147).

56   We now see that the lie about the rain is clarified by the fact that Moran's umbrella turns into a parasol here, and that the major threat is the sun rather than the rain.

57   Hugh Kenner cites this from *Murphy* in *Samuel Beckett: A Critical Study* (Berkeley: University of California Press, 1968), 133.

58   Bersani and Dutoit, *Arts of Impoverishment,* 41.

59   Begam, *Samuel Beckett and the End of Modernity,* 183.

60   For an extensive discussion of the "encounter" in terms of nineteenth-century theory, see David F. Bell, *Circumstances: Chance in the Literary Text* (Lincoln: University of Nebraska Press, 1993).

61   Leslie Hill accurately observes that "if the name may become a figure of singularity, it also reveals itself as impossible" ("The Name," 291) within language. But while this deconstructionist point is certainly relevant to *The Unnamable,* the opposition between the sacrificial and nonsacrificial extends beyond language, explicitly as we will see, into two varieties of silence (only one of which is defined dialectically in relation to language).

62 Girard has argued this point in "Perilous Balance: A Comic Hypothesis," in *To Double Business Bound: Essays on Literature, Mimesis, and Anthropology* (Baltimore: Johns Hopkins University Press, 1978).

63 And implies exhaustive speech, "the whole truth." The *OED* gives *con-fateri* (related to *fari*, to speak) as etymological origin of *confess*, noting that *fatari* means "to speak much."

64 Hence the accuracy of Arnold Heumakers's description of "le supplice de la parole" ("L'enfer abstraite de Samuel Beckett," *Samuel Beckett Today/Aujourd'hui* 1 [Amsterdam: Rodopi, 1992]: 82) in the work of art's "abstract hell," where "my crime is my punishment" (*The Unnamable*, 372). He adds wittily: "En réalité il ne s'agit pas d'un enfer, ni d'une abstraction non plus" (84).

65 Slavoj Žižek, *Enjoy Your Symptom: Jacques Lacan in Hollywood and Out* (New York: Routledge, 1992), 165ff.

7 Fashion Theory

1 Alan Hunt, in the *Governance of the Consuming Passions: A History of Sumptuary Law* (New York: St. Martin's Press, 1996), attempts to move "beyond imitation theory" of dress (Hunt, 49ff.). However, he regards imitation theory as "typically a view from above" (54), whereby social inferiors are thought to imitate their superiors, and later concedes that his own view of the "fundamental contradiction [of sumptuary regulation] involves some minimal acceptance of a social psychology of imitation" (102). His view of modern "'mass fashion' whose dynamic is not reducible to imitation" but rather "collective taste" (55), is far from incompatible with the present analysis, inasmuch as imitation (whether from "above," "below," or "sideways") is nevertheless an irreducible element in the propagation of fashion. That "people make decisions on their own account" (55) obviously does not mean they make them independently of others.

2 *Much Ado*, 3.3.114.

3 Roland Barthes, *The Fashion System*, trans. M. Ward and R. Howard (New York: Hill and Wang, 1983), 243.

4 Geoffrey Squire, *Dress and Society, 1560–1970* (New York: Viking, 1974), 41. Hunt confirms the point, citing René Konig's dating of the origin of premodern fashion to the rise of the urban middle class of the thirteenth century (Hunt, *Governance*, 47), and claiming that "the major long-term shift was the abandonment of the unisex long robes that had been dominant from Roman times" (45). One of his related theses is that sumptuary law was most active when Europe was on the brink of modernity (28). None of this, however, contradicts Daniel Roche's observation that "fashion can affect the most traditional of societies and the most fixed of costumes" (Roche, *The Culture of Clothing: Dress and Fashion in the Ancien Régime*, trans. Jean Birrell [Cambridge: Cambridge University Press, 1996], 42).

5 See Hunt, *Governance*, 217–18.

6 *Much Ado*, 2.1.59; 2.1.26ff.

7 *Much Ado*, 3.3.127ff.

8 *The Encyclopedia Britannica*, 1911 edition.

9 See the Arden edition of *Much Ado*, ed. A. R. Humphries (London: Routledge, 1981), 161.

10 *A Midsummer Night's Dream*, 3.1.185. In this play, Theseus also claims to have

been told the story of "the battle with the Centaurs, to be sung / *by an Athenian eunuch*" to his love Hippolyta, *"in glory of my kinsman Hercules"* (5.1.44–48, my emphases).

11 Kenneth Dover, *Greek Homosexuality* (Cambridge: Harvard University Press, 1979), 129.

12 *Much Ado*, 3.3.161–64.

13 Roche, similarly, stresses the general significance of the "order" of clothing-appearance inasmuch as "there, the mental becomes the corporeal, the individualized body displaying the fleeting traces of the person and clothing revealing the hidden correspondences between substance and spirit" (Roche, *Culture of Clothing*, 511).

14 I say "seemingly" because, aside from the fashionable resurgence of actual bodily mutilation, the prevalence of eating disorders in modern society is often attributed, in part, to the cruel demands of fashion. In this connection, an analysis could be made of eating metaphors in *Much Ado*, along the lines of Beckett's *Malone Dies*, with the pattern of *literalization of figure* in mind.

15 Though "nothing" is often vaginal in Shakespeare, it is also sometimes (as in Beckett) anal. I discuss the "law of the ass" as represented by Bottom in *A Midsummer Night's Dream* in "A Glance at SunSet: Numerical Fundaments in Frege, Wittgenstein, Shakespeare, Beckett," in *Mathematics, Science, and Postclassical Theory*, ed. Barbara Herrnstein Smith and Arkadi Plotnitsky (Durham: Duke University Press, 1997), 228–30.

16 *Othello*, 3.1.6–10. The mimetic violence of the Trojan War is described in *Troilus and Cressida* (2.2.6) as "hot digestion."

17 Barthes, *The Fashion System*, 259.

18 We will pursue this reciprocity more concretely in the third section, "Seeing through Clothes." Though Barthes writes here of contemporary fashion, Roche, for instance, detects a historical transition from bodies that "refer" to their clothes, in the hierarchical display of the *ancien régime*, to a contrary tendency linked to late-Enlightenment development of the fashion press: "The body was no longer a mannequin for the clothes but the secret reference in the various signs of fashion to its new reality" (Roche, *Culture of Clothing*, 496). He comments, however, that "the new coat bend[s] us to its shape before adapting to ours" (499).

19 *Much Ado*, 3.3.114ff.

20 *Much Ado*, 3.3.109–12.

21 *Much Ado*, 3.5.35–39.

22 "Today as in the past, clothing relates to our profound conception of the sacred, the [relation between] social and the individual" (Roche, *Culture of Clothing*, 510).

23 John Carl Flugel, *The Psychology of Clothes* (London: Hogarth Press, 1930).

24 Barthes, *Fashion System*, 289. We will return to this in the fourth section.

25 Roche observes that "for psychoanalysts, [modesty] implies the existence of a first tendency which it requires to repress, whereas historians assert that there are periods when the negative impulses triumph and others when they are in retreat" (*Culture of Clothing*, 36). Nevertheless, he concedes that "in the last analysis clothes may well respond to constant imperatives, whose anteriorities and priorities the historian is less prepared to discuss than the anthropologist or the psychoanalyst," and which are "more important from a theoretical point of view than to a medium-term historical analysis" (ibid., 35).

26 James Laver, in his *Modesty in Dress: An Inquiry into the Fundamentals of Fashion*

(Boston: Houghton Mifflin, 1969), cites the story of two Native Americans fighting in this manner, which—however questionable in fact—instantiates his display model (4).

27 Hilaire Hiler, *From Nudity to Raiment* (London: Simkin Marshall, 1929), 88–89.

28 Tooth extraction probably relates to the class of modesties surrounding eating. Just as sumptuary laws generally applied to food before they were introduced for dress (Hunt, *Governance*, 19), so-called primitive alimentary modesties are found where dress-concealment is minimal or nonexistent. As regards the relation of decoration and sacrificial violence more generally, it is not surprising that Mayan priests, for instance, adorned their hair with sacrificial blood (Hiler, *From Nudity to Raiment*, 245). Perhaps more surprising are Claude Lévi-Strauss's ambitious claims about the systematic relation, in a wide variety of (mainly South American) myth, between head-hunting and menstrual blood on the one hand, and red hair, pubic-hair ornament, and dress fringes on the other. Punning on links between cosmic and cosmetic orders, he suggests that a large number of such myths are structured by two mutually mediating conceptual triangles: scalping/quill-work/pubic hair, and sun/moon/stone (or earth) (*The Origin of Table-Manners*, trans. John and Doreen Weightman [New York: Harper and Row, 1978], 398). Both masculine and feminine blood are prominent in his claim to establish a general symbolic progression from scalping to pubic-hair fringes to stones that fertilize women when sucked, on one hand (389), and from a male nonmilitary wound to a war wound to a bleeding woman on the other (408). In his account of many myths (and not only South American ones) which link the end of cannibalism to the origin of scalping and hair ornament (377), the latter appear as attenuated and substitutive forms of sacrificial violence.

29 *Much Ado*, 4.1.122.

30 This is discussed, for instance, by the "Just Logos" in Aristophanes's *Clouds*.

31 Huddleston's introduction to Hilaire Hiler's *From Nudity to Raiment* (London: Simkin Marshall, 1929) praises him for presenting a number of conflicting theories, while falling for none of them. Since then, no consensus seems even vaguely to have been reached, and conflicting universalisms have given way in large part to fear of global theorization. Nevertheless, "clothing is a global social fact in the sense in which Mauss used the term, and it may be that analysis of global social facts goes some way to resolve the conflicts between opponents or partisans of serial or macroscopic studies and the defenders of *microstoria* or case studies" (Roche, *Culture of Clothing*, 503).

32 Hiler, *From Nudity to Raiment*, 129.

33 Ibid., 129–30. A similar inconsistency goes for the sumptuary law of modern Europe. In Bern of 1637, for instance, unmarried women were permitted a range of clothing denied to matrons, whereas in Siena the reverse held (Hunt, *Governance*, 223).

34 Hiler, *From Nudity to Raiment*, 122–23.

35 Hunt cites Jonathan Culler's notion of the "evasive complexity" of aesthetic codes in support of his contention that dress tends "toward transgressive violation or disruption of its own code" (Hunt, *Governance*, 62). However, as these examples suggest, the issue can by no means be restricted to "aesthetics."

36 This also goes for what Hunt calls the "fundamental contradiction" of sumptuary law, which, he concedes, "involves some minimal acceptance of a social psychology

of imitation" (Hunt, *Governance*, 102). "The kicker of sumptuary law is that not only is it beset by a fundamental contradiction but that contradiction sharpens as the position of those claiming privilege becomes less secure in their continued capacity to exercise it. This expresses itself in self-parody when, for example, the illicit status of some item generates its very attraction" (ibid., 104). Roche, similarly, claims that "sumptuary laws promoted the growth of fashion in France" (*Culture of Clothing*, 56). Hunt also discusses the "ambivalent existence" of the veil, on the one hand "exhibit[ing] piety and modesty, but on the other . . . signify[ing] allure by facilitating concealment of identity" (*Governance*, 223).

37 Roche, *Culture of Clothing*, 55.

38 Ibid., 35. See also, for example, Andrea R. Rugh, *Reveal and Conceal: Dress in Contemporary Egypt* (Syracuse: Syracuse University Press, 1986), 5; and Francoise Simon-Miller, "Commentary: Signs and Cycles in the Fashion System," in *The Psychology of Fashion*, ed. Michael R. Solomon (Lexington: Lexington Books, 1985), 75–76.

39 Hunt cites Harriane Mills and Diane Hughes on this opposition (*Governance*, 219).

40 Hunt notes that the opposition is frequently "cast within an essentialist view of sex difference" (ibid., 219), criticizing Flugel's Freudian theory for making the similar unsubstantiated (indeed patently false) claim that "women . . . introduced the principle of the deliberate reinforcement of the attractions exercised by clothes and nakedness" (ibid., 221–22). He also criticizes "radical feminism, in which women are constructed as passive victims of an all-powerful male compulsion," arguing that "neither of these polarities can grapple with the coexistence of display and concealment, perhaps the best exemplification of which is the way in which female modesty is never simply denial or purity, but is itself a complex form of eroticization" (222).

41 "It should not be thought that the erotic and the economic roles are always distinct; the eroticization of wealth plays a significant part of my story" (Hunt, *Governance*, 65).

42 A parallel may be drawn here with Kenneth Burke's conception of the "rhetoric of courtship"—which is modestly self-inhibiting, self-frustrating, even "masochistic," but a constitutive part, according to Burke, of all semiological seduction and social hierarchy (see, for example, Burke, *A Rhetoric of Motives* [New York: Prentice-Hall, 1950], 177, 269).

43 Baudrillard discusses this general tendency in *L'echange symbolique et la mort* (Paris: Editions Gallimard, 1976). Hunt cites Diane Hughes's study of the social history of the earring more particularly, which "shows how the earring was imposed upon prostitutes and Jewesses as 'marks of infamy' but came to acquire the status of marks of distinction" (Hunt, *Governance*, 65). Moreover, this "*produced* [rather than merely reflected] a degradation discourse linking prostitutes and Jewesses as both 'foreign' and immoral" (65, my emphasis).

44 Hunt, *Governance*, 63.

45 Such shamans frequently claim to have been killed and dismembered in their past lives, and their qualifications for treating mental illnesses often stem from their having once suffered from such illnesses. A strikingly mimetic disorder, called "arctic hysteria," is said to be characterized by obsessive imitation of others, sometimes while muttering obscenities.

46 Angela Carter, *The Sadeian Woman and the Ideology of Pornography* (New York: Pantheon Books, 1978), 20–21.

47 Anne Hollander, *Seeing through Clothes* (New York: Avon, 1980), 315.

48 Ibid., 83–236. Hunt agrees that Hollander "most convincingly demonstrates even in the artistic convention of the nude, the naked body is always significantly clothed" (*Governance*, 61).

49 Hollander, *Seeing through Clothes*, 157ff.

50 Ibid., 181–83.

51 Dover, *Greek Homosexuality*, 68.

52 Ibid., 71.

53 Ibid., 69, 73.

54 Ibid., 115.

55 Ibid., 195, cites the Spartan poet Tyrtaios.

56 Though exposition of the sacrificial dimension of dress origins is beyond the scope of this analysis, it is worth noting that Lévi-Strauss's three-volume *Introduction to the Science of Mythology* cites many dress-origin myths (and, to a lesser extent, dress practices) that are most suggestive in this regard. As for the relation between dress and literal violence, we may cite Herodotus's quasi-historical account of the transition from Ionic (or Carian) fashions that succeeded the relatively simple styles of Doric dress. Ethel Abrahams claims that Herodotus's dating of this transition at 568 B.C. is faulty, but his story nevertheless provides a striking identification of dress with both violence and its inhibition. According to him, only one man returned from a disastrous Athenian expedition against the Aeginetans in which the Athenians attempted to steal their enemies' divine statues, but were mysteriously overcome by "madness . . . so that they slew one another" (Maria Millington Evans, *Chapters on Greek Dress* [London: Macmillan, 1893], 28). On the return of the sole survivor, the Athenian women killed him out of fury that he was without their husbands, using the pins and clasps of their garments. Henceforth, says Herodotus, Ionic dress was adopted, which had no use for such dangerous pins (while the Aeginetans made their own pins larger than ever in triumphant rivalry).

57 Hollander, *Seeing through Clothes*, 98.

58 Ibid., 315 (my emphasis).

59 Ibid., 448.

60 Roche claims, for example, that "historians are still unable to explain what lay behind the change from the Rabelaisian cod-piece to the sansculottes trousers, from flamboyant exhibition to deceptive disappearance" (*Culture of Clothing*, 36).

61 Squire, *Dress and Society*, 132. As early as 1657, a Nurnberg law complained that fashion had made it virtually impossible to tell the classes apart (Hunt, *Governance*, 121). Roche observes that "before the sixteenth century, the link between social distinction and sartorial difference was constantly affirmed. Between the sixteenth and the eighteenth centuries, things grew more complicated: first, as a result of the development of intermediate groups . . . and the spread of distinctive imitation; second, because of the migration from the country to the town, and probably also to some extent a real upward and downward social mobility, accentuated movement" (*Culture of Clothing*, 39).

62 Squire, *Dress and Society*, 126.

63 Roche, *Culture of Clothing*, 91.

64 Laver, *Modesty in Dress*, 134.

65 Hollander, *Seeing through Clothes*, 216–17.

66 Though he stresses the increasing medicalization of the relations between bodies and clothes at this period (464), Roche notes that Rousseau's influential insistence that children be dressed healthily (and liberated, for example, from the "Gothic shackles" of whalebone corsets) did not entail proposing "special clothes for children (something Rousseau hardly discussed)." Rather, "new ideas about the sanctity of childhood . . . [and their consequent] new autonomy resulted, in the long term," in such special clothes (*Culture of Clothing*, 217–18).

67 Squire, *Dress and Society*, 135.

68 Roche, *Culture of Clothing*, 499. Roche further observes in this context that "in sum, there was a general order [to fashion], all the more effective in that it enjoyed all the appeal of play and caprice" (499).

69 Ibid., 62. This goes for men too, as illustrated by the fact that the eldest son, in the new order of French dress, was not allowed to wear the fashionable, fancy clothes permitted to his siblings (ibid., 59).

70 As Roche claims that children's clothes created a new frontier between rich and poor, the latter still dressed like miniadults (*Culture of Clothing*, 116–17).

71 Ibid., 140.

72 Barthes, *The Fashion System*, 241.

73 Roche makes a further connection between childhood and underwear in the eighteenth century: "Through its intermediate position and its proximity to the body, which made it a sort of second skin, linen underwear acquired a carnal value which was emphasized by the ritual of socialization. It was one of the ways by which children won their autonomy" (*Culture of Clothing*, 154).

74 Hollander, *Seeing through Clothes*, 133.

75 Laver, *Modesty in Dress*, 135.

76 Hollander, *Seeing through Clothes*, 212.

77 Ibid., 212–13.

78 At the end of the seventeenth century (in France) women had no more underwear than men. Undershirts were often more or less sexually undifferentiated, and men owned more stockings than women (Roche, *Culture of Clothing*, 163).

79 "It was pornographic works of art that now showed female nudity emerging from lacy undergarments, whereas in 1700 the same motif had appeared in formal portraits of duchesses" (Hollander, *Seeing through Clothes*, 213).

80 Ibid., 134, 213. Roche confirms the connection between "the cult of underwear" and "the secret exaltation of the corset, the mystique of the tortured body" (*Culture of Clothing*, 62). Hollander's emphasis on the fetishization of black underwear which began during the late nineteenth century and has lasted to the present (*Seeing through Clothes*, 133) may be contrasted, incidentally, with Casanova's hatred of female drawers, especially black ones (Roche, *Culture of Clothing*, 414).

81 Similarly, Francoise Simon-Miller cites Ernst Dichter, who "points to the growing importance of the 'innerfeel' of lining, pockets, and other elements constituting the inside of clothing" (Simon-Miller, "Commentary," 78).

82 Barthes, *The Fashion System*, ix.

83 Ibid., 294.

84 Ibid., 288.

85 Ibid., 10.

86 Ibid., 300.

87 Hunt, *Governance*, 63; Roche, *Culture of Clothing*, 517.

88 Barthes, *The Fashion System*, 253, 242, 241, 245, 256.

89 Ibid., 272.

90 Ibid., 256.

91 Ibid., 14.

92 Ibid., 15.

93 Ibid., 273 (my emphasis).

94 Ibid., 271.

95 Ibid., 282.

96 Ibid., 289 (my emphasis).

97 Ibid., 289.

98 Ibid., 296.

99 Ibid., 293 (I have inserted this example).

100 Ibid., 294.

101 Ibid., 294.

102 Hunt, *Governance*, 44.

103 Barthes, *The Fashion System*, 296.

104 Ibid., 299.

105 Alasdair MacIntyre, *After Virtue* (Notre Dame: University of Notre Dame Press, 1984), 97.

106 Ibid., 104.

107 To take a simple case: the reduction of bathing suits to one or two overpriced elements—indeed the limited abolition of bathing suits altogether in favor of nudity—might have been anticipated by anyone who anticipated the general sexual mores of our day. Such a person might also have predicted the "arbitrary" line that currently separates legal nudity on beaches from criminal nudity only a few feet away on the street. The ultimate arbitrariness of the *principle* of the sartorial cut and sartorial law by no means precludes its practical predictability.

108 Barthes, *The Fashion System*, xii.

109 Ibid., 297.

110 Ibid., 234.

111 Roche, *Culture of Clothing*, 69–70.

112 John Maynard Keynes as cited by Jean-Pierre Dupuy in "Self-Reference in Literature," *Poetics* 18 (1989): 509.

113 Hiler, *From Nudity to Raiment*, 137.

114 Roche, *Culture of Clothing*, 498, 45. The tendency to stress the reverse pattern of causality, as Barthes does, may be connected to the fact that "while historians and economists have tended to concentrate on production, consumption and its social mechanisms have suffered relative neglect" (ibid., 501).

115 Ibid., 516 (my emphasis), 518.

116 Barthes, *The Fashion System*, 286.

117 Ibid., 285.

118 Ibid.

119 Ibid.

120 Ibid., 286.

121 Ibid., xi (my emphases).

122 Squire, *Dress and Society*, 39.

123 Roche, *Culture of Clothing*, 297, 328.

124 Ibid., 497.

125 Hunt, *Governance*, 55.

126 Aside from designers and models themselves, Andy Warhol's mechanically mimetic Monroes are convenient (if uninteresting) emblems of this merger.

Conclusion

1 Mihai Spariosu, "Mimesis and Contemporary French Theory," in *Mimesis in Contemporary Theory: An Interdisciplinary Approach*, vol. 1: *The Literary and Philosophical Debate*, ed. Spariosu (Philadelphia/Amsterdam: John Benjamins Publishing, 1984), 88.

2 Ibid., 99.

3 I treat this topic in "Sacrificial Materialism in Kierkegaard and Adorno" (forthcoming in *Idealism without Absolutes: Philosophy and the Limits of Romanticism*, ed. Arkady Plotnitsky [Albany: SUNY University Press]).

4 Paul de Man, "Hegel on the Sublime," in *Aesthetic Ideology*, ed. Andrzej Warminski (Minneapolis: Minnesota University Press, 1996), 113.

5 Ibid., 114.

6 Ibid.

7 Ibid., 117.

8 J. Hillis Miller, "An Open Letter to Professor Jon Weiner," in *Responses: On Paul de Man's Wartime Journalism*, ed. Werner Hamacher, Neil Hertz, and Thomas Keenan (Lincoln: University of Nebraska Press, 1989), 339.

9 De Man, "The Concept of Irony," in *Aesthetic Ideology*, 183.

10 De Man, "Dialogue and Dialogism," in *The Resistance to Theory* (Minneapolis: Minnesota University Press, 1986), 106ff.

11 De Man, "Hegel on the Sublime," 118.

12 Leo Strauss, *The City and Man* (Chicago: Chicago University Press, 1964), 52.

13 De Man, "Hegel on the Sublime," 106, 115.

14 Spariosu, "Mimeis," 88.

15 As noted in chapter 6, Žižek's recommendation occurs in his book titled *Enjoy Your Symptom: Jacques Lacan Hollywood and Out* (New York: Routledge, 1992).

16 Ian Hacking, *Rewriting the Soul: Multiple Personality and the Sciences of Memory* (Princeton: Princeton University Press, 1995), 260ff.

17 Max Horkheimer and Theodor W. Adorno, *Dialectic of Enlightenment*, trans. John Cumming (New York: Continuum, 1999), 56.

18 I discuss this at greater length in "Music Theory in Late Kafka," *Angelaki* 3.2 (1998): 169–81.

19 I hope I will not be misunderstood when I point out that the potentially sacrificial character of that distinction is perhaps most clearly, if problematically, evidenced in current U.S. abortion law, which predicates a definition of legal killing on an interpretation of the law concerning privacy.

Appendix

1 I cannot summarize McKenna's "propaedeutic effort throughout to explicate Derrida and Girard via each other" in *Violence and Difference: Girard, Derrida, and*

Deconstruction (Urbana: University of Illinois Press, 1992), 13—a brave effort, since he claims that Derrida mentions Girard only "but once, dismissively" (177). Among other things, McKenna cites Derrida's claim that "the only referent that is absolutely real is . . . of the scope or dimension" of total violence and the destruction of "all symbolic capacity" (111) as analogous to Girard's insistence on undifferentiated violence as the ultimate "referent" of sacrificial systems generally.

2 See Paul de Man, "The Contemporary Criticism of Romanticism," in de Man, *Romanticism and Contemporary Criticism: The Gauss Seminars and Other Papers*, ed. E. S. Burt, Kevin Newmark, and Andrzej Warminski (Baltimore: Johns Hopkins University Press, 1993), 18.

3 De Man, "The Contemporary Criticism of Romanticism," 10.

4 Ibid., 22.

5 Ibid.

6 See de Man's preface to *Allegories of Reading*.

7 Cited by J. Hillis Miller in "On Edge: The Crossways of Contemporary Criticism," in *Romanticism and Contemporary Criticism*, 122.

8 See "Hegel on the Sublime," in *Aesthetic Ideology*, 113.

Bibliography

Acheson, James. *Samuel Beckett's Artistic Theory and Practice*. New York: St. Martin's, 1997.

Adorno, Theodor W. *Aesthetic Theory*. Edited and translated by Robert Hullot-Kentor. Minneapolis: University of Minnesota Press, 1997.

——. *Kierkegaard: Construction of the Aesthetic*. Translated by Robert Hullot-Kentor. Minneapolis: University of Minnesota Press, 1989.

——. *Notes to Literature*. Vol. 1. Edited by Rolf Tiedernmann. Translated by Shierry Weter Nicholson. New York: Columbia University Press, 1991.

Adorno, Theodor W., and Max Horkheimer. *Dialectic of Enlightenment*. Translated by John Cumming. New York: Continuum, 1999.

Anscombe, G. E. M. *An Introduction to Wittgenstein's "Tractatus."* London: Hutchinson Library, 1963.

Anzien, Didier. "Beckett and the Psychoanalyst." *Journal of Beckett Studies* 4.1 (1991): 23–34.

Armstrong, Katherine. *Defoe: Writer as Agent*. Victoria, B.C.: University of Victoria, 1996.

Astro, Alan. *Understanding Samuel Beckett*. Columbia: South Carolina University Press, 1990.

Baker, Phil. "The Stamp of the Father in *Molloy*." *Journal of Beckett Studies* 5.1–2 (1996): 143–55.

Balzac, Honoré de. *Louis Lambert*. In *Honoré de Balzac*, vol. 25. New York: Peter Fenelon Collier and Son, 1900.

Barnes, J. A. *A Pack of Lies: Towards a Sociology of Lying*. New York: Cambridge University Press, 1994.

Barthes, Roland. *The Fashion System*. Translated by M. Ward and R. Howard. New York: Hill and Wang, 1983.

Bataille, Georges. *Les Larmes d'Eros*. Paris: Pauvert, 1961.

Baudrillard, Jean. *L'exchange symbolique et la mort*. Paris: Editions Gallimard, 1976.

Beck, Lewis White. *A Commentary on Kant's Critique of Practical Reason*. Chicago: Chicago University Press, 1966.

Beckett, Samuel. *The Expelled and Other Novellas*. London: Penguin, 1980.

——. *First Love and Other Shorts*. New York: Grove Press, 1974.

——. *Molloy*. Paris: Editions de Minuit, 1951.

——. *Molloy, Malone Dies, The Unnamable*. London: Calder Publications, 1994.

——. *No's Knife: Collected Shorter Prose, 1945–1966*. London: Calder and Boyars, 1967.

——. *Proust and Three Dialogues with Georges Duthuit*. London: John Calder, 1987.

——. *Stories and Texts for Nothing*. New York: Grove Press, 1967.

Begam, Richard. *Samuel Beckett and the End of Modernity*. Stanford: Stanford University Press, 1996.

——. "Splitting the Différance: Beckett, Derrida, and the Unnamable." *Modern Fiction Studies* 38.4 (1992): 873–92.

Bell, David F. *Circumstances: Chance in the Literary Text*. Lincoln: University of Nebraska Press, 1993.

Bell, Ian. *Defoe's Fiction*. London: Croom Helm, 1985.

Ben-Zvi, Linda. *Samuel Beckett*. Boston: Twayne, 1986.

Bernal, Olga. "Samuel Beckett: l'ecrivain et le savoir." *Journal of Beckett Studies* 2 (summer 1977): 59–62.

Bersani, Leo, and Ulysse Dutoit. *Arts of Impoverishment: Beckett, Rothko, Renais*. Cambridge: Harvard University Press, 1993.

Bishop, Tom, and Raymond Federman, eds. Samuel Beckett issue of *Cahier L'Herne*. Paris: Editions Cahier L'Herne, 1976.

Bloom, Harold, ed. *Samuel Beckett's "Molloy," "Malone Dies," "The Unnamable."* New York: Chelsea, 1988.

Boardman, Michael. *Defoe and the Uses of Narrative*. New Brunswick: Rutgers University Press, 1983.

Bok, Sissela. *Lying: Moral Choice in Public and Private Life*. New York: Pantheon, 1978.

Booker, Keith M. "The Bicycle and Descartes: Epistemology in the Fiction of Beckett and O'Brien." *Eire-Ireland* 26.1 (1991): 76–94.

Brater, Enoch. *Why Beckett*. London: Thames and Hudson, 1989.

Breton, André. *Manifestes du surréalisme*. Edited by Jean-Jacques Pauvert. Paris: Gallimard, 1975.

Bryden, Mary. "Figures of Golgotha: Beckett's Pinioned People." In *The Ideal Core of the Onion*, ed. John Pilling and Mary Bryden, 45–62. Reading, Eng.: Beckett International Foundation, 1992.

——. *Women in Samuel Beckett's Prose and Drama: Her Own Other*. Lanham, Md.: Barnes, 1993.

Buber, Martin. *Good and Evil: Two Interpretations*. New York: Charles Scribner and Sons, 1952.

Buning, Marius. "Allegory's Double Bookkeeping: The Case of Samuel Beckett." *Samuel Beckett Today/Aujourd'hui* 1 (1992): 69–77.

Burke, Kenneth. *A Rhetoric of Motives*. New York: Prentice Hall, 1950.

Butler, Lance St. John, ed. *Critical Essays on Samuel Beckett*. Aldershot, U.K.: Scolar Press, 1994.

Butler, Lance St. John, and Robert Davis. *Rethinking Beckett: A Collection of Critical Essays*. London: Macmillan, 1990.

Carter, Angela. *The Sadeian Woman and the Ideology of Pornography*. New York: Pantheon Books, 1978.

Cavell, Stanley. *Must We Mean What We Say?* Cambridge: Cambridge University Press, 1969.

Coetzee, J. M. *Foe*. London: Penguin, 1987.

Connor, Steven. "Beckett's Animals." *Journal of Beckett Studies* 8 (1982): 29–44.

Curtis, Laura. *The Elusive Daniel Defoe*. London: Vision and Barnes and Noble, 1984.

Defoe, Daniel. *A General History of the Pirates*. London: T. Warner, 1724.

——. *A General History of the Robberies and Murders of the most notorious Pyrates*. London: Ch. Rivington, J. Stone, and J. Lacy, 1724.

——. *The History and Remarkable Life of the Truly Honourable Col. Jacque, commonly call'd Col. Jack*. London: J Brotherton, 1720.

——. *The History of Colonel Jack*. London: William Clowes and Sons, 1974.

——. *Memoirs of A Cavalier: Or A Military Journal of the Wars in Germany And the Wars In England, From the Year 1632, to the Year 1648*. London: A. Bell, J. Osborn, W. Taylor, and T. Warner, 1720.

——. *The Memoirs of Major Alexander Ramkins, a Highland-Officer, now in prison at Avignon*. London: R. King; W. Boreham, 1719.

——. *Moll Flanders*. Edited by Edward Kelly. New York: Norton Critical Edition, 1973.

——. *Robinson Crusoe*. Edited by Michael Shinagel. New York: W. W. Norton, 1975.

——. *The Serious Reflections During the Life and Surprising Adventures of Robinson Crusoe*. London: B. Yeats and J. M. Dent, 1985.

De Man, Paul. *Aesthetic Ideology*. Edited by Andrzej Warminski. Minneapolis: Minnesota University Press, 1996.

——. *Allegories of Reading: Figural Language in Rousseau, Nietzsche, Rilke, and Proust*. New Haven: Yale University Press, 1978.

——. *Critical Writings, 1953–1978*. Edited by Lindsay Waters. Minneapolis: University of Minnesota Press, 1989.

——. *The Resistance to Theory*. Minneapolis: Minnesota University Press, 1986.

——. *Romanticism and Contemporary Criticism: The Gauss Seminars and Other Papers*. Edited by E. S. Burt, Kevin Newmark, and Andrzej Warminski. Baltimore: Johns Hopkins University Press, 1993.

Derrida, Jacques. *La Dissemination*. Editions du Seuil, 1972.

——. *La Verité en peinture*. Paris: Flammarion, 1978.

——. *Writing and Difference*. Translated by Alan Bass. Chicago: University of Chicago Press, 1978.

Dettmar, Kevin J. H., "The Figure in Beckett's Carpet: *Molloy* and the Assault on Metaphor." In *Rethinking Beckett: A Collection of Critical Essays*, ed. Lance St. John Butler and Robert Davis. London: Macmillan, 1990.

Djikstra, Bran. *Defoe and Economics: The Fortunes of Roxana in the History of Interpretation.* Houndsmills: Basingstoke, Hampshire, 1987.

Dover, Kenneth. *Greek Homosexuality.* Cambridge: Harvard University Press, 1979.

Dukes, Gerry. "Quarrying the Trilogy." *Samuel Beckett Today* 2 (1993): 197–203.

Dumouchel, Paul, and Jean-Pierre Dupuy. *L'Enfer des choses: René Girard et la logique de l'économie.* Paris: Seuil, 1979.

Dupuy, Jean-Pierre. "Self-Reference in Literature." *Poetics* 18 (1989): 491–515.

Durkheim, Emile. *The Elementary Forms of Religious Life.* Translated by Joseph Ward Swain. London: George Allen and Unwin, 1915.

Erickson, Robert A. *Birth, Sex, and Fate in Eighteenth-Century Fiction.* New York: A.M.S. Press, 1986.

Esslin, Martin, ed. *Samuel Beckett: A Collection of Critical Essays.* Englewood Cliffs, N.J.: Prentice Hall, 1965.

Evans, Maria Millington. *Chapters of Greek Dress.* London: Macmillan, 1893.

Faller, Lincoln. *Crime and Defoe: A New Kind of Writing.* Cambridge: Cambridge University Press, 1993.

Feibleman, James. *Inside the Great Mirror: A Critical Examination of Russell, Wittgenstein, and Their Followers.* The Hague: M. Nijhoff, 1973.

Flugel, John Carl. *The Psychology of Clothes.* London: Hogarth Press, 1930.

Ford, Charles V. *Lies! Lies!! Lies!!! The Psychology of Deceit.* Washington: American Psychiatric Press, 1996.

Foucault, Michel. *The History of Sexuality.* Vol. 1. Translated by Robert Hurley. Layton, Utah: Peregrine Smith Books, 1984.

Furbank, P. N., and W. R. Owens. *The Canonization of Daniel Defoe.* New Haven: Yale University Press, 1988.

Garber, Marjorie. *Vested Interests: Cross-Dressing and Cultural Anxiety.* New York: Routledge, 1992.

Girard, René. *Deceit, Desire, and the Novel.* Translated by Yvonne Freccero. Baltimore: Johns Hopkins University Press, 1965.

——. *A Theater of Envy: William Shakespeare.* New York: Oxford University Press, 1991.

——. *"To Double Business Bound": Essays on Literature, Mimesis, and Anthropology.* Baltimore: Johns Hopkins University Press, 1978.

——. *Violence and the Sacred.* Translated by Patrick Gregory. Baltimore: Johns Hopkins University Press, 1977.

Gontarski, S. E., ed. *On Beckett: Essays and Criticism.* New York: Grove, 1986.

Goodman, Nelson. *Fact, Fiction, and Forecast.* 4th edition. Cambridge: Harvard University Press, 1983.

——. *The Languages of Art: An Approach to a Theory of Symbols.* Indianapolis: Hackett Publishing, 1986.

——. *Ways of Worldmaking.* Indianapolis: Hackett Publishing, 1978.

Habermas, Jürgen. *The Theory of Communicative Action.* Translated by Thomas McCarthy. Boston: Beacon Press, 1984.

Haig, Stirling. *Stendhal: The Red and the Black.* Cambridge: Cambridge University Press, 1989.

Hammond, J. R. *A Defoe Companion.* Lanham, Md.: Barnes & Noble, 1993.

Harrod, R. F. "Utilitarianism Revised." *Mind* 45 (1936): 137–56.

Henning, Sylvie Deberec. *Beckett's Critical Complicity: Carnival, Contestation, and Tradition.* Lexington: University of Kentucky Press, 1988.

Hesla, David. *The Shape of Chaos: An Interpretation of the Art of Samuel Beckett*. Minneapolis: University of Minnesota Press, 1971.

Heumakers, Arnold. "L'enfer abstraite de Samuel Beckett." *Samuel Beckett Today/ Aujourd'hui* 1 (Amsterdam: Rodopi, 1992): 79–85.

Hiler, Hilaire. *From Nudity to Raiment*. London: Simkin Marshall, 1929.

Hill, Leslie. "The Name, the Body, 'The Unnamable.'" *Oxford Literary Review* 6.1 (1983): 52–67.

Hollander, Anne. *Seeing through Clothes*. New York: Avon, 1980.

Hubner, Kurt. *Critique of Scientific Reason*. Translated by Paul R. Dixon and Hollis M. Dixon. Chicago: University of Chicago Press, 1983.

Humphries, Jefferson. *The Red and the Black: Mimetic Desire and the Myth of Celebrity*. Boston: Twayne Publishers, 1991.

Hunt, Alan. *Governance of the Consuming Passions: A History of Sumptuary Law*. New York: St. Martin's, 1996.

Hutchings, William. " 'Shat into Grace' Or, A Tale of a Turd: Why It Is How It Is in Samuel Beckett's *How It Is*." *Papers on Language and Literature* 21.1 (1985): 64–87.

Jayne, Edward. *Negative Poetics*. Iowa City: University of Iowa Press, 1992.

Jefferson, Ann. *Reading Realism in Stendhal*. Cambridge: Cambridge University Press, 1988.

Kafka, Franz. *Complete Stories*. Edited by Nahum N. Glatzer. New York: Schocken Books, 1971.

—. *Gesammelte Schriften*. Edited by Max Brod. Vol. 5: *Beschreibung eines Kampfes, Novellen, Skizzen, Aphorismen aus dem Nachlass*. New York: Schocken Books, 1946.

—. *The Trial*. Translated by Willa and Edwin Muir. New York: Schocken Books, 1984.

Kahn, Madeleine. *Narrative Transvesticism: Rhetoric and Gender in the Eighteenth-Century English Novel*. Ithaca: Cornell University Press, 1991.

Kant, Immanuel. *Perpetual Peace*. Edited and translated by Lewis White Beck. Indianapolis: Library of Liberal Arts, 1967.

Kennedy, Andrew. *Samuel Beckett*. Cambridge: Cambridge University Press, 1989.

Kenner, Hugh. *A Reader's Guide to Samuel Beckett*. New York: Farrar, Straus, and Giroux, 1973.

—. *Samuel Beckett: A Critical Study*. Berkeley: University of California Press, 1968.

Kierkegaard, Søren. *Either/Or*. Vol. 1. Translated by David F. Swenson and Lillian Marvin Swenson. Revised by Howard A. Johnson. Princeton: Princeton University Press, 1959.

Laver, James. *Modesty in Dress: An Inquiry into the Fundamentals of Fashion*. Boston: Houghton Mifflin, 1969.

Lévi-Strauss, Claude. *The Origin of Table-Manners*. Translated by John and Doreen Weightman. New York: Harper and Row, 1978.

Lewis, M., and C. Saarni, eds. *Lying and Deception in Everyday Life*. New York: Guilford, 1993.

MacIntyre, Alasdair. *After Virtue*. Notre Dame: University of Notre Dame Press, 1984.

Martineau, Henri. *L'oeuvre de Stendhal*. Paris: 1945.

McGinnis, Reginald. *La Prostitution sacrée: essai sur Baudelaire*. Paris: Belin, 1994.

—. "Samuel Beckett: Un pelerinage au-dela du romanesque." *L'Atelier du roman* 16 (winter 1998–99): 111–22.

McKenna, Andrew. *Violence and Difference: Girard, Derrida, and Deconstruction*. Urbana: University of Illinois Press, 1992.

Meche, Jude R. *Obsessive-Compulsive Behavior in Samuel Beckett's Trilogy*. Huntington, W.V.: University Editions, 1995.

Menzies, Janet. "Beckett's Bicycles." *Journal of Beckett Studies* 6 (autumn 1980): 97–105.

Miller, Gerard R., and James B. Stiff. *Deceptive Communication*. Newbury Park, Calif.: Sage Publications, 1993.

Miller, J. Hillis. "An Open Letter to Professor Jon Weiner." In *Responses: On Paul de Man's Wartime Journalism*, ed. Werner Hamacher, Neil Hertz, and Thomas Keenan. Lincoln: University of Nebraska Press, 1989.

——. *Romanticism and Contemporary Criticism*. Edited by Morris Eaves and Michael Fischer. Ithaca: Cornell University Press, 1986.

Miller, Lawrence. *Samuel Beckett: The Expressive Dilemma*. New York: St. Martin's, 1992.

Mitchell, Robert W. "Animals as Liars: The Human Face of Non-Human Duplicity." In *Lying and Deception in Everyday Life*, ed. Michael Lewis and Carolyn Saarni. New York: Guilford Press, 1993.

Montaigne, Michel de. *The Complete Essays of Montaigne*. Translated by Donald M. Frame. Stanford: Stanford University Press, 1958.

Mooney, Michael E. "*Molloy*, Part I: Beckett's 'Discourse on Method.'" *Journal of Beckett Studies* 3 (summer 1978): 40–55.

Moorjani Angela. "A Cryptoanalysis of Beckett's *Molloy*." In *The World of Samuel Beckett*, ed. Joseph H. Smith. Baltimore: Johns Hopkins University Press, 1991.

O'Brien, Flann. *The Third Policeman*. New York: Plume Press, 1976.

O'Connor, Steven. "Beckett's Animals." *Journal of Beckett Studies* 8 (1982): 29–44.

O'Hara, J. D. "Jung and the 'Molloy' Narrative." In *The Beckett Studies Reader*, ed. S. E. Gontarski. Gainesville: University of Florida Press, 1993.

Pavel, Thomas. *Fictional Worlds*. Cambridge: Harvard University Press, 1986.

Peirce, Charles Sanders. *Philosophical Writings of Peirce*. Edited by Justus Buchler. New York: Dover Publications, 1955.

Prendergast, Christopher. *The Order of Mimesis: Balzac, Stendhal, Nerval, Flaubert*. New York: Cambridge University Press, 1986.

Pringent, Christian. "A Descent from Clowns." *Journal of Beckett Studies* 3.1 (1993): 1–19.

Rabinovitz, Rubin. "Repetition and the Underlying Meanings in Samuel Beckett's Trilogy." In *Rethinking Beckett: A Collection of Critical Essays*, ed. Lance St. John Butler and Robert Davis, 31–67. London: Macmillan, 1990.

Read, David. "Artistic Theory in the Work of Samuel Beckett." *Journal of Beckett Studies* 8 (1982): 7–22.

Ricks, Christopher. "Lies." *Critical Inquiry* 2 (autumn 1975): 121–42.

Riva, Raymond T. "Beckett and Freud." *Criticism* 12 (1970): 120–32.

Roche, Daniel. *The Culture of Clothing: Dress and Fashion in the Ancien Régime*. Translated by Jean Birrell. Cambridge: Cambridge University Press, 1996.

Rogers, Pat. *Robinson Crusoe*. London: George Allen and Unwin, 1979.

Rorty, Richard. *Consequences of Pragmatism (Essays: 1972–1980)*. Minneapolis: University of Minnesota Press, 1982.

Rugh, Andrea R. *Reveal and Conceal: Dress in Contemporary Egypt*. Syracuse: Syracuse University Press, 1986.

Seidler, Michael. *Robinson Crusoe: Island Myths and the Novel*. Boston: Twayne Publishers, 1991.

Serres, Michel. *Les Origines de la géométrie*. Paris: Flammarion, 1993.

Sheringham, Michael. *Beckett: Molloy*. London: Grant and Cutler, 1985.

Shklar, Judith N. *Ordinary Vices*. Cambridge: Harvard University Press, 1984.

Simon-Miller, Françoise. "Commentary: Signs and Cycles in the Fashion System." In *The Psychology of Fashion*, ed. Michael R. Solomon. Lexington: Lexington Books, 1985.

Smith, Barbara Herrnstein. *On the Margins of Discourse: The Relation of Literature to Language*. Chicago: University of Chicago Press, 1978.

Smyth, John Vignaux. "A Glance at SunSet: Numerical Fundaments in Frege, Wittgenstein, Shakespeare, Beckett." In *Mathematics, Science, and Postclassical Theory*, ed. Barbara Herrnstein Smith and Arkady Plotnitsky. Durham: Duke University Press, 1997.

——. "Music Theory in Late Kafka." *Angelaki* 3.2 (1997): 169–81.

——. "Sacrificial Materialism in Kierkegaard and Adorno." In *Idealism without Absolutes: Philosophy at the Limits of Romanticism*, ed. Arkady Plotnitsky. Albany: State University of New York Press. Forthcoming.

Smyth, John Vignaux, and Reginald McGinnis. "Irony." In *The Encyclopedia of Aesthetics*, ed. Michael Kelly. Vol. 2. Oxford: Oxford University Press, 1998.

Solomon, Robert C. "What a Tangled Web: Deception and Self-Deception in Philosophy." In *Lying and Deception in Everyday Life*, ed. Michael Lewis and Carolyn Saarni. New York: Guilford Press, 1993.

——, ed. *The Psychology of Fashion*. Lexington: Lexington Books, 1985.

Spariosu, Mihai, ed. *Mimesis in Contemporary Theory: An Interdisciplinary Approach*. Vol. 1, *The Literary and Philosophical Debate*. Philadelphia: John Benjamins Publishing, 1984.

Squire, Geoffrey. *Dress and Society, 1560–1970*. New York: Viking, 1974.

Steele, Valerie. *Fetish: Fashion, Sex, and Power*. New York: Oxford University Press, 1996.

Stendhal (Henri Beyle). *Le Rouge et le noir: Chronique du XIXe siècle*. Edited by Henri Martineau. Paris: Garnier Frères, 1960.

——. *Lucien Leuwen*. Edited by Henri Martineau. Paris: Gallimard, 1973.

——. *Red and Black*. Edited and translated by Robert Adams. New York: W. W. Norton, 1969.

——. "Sur *Le Rouge et le noir*." In *Le Rouge et le noir*, ed. Henri Martineau, 509–27. Paris: Garnier Frères, 1960.

Strauss, Leo. *The City and Man*. Chicago: University of Chicago Press, 1964.

——. *Socrates and Aristophanes*. Chicago: University of Chicago Press, 1966.

Taussig, Michael. *Mimesis and Alterity: A Particular History of the Senses*. New York: Routledge, 1993.

Toyami, Jean Yamasaki. *Beckett's Game: Self and Language in the Trilogy*. New York: Peter Lang, 1991.

Trezise, Thomas. *Into the Breach: Samuel Beckett and the Ends of Literature*. Princeton: Princeton University Press, 1990.

Wittgenstein, Ludwig. *Remarks on the Foundations of Mathematics*. Edited by G. H. von Wright and G. E. M. Anscombe. Translated by G. E. M. Anscombe. Oxford: Oxford University Press, 1989.

——. *Tractatus Logico-Philosophicus*. Translated by D. F. Pean and B. F. McGuinness. London: Routledge, 1974.

Žižek, Slavoj. *Enjoy Your Symptom: Jacques Lacan in Hollywood and Out*. New York: Routledge, 1992.

Index

BJ 1421 .S66 2002
Smyth, John Vignaux
Habit of Lying.

John Vignaux Smyth is Professor and Chair of English,
Portland State University. He is the author of *A Question
of Eros: Irony in Sterne, Kierkegaard, and Barthes* (Florida
State University Press, 1986).

Library of Congress Cataloging-in-Publication Data

Smyth, John Vignaux.
The habit of lying : sacrificial studies in literature, philosophy,
and fashion theory / John Vignaux Smyth.
Includes bibliographical references and index.
ISBN 0-8223-2809-7 (cloth : alk. paper)
ISBN 0-8223-2821-6 (pbk. : alk. paper)
1. Truthfulness and falsehood. 2. Deception. 3. Fiction. I. Title.
BJ1421 .S66 2002   177'.3—dc21   2001047511